Public Administration: an introduction

Public Administration: an introduction

Stuart MacRae and Douglas Pitt

Pitman

PITMAN PUBLISHING LIMITED
39 Parker Street, London WC2B 5PB

Associated Companies
Copp Clark Pitman, Toronto
Fearon Pitman Publishers Inc, San Francisco
Pitman Publishing New Zealand Ltd, Wellington
Pitman Publishing Pty Ltd, Melbourne

© Stuart MacRae and Douglas Pitt 1980

First published in Great Britain 1980

Text set in 10 on 12pt Times by George Over Limited, London and Rugby.
Printed and bound in Great Britain
at The Pitman Press, Bath

ISBN 0 273 01270 3

Contents

Acknowledgement

The authors and publishers would like to thank the Central Statistical Office and the Department of Industry for giving their permission for the inclusion in the text of certain tabulations and diagrams. They are also indebted to Mr N Price, Treasurer of Stratford-on-Avon District Council, for allowing his rating statement to be reproduced.

Preface

Anyone writing a book about public administration has first to ask himself some very fundamental questions regarding the nature of his subject. For what purpose is the book intended, for example? How will it differ from other textbooks on related subjects like constitutional law or administrative law? Most fundamental of all: in what sense is the term public administration itself to be understood?

We have given thought to these questions and it seems important at the outset to state as clearly as we can what we have tried to do. The book is an introductory outline to a theme which in one sense is as topical and immediate as this morning's papers, and in another, as old as antiquity. It is about the processes and procedures of government as they are discernible here and now, and while much of it deals with institutions and organisations, we have also endeavoured to probe beneath the surface of events to look for underlying principles; as well as being descriptive our book is analytical.

Public Administration: an introduction has been written specifically with the needs of certain groups of students in mind, including those following the course module in Public Administration prescribed by the Business Education Council and those reading for the Diploma in Public Administration. The book will also be useful for students of professional bodies such as the Institute of Health Service Administrators and for those taking first year university and polytechnic courses in Administration or Politics.

Since this is intended as an introductory text the short and compact treatment attempts to deal in a relatively straightforward and abbreviated way with ideas which are not at all straightforward, but instead are rather complex. Inevitably, some aspects have received less emphasis than perhaps they deserve: key issues like centrality and control have had to compete with others like democratic participation and environment. We have been very conscious of this problem of balance and at the end of each chapter suggestions for further study may prompt readers to delve more deeply into those aspects of the subject in which they may have developed a particular interest. With this same aim in view we have added an Appendix which suggests a number of assignments based on the material in the book. These may be used as teaching aids in tutorials or for self-assessment by students who are working on their own.

Though obviously grounded in the law, the administrative institutions and practices discussed are a very practical response to the everyday problems of government. They are to be thought of as a total response rather than a series of isolated adaptations. In this sense the book tries to answer the question: how is Britain governed in the 1980's? There is a need here for as much objectivity and "distancing" as we have been able to muster.

British public administration today is much less intact than is commonly supposed. For one thing, there is a powerful centrifugal impulse towards devolved administration prompted by nationalist movements and aspirations in different parts of the country which cannot easily be ignored. For another, there is a certain shift towards continental Europe and significant areas of our national life are now governed by policies evolved not in London but in Brussels. These trends have been observed and discussed.

The great administrative reforms which took place in central and local government in the 1960's and 1970's and the steady increase in the number of public corporations during the past twenty years also constitute good reasons for introducing a new treatment of public administration at the present time. Changes like these reflect the dynamic and transitional nature of the subject and, indeed, change is one of the major themes of the book.

The other theme is permanence, for in the midst of all the natural and sometimes explosive adjustments to the changing needs of society, there is a constant core element which does not change. It is this element which gives to British public administration its unique and quintessential quality.

University of Strathclyde
1980

The same things come back, but under different names and colours.

Francesco Guicciardini

1
The nature of public administration

Beginnings

Searching for beginnings in a subject which is so characterised by change is difficult. Perhaps the most obvious point of departure is the land itself, for where nearly everything else has altered, the land mass has not. For as far back in time as one cares to go the land of Britain, for example, has remained much the same as it is now: an island off the continent of Europe fringed with numerous smaller islands. Thus it was when the Celts found it and so it was when the Romans came and later the Vikings and the Normans after them.

These occupiers cultivated Britain, made it their home and divided it up for easy government. The five Roman provinces, the Saxon kingdoms, the Norman counties, the shires, the parishes: all in their day served a basic purpose of setting boundaries within which common laws and usages could operate to establish civilised life styles under the control of a central power.

Today, the land areas of England, Scotland and Wales together with Northern Ireland form the United Kingdom, a country of some 56 million people, differentiated over standard regions[1] (and in numerous other groupings) under the supreme authority of Parliament at Westminster. The processes and procedures which help these united people to organise themselves and discipline their actions so as to live an ordered and prosperous existence are referred to as public administration.

This book begins by asking some basic questions: what does the term "public administration" mean? Is it worthy of study? Should it be distinguished from "private administration"? How and why is it studied? The characteristic features of public administration will now be examined.

It is by now a common assumption that administration is an important activity in modern industrial societies. This is an administrative age in

1 East Anglia, East Midlands, Northern, North-West, South-East, South-West, West Midlands, Yorkshire and Humberside, Scotland, Wales and Northern Ireland. These are also European Community regions.

which administration-as-an-activity confers undoubted benefits on society and affects the lives of all individuals. Unlike simpler societies, ours is dependent on organisations for such benefits. Each day products are consumed and materials and services (such as housing, electricity, health services and education facilities) provided by organisations which individuals could never hope to provide for themselves.

Each of us is an administrative person since a considerable part of our lives is spent in organisations. With some exceptions, we are born in organisations, educated in organisations and we die in organisations; the organisation is all-pervasive. Even if we escape membership of organisations, we are unlikely to escape their influence for they are part and parcel of our society: not for nothing have some writers chosen to call this the "Age of Organisation".

Organisations are so prominent in present society because they provide certain desirable services and commodities. But what are they? How are they constructed? What do they do? After investigating the distinguishing features of "administration" and "organisation" this chapter argues that the two are inter-linked.

Organisations

The following definition of organisations may be helpful: "organisations are social units deliberately constructed and re-constructed to seek specific goals". This definition highlights three important features of organisations. Firstly, they are social groupings. Although one-man organisations are often referred to in connection with small businesses in which the owner manages the business and performs the role of worker, organisations are normally considered to comprise groups of individuals working together to achieve some purpose.

Organisations are identified by their goals, thus, the term "hospital" is identified with the object of healing the sick, "prison", with the incarceration of people guilty of socially undesirable conduct and the "factory", with the production of goods in demand by society. These three organisations, selected at random from many, have certain features in common. They are not aimless collections of human beings; all exist with defined objects in view and all are constructed deliberately to achieve some social goal or objective.

The world of organisations is not clear-cut. Although organisations have a purpose, the exact nature of that purpose may be obscured or the original purpose of the organisation changed. Voluntary organisations often change their goals when their original goal is deemed to have been met. The American Veterans' Association, for example, set up to look after the welfare of US ex-Servicemen, has been obliged to widen its objectives to carry out broader social functions as the number of ex-Servicemen diminishes. Problems also arise when the question is asked "whose purpose is the organisation trying to achieve?" Disagreements over goals often arise between the owners of an organisation, its managers and the workers.

An important characteristic of organisations is that they are engaged on the rational pursuit of a goal, purpose or objective. The word "rational" here implies that organisations are a product of human reason since they are deliberately set up to pursue objectives. "Rational" can also imply that an effort will be made to build the organisation in such a way that its purposes are efficiently achieved. Organisations are expected to function efficiently by achieving their purpose at the least possible cost and with the best use of resources. In practice, however, the efficiency of organisations varies.

The second point is that organisations have a distinct structure. The term "organisation" suggests a high degree of co-operation between the individuals and groups within it. Indeed, an organisation in which co-operation is non-existent could hardly be described as an "organisation" at all. Co-operation is made easier by the use of a structure. This often takes the form of a "hierarchy of authority". A typical hierarchical structure is shown in *Fig. 1.*

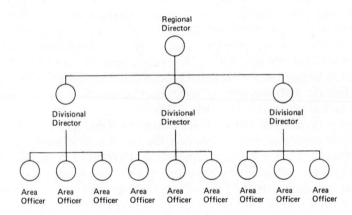

Fig. 1 A typical hierarchical structure in an organisation

The term "hierarchy" refers to a set of offices and office-holders in an organisation. Those situated at the top of the hierarchy in strategic positions (such as the regional director in *Fig. 1*) are considered to be the most important people within the organisation. Their important position in the hierarchy gives them key responsibility for taking decisions and giving orders within the organisation. They are thus able to give coherence and direction to the organisation by issuing commands and offering advice to those below them in the hierarchy.

"Organisation" also suggests an element of control which is essential for two reasons. Firstly, control is used to obtain the required degree of co-operation necessary for the achievement of goals. Secondly, it is necessary for supervising performance and assessing the success or failure of the organisation in achieving these goals.

The third point is that organisations do not work in isolation. The society in which they function is the environment which surrounds them. Thus, the organisation may be seen as importing men, materials and money from the environment and converting them into "outputs". In the case of manufacturing organisations, raw materials from the environment are processed into products. Schools may import the uneducated and turn out the educated; hospitals may import the sick and turn out the healthy. The importance of an organisation's "environment" is now widely recognised and this will be dealt with later.

Administration

Many words have a variety of meanings which can cause confusion, so it is extremely important to establish in which sense a particular term is being used. The word "bureaucracy", commonly used with reference to government and large private organisations, is a good example. It is commonly encountered in discussions about the failure of a particular organisation: an old age pensioner is prevented from receiving a pension payment one week at the Post Office because there is something minutely irregular about the way that he has signed the form; an applicant at a Department of Health and Social Security Office is referred to another government agency which, in turn, refers him back to the original office.

Everyone is familiar with personal examples of this kind of problem and is swift to condemn the organisation for its "bureaucracy" and "red-tape". One meaning of the word bureaucracy has thus become quite clearly identified in the public mind with slowness and inefficiency. Another very different meaning is used by social scientists to refer not to the negative consequences of all large organisations, but to a particular type of organisation (see Chapter 4).

Even more care must be taken with the word "administration". Andrew Dunsire suggests that there are at least 15 meanings of the word as it is commonly used. Two alternative meanings will be examined, since it is essential in the study of public administration to recognise these important differences in usage.

Dunsire shows that ambiguity surrounding the word is not new. "Administration" is, in origin, a Latin word and the Romans used it in two ways. The first suggests that "administration" occurs after a decision on policy has been taken, thus "policy" decisions are separate from "administrative" decisions. For example, a student may wish to travel cheaply from Scotland to France. Several choices clearly present themselves. He could fly, go by train/boat, car/boat, car/hovercraft, etc. Having investigated the cost and convenience of the various modes of transport by referring to airline tariffs and railway timetables, he may make a decision to travel by train/boat. In so doing he has formulated a policy for travelling which will serve his purposes.

Now, however, another decision must be made. The student's policy decision must be translated into administrative action. He must consider everything that must be done to enable him actually to travel to France; he must check that his passport is in order, purchase tickets and buy travellers' cheques or foreign currency. Finally, he must arrange things so that he can be at the station on the appointed day at the appropriate time. These are "administrative" acts.

The terms "policy" and "administration" in the above example are of key importance. "Policy" is being used to refer to decisions about goals or objectives. The student's decision to go to France was made according to a set of values. He may have wanted a holiday. Why France? He may prefer French snails to German sausages, or French culture to Scandinavian culture. **Policy-making**, in this sense, is about deciding on priorities and establishing preferences. The act of policy-making in the above example precedes the act of administration; there would be little point in purchasing a ticket before deciding upon a destination. "Administration" in this context can only take place after the act of decision.

"Administration" and "policy" must also be examined in an organisational setting. Decision-making, or establishing "policy" preferences is an inevitable part of organisational life. The view, expressed above, that organisations pursue goals implies that decisions are being taken. Someone must decide what goals are to be pursued and establish methods of judging the importance of those goals. However, a means to achieve those goals must also be established: a decision to sell more fridges and less television sets must be accompanied by the appropriate administrative machinery for carrying this decision into effect.

This first meaning of the term "administration" illustrates its relatively subordinate role in relation to "policy"; "administration" implies an element of serving. Policy-making in organisations is widely considered a more important function than the act of putting policy into effect. This is generally reflected in the higher status and salaries of policy-makers as compared with those of policy-executors (administrators). An important assumption has been made, namely that policy-making and administration are not only separate functions in organisations but they are also performed by separate groups of people.

The second use of the term "administration" challenges this assumption. It stresses that administration is not to be seen as a subordinate activity. The distinction can no longer be made between policy and administration as in the first usage; now the "administrator" is seen as someone who not only executes decisions taken by others, but is himself the source of much decision-making.

Used in this latter sense, "administration" refers not only to the means to be used to put decisions into effect, but to the aims of the policy itself. In fact, the term "administrator" is used to describe the key decision-making person in many organisational settings. In American hospitals, for example, the administrator is the head of the organisation and responsible for making many of the most important decisions about the way resources are to be used. Used in this way, the term "administration" is very close to "management": managers in organisations not only have to set up the machinery for putting decisions into effect; they are also the key decision-makers.

Why are definitions so important? The various uses of the term "administration" encourage one to consider the important problems which will recur in any survey of public administration. The way the subject is approached will depend upon which view of administration is adopted.

Administration and organisation

The connection between organisations and administration is significant. The analysis of administration and policy-making suggests that certain important activities are bound up with the notion of administration. The example of the trip to France suggests that administration is, in some sense, connected with the activity of decision-making. Whether the administrator plays a part in the decision-making process or merely executes decisions taken by others, the activity, "administration", implies that a decision has been taken.

In a complex industrial society such as ours, decisions which are often extremely complex and far-reaching have to be made. Everyone makes decisions but some people are clearly in far more important decision-making positions than others. Their decisions may affect the lives of communities and ultimately of the society itself. What is becoming more and more clear is that the vast bulk of important decision-making takes place within an organisational setting. Decisions to invest in a new industry may be taken by bankers and financiers in financial institutions in the City of London. Decisions to develop North Sea oil will be made by industrialists in large multi-national corporations. Decisions to develop a particular type of atomic reactor for the electricity industry will be taken by politicians and civil servants in the Department of Energy. These decisions will all be made within organisations. Increasingly, decisions are made in organisations rather than by individuals acting singly. Such decisions result in administrative activity since they need, at some stage, to be carried out.

"Organisation" and "administration" are thus inseparable; both are concerned with means and ends. Whichever meaning of the term "administration" is adopted, organisation provides the framework for administration in contemporary society. The following definition of administration is therefore appropriate:

Administration is the co-ordination of men and materials within organisations for the accomplishment of identifiable purposes.

The nature of "public" administration

As with "administration", the co-ordination of men and materials is also involved in the activity of "public administration". Like administration in private organisations, public administration is concerned with accomplishing "identifiable purposes". The differences and similarities between "public" and "private" organisations are dealt with later. This section simply outlines the meaning of the term "public".

There are two ways in which the term "public" can be used. Public administration is concerned with the purposes of society as a whole, as opposed to groups within it such as trade unions, businesses and the like. Public administration is concerned, therefore, with the purposes of the State.

The State is uniquely placed in a society: it operates in the name of the land and its people. In terms of policy and administration, it "possesses" a specialised group of people—the "Government"—who establish its priorities. The Government, therefore, can be said to provide policies for society aimed at establishing the goals or ends of that society whilst public administration is concerned with achieving them. Public administrators deal with the activities of the State as compared with private administrators who are concerned with the goals of non-State organisations.

This view of the Government and administrative system corresponds to the first of the two meanings of administration considered above. Here, administration is seen as a subordinate activity which comes after policy-making. Again, the assumption is that those carrying out the function of policy-making are separate from those carrying out the functions of administration. However, this is rather a dubious assumption.

The second sense of the term "public" does not contrast it with the term "private". This usage contrasts public with secret, or closed. Public, here, means open to scrutiny. This is a very important use of the term. The next chapter examines the environment of public organisations and the fact that many people believe that Government administration should be open to public view in a way that private organisations are not. One of the values affecting public administration is that of public accountability.

Public versus private

The link between administration and organisation has been shown, and the argument put forward that the two are inseparable. However, there are considerable differences between organisations. One important difference is widely held to be their public and private natures. It is commonly assumed, for example, that Government organisations differ from privately-owned organisations in certain respects. Often, but not invariably, Government organisations are contrasted poorly with non-Government organisations, and privately-owned organisations are widely viewed as being more efficient than publicly-owned ones.

Government organisations are often characterised as "bureaucratic"— the word being used in its derogatory sense. Privately-owned organisations are often seen as taking speedier and more effective decisions than their publicly-owned counterparts. The questions arising are: does administration really vary in private and public organisations? Do differences in ownership affect the way in which administration is conducted? Do differences in goals affect the administrative process within organisations?

Public and private: differences

The expressions "public sector" and "private sector" are now very commonplace. The first refers to a system of organisations concerned with achieving State purposes. Public sector organisations include Government Departments and nationalised industries, both the subjects of later chapters. There is tremendous variety within this sector. The term private sector, on the other hand, is used as a collective phrase referring to organisations which are neither State-owned, nor operating specifically to achieve State goals.

A popular view of the private organisation is that it is built on the enterprise of an individual or a family, the typical example of such an organisation being the business firm. Another linked view of such organisations is that they are headed by an entrepreneur, and ownership and control of the business are in his hands. Such a view of the business firm is much loved by classical economists, and whole industries are sometimes portrayed as being organised in this way. Competition takes place between the firms and as a result everybody benefits. Efficiency is rewarded and inefficiency is punished. Such a view of private business organisations is no longer appropriate; the day of the individual entrepreneur, with notable exceptions, is over. However, this model is a useful means of illustrating the widely reported differences between the public and the private sectors.

The first test of this difference is known as the **cui bono** test. This asks the question: who benefits from the organisation? Or, put another way, whose goals does the organisation serve? The main beneficiary of the firm which is headed by a single individual and financed by his money is the owner/manager. The owner usually invests time and effort in establishing a business in the hope of making a profit. Profit is seen as the main motivating force of a private enterprise economy. The administration of such a firm is concerned with the management of men, materials and the like, in such a way as to make it possible and practical to make a profit. Administration here is also concerned with the problem of "efficiency".

When the cui bono test is applied to the State organisations of the public sector, different results are obtained. For instance, it is difficult to recognise who the prime beneficiaries of many public sector organisations are. Is the prime beneficiary of the Department of Social Security the Minister in charge of it? Is it an individual applicant for welfare benefit at the counter of a local branch of the Department?

The prime beneficiary of any public organisation is the public-at-large: public organisations serve the public interest. Some writers have suggested that these organisations should be known as "commonweal" organisations to reflect this commitment to the general community. The question of what the organisation is doing also causes problems. Here, clear and interesting differences between the private and public organisation arise.

Publicly-owned organisations which together make up the public sector perform a wide variety of functions. For example, the Ministry of Defence provides the country with a nuclear defence capability which includes the manufacture of submarines and rockets and their subsequent deployment: it is a long way from this James Bond world to the counter of the local Post Office where the main concern of its employees may be the payment of State pensions, yet both are Government activities performed by public sector organisations. This variety is extremely important for, while some functions performed by such organisations resemble those run by individual owner-managers, many activities performed by public sector organisations are completely different.

An important difference between the public and the private sector organisation is shown by the emphasis on profit. Whilst it is relatively easy for the individual entrepreneur to assess the profitability of his enterprise, it will be difficult if not impossible for the public organisation to do this. How can the profitability of a nuclear submarine or a housing policy be measured? Other difficulties also emerge. The public organisation may have to take into account social costs which do not have to be faced by the private firm. The Government may have to provide costly, unprofitable services for the community, since their absence would involve social hardship for certain groups or dangers, such as the possibility of foreign invasion.

It is not true that profit tests can never be applied in government but the application of profit tests in some areas may be much more difficult than for the private firm. Although administration in public organisations may be concerned with questions of efficiency, it will have to deal with other factors which may override profit and efficiency goals. One of these factors is "public accountability".

Profit may be less important than ensuring that the organisation is controlled by the public through Parliament. Parliament wants to ensure not only that organisations are efficient, but also that they operate impartially, fairly, and with due regard to the wishes of those who are elected to control them. These demands will be borne in mind by those running such organisations, and greater consideration will be given to them than is the case in the private company.

Administration in the public organisation is inevitably much more complicated than in the private company. In the former, a constant process of adjustment must be made between the sometimes conflicting demands made upon it. Demands for fair treatment may conflict with demands for efficiency in the provision of services, and profitability is only one test among many of the way a public sector organisation is performing.

Private and public: similarities

Private businesses have tended to grow in size. The economy is dominated by large firms, and the process of ownership has become separate from the process of control. The owner-manager has become more rare, and the idea of an individual providing capital to finance the organisation has been replaced by the idea of capital being provided by large groups of shareholders. The "private" company has largely, though not completely, been replaced by the "public" company: that is, basically, a company whose money is raised through the Stock Exchange.

This change is extremely important. The individual owner or shareholding group can no longer be said to retain day to day working control of the organisation. Control has passed into the hands of professional managers who are skilled in the task of administration. Consequently, administration has become far more complex in private organisations and in their day to day running they have become more like public sector organisations.

New management groups have come to recognise that they, too, have wider responsibilities in society. Profit is still important in this type of organisation, but so, too, is the need to treat employees fairly and take account of the effect of the firm's activity on the community it serves and the environment in which it functions. Such objectives must be balanced against a goal of out-and-out pursuit of profit.

The point is this: any comparison of decision-making and administration in private organisations with the more complex public organisations such as Government Departments, shows that things may be much more complex in the private organisation than at first appears. In this sense, private and public organisations are more alike than might be imagined.

If private and public organisations have become more alike, this is not a one-way process. The private organisation has taken on some of the characteristics of the public sector organisation, but another process has also led to greater similarity between the two. In recent years there has been a popular call for the public sector to adopt methods and working practices akin to those used in private business. This process will be examined in greater detail in Chapter 7. The Conservative Government elected to office in 1970 was convinced that the public sector could, with advantage, import "business talent" from outside the Civil Service to enable more efficient running of important areas of public life. The previous Labour Government (1964–70) appointed the Fulton Committee to inquire into the methods and working of the Civil Service and it concluded that if the concept of profit was applied to parts of the Civil Service it would encourage greater efficiency.

Not quite Government, not quite private

Great changes have occurred in the nature and scope of Government work in the last 50 years. Before the era of the Welfare State, the role of Government in society was that of nightwatchman. This suggests that the function of Government was to provide the conditions in which private enterprise could flourish i.e. Government should be restricted to questions of external security (ensuring that the country was defended) and internal law and order (ensuring that peace and stability was secured).

Over the years, demands made by all groups in society for these activities to be extended resulted in two major changes. Firstly, Government has extended its activities directly. Government Departments have been set up to administer new areas of policy concerned with pensions, employment benefits, the National Health Service and the like. On the other hand, Government activity has also extended indirectly. This is particularly evident in the continuing attempts by Governments to control the level of economic activity in the country. Governments have extended control over the private sector by taxation policy, monetary policy and, recently, by the investment of money in private organisations in return for a say in the running and organisation of key firms such as British Leyland.

Public investment in private companies is extremely important, for the status of some organisations has become less clear-cut in the process. For example, it is no longer possible to describe organisations which are jointly owned by Government and private enterprise as wholly private. Similarly, some organisations in the public sector have been set up with a structure quite unlike that of the straightforward Government Department. They have a degree of independence from Parliamentary and Ministerial control over and above that of the traditional Department. Organisations which are difficult to classify as wholly private or wholly public can be classified as "quasi-private" or "quasi-public" (quasi meaning "not quite"), depending on how similar to the private or public organisation they are in structure and working. An example of a quasi-private organisation is British Leyland and an example of a quasi-public one is the British Tourist Authority.

This private/public distinction is important. Many writers have suggested that Government organisations and non-Government organisations have become more alike. They resemble each other in structure (both are "bureaucratic") and with Government deeply involved in many major private companies, public and private organisations have also come to have similar goals. Large private companies no longer pursue narrow, group interests but are, in a real sense, involved in the goals of the State. The phrase "what is good for British Leyland is good for Britain" is not hollow.

Politics and administration

While administration is an activity (or set of activities) which is carried out in both private and public organisations, public administration is different from administration in the private organisation. For example, administration in public organisations is subject to more political direction than in business.

Politics is concerned with the broad question of Government in society. The Government is entrusted with the function of establishing the values and priorities by which society is run. As such, the Government may be seen as the final authority in the State. In a democratic society, Government is given the authority in the name of the people, to lay down the rules and codes which govern our daily lives. Chapters 2 and 3 examine in greater detail the structure and working of the political process in Britain and the way in which codes and values are established. The point here is that administrative officials are subject to the overall control of the political Executive (Cabinet and Ministers) and the Legislature (Parliament). This greatly affects the administrative process within public organisations. Public administration is also open to public criticism. The public administrator must therefore *be seen* to be working fairly and openly within the law. This inevitably encourages a self-protective attitude on his part.

Earlier, a distinction was made between the two meanings of the term administration. One meaning implies that administrators simply provide the means for putting decisions into effect. This is called an instrumental view of administration. It is quite common for people to argue that such a view of administration is applicable to the organisations in the public sector. Administrative officials within that sector put into effect decisions made by important people, particularly MPs and Government Ministers. They make the decisions; the administrative staff then carry them out.

However, it is not really so easy to separate the roles of decision-maker and decision-applier, since politics and administration merge. This is interesting for it raises fundamental questions about the constitutional roles and responsibilities of civil servants who are key figures in the administrative process. While it is possible to separate the "political" from the "administrative" in theory, it becomes very much more difficult in practice.

This chapter concludes by exploring two questions. Firstly, how important is the system of public administration? Secondly, what are the parts which make up the administrative process and what values and expectations govern them?

The importance of public administration

The system of public administration in a country such as Britain is extremely important. The nature of Government activity has changed so that it now affects many aspects of our daily lives. Government Departments alone are responsible for controlling a total public expenditure of £58 000 million. This accounts for 53% of the gross national product.

The increase in Government functions alone is very noticeable, but other important questions arise in the analysis of public administration which go to the very heart of our democratic way of life. Civil servants, for example, are not elected, yet they greatly control the way in which we live. Analysis of public administration cannot be confined to a description of the organisations which make up the public sector. It inevitably involves questions of control, accountability and openness, and a study of public administration will provide an insight into questions like these.

Public service organisations are not to be seen as separate and isolated; they form part of a complex system of administration. Thus, certain central Departments exert influence over local authorities, local authorities exert influence over central Departments, advisory bodies work closely with Government Departments and so on. (The nature of many of these relationships will be made clearer in later chapters). A brief statement about the respective roles of each of these types of organisation will provide a useful background to further analysis.

Central administration

Departments of State

The Government Department is, without doubt, the most important unit of administration at central government level. It is also the oldest; some Departments may be traced back hundreds of years. Departments—or Ministries as they are sometimes called—are headed by members of Parliament (either Lords or Commons) holding a Ministerial appointment. The Ministerial head of the Department exercises control over the Department either directly, or indirectly through a board of appointed officials (e.g. the Board of Customs and Excise, the Board of Inland Revenue).

The Department is the main administrative agency of the State at central government level. The system of Departments has grown up over a long period of time and reflects historical changes which have taken place in the nature and scope of Government functions. (See Chapter 5.)

Advisory bodies

These, as the name implies, exist for the purpose of offering advice to Ministers on particular problems or areas of administration. They are loosely attached to Departments. The National Economic Development Council and the Advisory Committee on the Supply and Training of Teachers are two examples of such bodies.

Non-Departmental or ad hoc agencies

This covers a wide variety of bodies—a complex assortment of organisations. Some of these are national in scope, as is the Countryside Commission, and others, like the Scottish Tourist Board, are not. One of the most important features of the ad hoc body is that it has a degree of autonomy or independence from direct Ministerial control. However, such freedom as they possess can cause difficulties within the administrative system.

The most important single group of organisations within this ad hoc category is the nationalised industries. (These are examined in more detail in Chapter 13.) Such organisations are most interesting because they operate commercial services; they may be described as quasi-public organisations. The success of such agencies is judged partly on the basis of profit, and they are deliberately constructed so as to function largely as a business.

Local administration

Few societies operate through a completely "centralised" administrative system. In democratic societies, the demands for some form of local administration are widespread and, by now, traditional. Central government is often characterised as remote and inaccessible. Indeed, "centralism", like "bureaucracy", has distinctly unpopular connotations.

Local administration can assume different forms. "Deconcentrated" administration refers to a system in which, though the responsibility for administration rests with central government, convenience demands that important decision-making and administrative action is made in local offices, or regional centres. Departments such as the Department of Health and Social Security maintain a network of local offices which process claims for health benefit and supplementary benefit. Some of the ad hoc bodies mentioned above also maintain local and regional offices, for example, the Post Office.

"Decentralised" administration, on the other hand, is largely independent of direct central control. The staff of a decentralised unit of administration are separate from the staff of central government. Moreover, the decentralised organisation is not the mere instrument of national Government. The most important form of decentralised administration in this country at present is local government. Local government organisations provide a large number of services to society, such as social work, education and cleansing. The local administrative officials are responsible—in a way that the local representatives of central government organisations are not—to locally elected, "lay" politicians. Local government is an important part of democratic self-government.

Values and expectations

The above represent some of the most important organisations which, together, make up the system of public administration in Great Britain. Each will be considered in more detail throughout the book. This chapter concludes with a reminder of the context within which public administration is conducted.

a) The prime function of public administration is service to the public and safeguarding the public interest.

b) The public administrator's discretion and freedom of action is limited. Much more than in business, the public administrator is subject to laws and regulations designed to prevent abuse or misuse of power.

c) The criteria for judging success and failure are not clear-cut. No simple test of efficiency by itself is sufficient.

d) The public administrator is constantly in the public eye.

e) The concepts of fairness, justice, and impartiality are extremely important limitations on the activity of public officials.

f) The public administrator works for, with, and under the direction of politicians.

These important "environmental" factors will be discussed in Chapters 2 and 3.

Suggestions for further reading

A Dunsire, *Administration: The Word and the Science,* Martin Robertson, 1973
A Etzioni, *Modern Organisations,* Prentice Hall, 1964
A N Gladden, *A History of Public Administration,* Frank Cass, 1972
A H Hanson and M Walles, *Governing Britain,* Fontana, 1976
J Stanyer, *Understanding Local Government,* Fontana, 1976

Questions

1 Define "administration".
2 What is an organisation?
3 Identify the so-called public sector.
4 Apply the cui bono test to the British Museum.
5 What is the main function of public administration?

2
The environment and the public sector

The environment

Public administration comprises a set of activities and organisations concerned with achieving the major purposes of the State acting on society's behalf. As such, public administration does not operate in a vacuum; on the contrary, these activities and organisations are deeply imbedded in the social and cultural environment. The cultural norms and values of society limit the activities of public officials and the methods which they can adopt to pursue their goals.

The importance of the environment of public administration has recently been outlined by two American writers:

"It is from the environment that the public administrator perceives the problems to be resolved, the alternative possibilities within which choices can be made, the resources to be employed, and the support and opposition to policies and programmes. Further, within the environment are found the clients to be served or regulated, the market forces which establish the costs for the goods and services produced by government, special interest groups that have a particular concern about what the public administrator does, and other public and private institutions that may offer support or opposition. Finally, it is within the environment that the consequences of public administration are to be judged 'right' or 'wrong' ".[1]

The environment of public administration in Britain is an issue which has long interested students of organisation. The question is: how is the administration to be made accountable to the people it is supposed to serve? One of the most influential social thinkers of recent years—Max Weber, a German sociologist—devoted considerable attention to this question. He was interested in the relationship between public officials— "bureaucrats" as they are sometimes known—and the elected politician who, in theory, controls the system of government and represents the interests of the community.

1 Ivan L Richardson and Sidney Baldwin, *Public Administration*, Columbus, Charles Merrill, 1976, p.24.

This question has been considered by many writers since Weber wrote at the beginning of the century, which suggests that it is still of great significance. Indeed, as recently as 1977, a sub-committee of the prestigious House of Commons Expenditure Committee investigated in detail questions relating to the influence of public officials over elected politicians. The power and influence of public "servants" is a favourite topic of discussion amongst students of Government administration.

That this debate goes on at all is a healthy sign that democracy in Britain is being safeguarded. The view attributed to the Labour politician Douglas Jay that "the man in Whitehall knows best"—that we can safely leave decision-making to the civil servants in London—is not a view shared by many people in Britain. The so-called "man in the street" is wise to distrust the "bureaucracy", though too much suspicion of public officials can be as destructive of democracy as too little.

It has been said that the price to be paid for democracy is eternal vigilance. People must be constantly on their guard to safeguard basic freedoms—freedom of speech, freedom of assembly and the like. Public administration must therefore be subject to restrictions and limitations.

Public administration—the democratic background

Most books on British government suggest that Britain is a democratic country. Government is subject to a high degree of control by the citizens, takes into account public opinion and does not act in an arbitrary manner towards the individual or minority groups in society. Commentators on British politics generally agree that for a long time British society has been based on an agreed set of values about the way Government should make decisions and how they should be administered. At the time of writing, there is less confidence that these are enduring characteristics of society.

Until fairly recently, political debate and administrative activity have both taken place in British society within a cultural setting which has encouraged the search for peaceful ways of resolving disputes and settling differences. A set of political ideals has developed which has placed a high value on the virtues of representative and responsible government.

In 1963 two American political scientists, G Almond and S Verba[2], carried out a detailed examination of attitudes towards government in Great Britain and compared them with those of other countries in Europe and the Americas. They found a high degree of "trust relations" in Britain—a widespread belief amongst citizens that the Government could be relied upon to act in a restrained and responsible way and, importantly, that the Civil Service was a body of public officials attentive to the wants of the public and responsive to their reasonable demands for service. Professor Samuel Finer has argued that this indicated widespread agreement about the way government should be conducted in Britain. In other

2 G Almond and S Verba, *The Civic Culture*, Princetown University Press, 1963.

words, there was a belief that the institutions of Government served the population reasonably well.

Professor Finer's assessment, written in 1970, appears on initial consideration to have been rendered outdated by events. Pressure for devolution has gained momentum since he wrote, and widespread criticism has been directed, over the last decade, to the organisation of central and local administration. Certain individuals and groups hold that the electoral process—arguably the foundation of a democratic system—is unjust and consistently discriminates against minor parties.

However, the basic integrity of democracy in Britain is not being attacked with a view to introducing a completely different form of government. All the reforms and proposals which have been put forward since the 1960's have been aimed at improving the system. Even the most radical arguments, for example, for the separation of parts of the United Kingdom and the establishment of devolved Assemblies in Scotland and Wales could be seen as ultimately resulting in the greater effectiveness of the democratic political system of the British Isles.

The question: "what is democracy?" is important. A related question is: "how does democracy affect the working of public administration?" Broadly speaking, government in Britain operates in a framework of general consent and agreement which may be described as democratic. "Democracy" is a very slippery idea: it can be defined in many ways and there is argument about whether, in practice, it exists at all. Nevertheless, democracy implies the following assumptions:

Representativeness

This characteristic feature of democracy implies that the wishes of the people are reflected in the decisions taken in their name. In a large modern system of government—such as that in Britain—it is not possible for every member of the society to take part in the decision-making process. Hence "representatives" must be chosen—by election—to govern on behalf of the mass of the population. Parliament is the supreme representative body in the British system of government.

Responsibility

This aspect of a democratic political system is particularly relevant to an understanding of public administration in Britain.

Political office-holders are not only representative of the public because they have been elected by them, they are also responsible to the public; they can regularly be held to account for their supervision of the country's political affairs. If "representativeness" implies that the decisions taken by political office-holders are broadly in line with the view of the community, then "responsibility" implies that they can be held to account for their stewardship of the nation's affairs.

The political office-holders are thus responsible for the administration of policies once they have been decided, and they are also responsible for the activities of civil servants and other public officials over whom they have control. In this way, the administration of the country is held accountable to the electorate through its politically elected heads. This value—responsibility—binds the public administrative system to Parliament. The electorate is sovereign; it has final, if indirect, control over the public officials who exercise authority in its name.

These two principles, representativeness and responsibility, form the basis of a system of democratic government. Democracy, responsible and representative, is a system in which the ordinary people, through their representatives, may influence and ultimately control what public administrators do.

Constitutionalism and the rule of law

No democracy can function without limits being placed on the activities of political and administrative office-holders. Constitutionalism implies that no Government or set of officials can alter either the basic "rules of the game" or the principles of government on which the State and society function, without reference to the electorate. Politicians and officials must be prevented from acting in an arbitrary and dictatorial manner.

Similarly, the so-called rule of law ensures that the same office-holders do not act as judge and jury in their own cause. The powers of Government are conditioned by law. In a democracy the Courts play an important role in judging the legality or illegality of political and administrative action. In a recent case[3] the Courts overturned the Secretary of State's decision to direct a local authority to introduce comprehensive education on the grounds that correct legal procedure had not been observed.

In any system of government, a **Constitution** is a set of codes or rules governing the distribution of powers and duties between its various parts. The Constitution defines the relationships which exist between the parts of Government and the public. Consideration of the workings of the Constitution is therefore the first step in a more detailed examination of the various organisations which together make up "Government".

A distinction must be made between countries having a written Constitution and those having an unwritten Constitution. A written Constitution is one which is contained in one or a small number of documents. Amendment of such a document is made deliberately difficult—the Constitution acts as the basic guarantor of individual rights and lays down the fundamental rules within which Government should operate. Usually, a special amendment procedure is available, ensuring that widespread agreement is reached before constitutional change is made. Written Constitutions provide for the Constitution to be interpreted by a court specially designed for the purpose. America has a written Constitution which is subject to interpretation in this way by the Supreme Court.

3   The Secretary of State for Education versus Tameside Metropolitan Borough.

In a strict sense, Britain does not have a written Constitution. No one document lays down the basic powers and obligations of the Government or outlines the rights and duties of individual citizens. However, neither is Britain's Constitution completely unwritten. Identifiable—codified— constitutional rules are contained in various statutes. Admittedly, the sources of Britain's Constitution are various:

Statutes

Acts of Parliament are an important source of constitutional practice. This is especially true of certain outstanding legislative enactments, for example, Magna Carta 1215, Bill of Rights 1688, Franchise Act 1832.

Conventions

These are rules which do not have the force of law, but nevertheless are considered binding. They are usually supported by custom and public opinion. It is a convention that if a Minister disagrees with an aspect of Government policy, but chooses not to resign, he will not make his disagreement public.

Judicial precedent

The Courts of law have an important part to play in interpreting Parliamentary statutes. Legal decisions taken in Court cases are one way of establishing precedents which will bind future behaviour.

Informed advice

Certain books on the Constitution have become "authorities" on constitutional practice and are widely consulted. One of the most celebrated of these for many years was A V Dicey's *Law of the Constitution.*

One of the most interesting features of British constitutional practice is its flexibility. The absence of a special amendment procedure in a written constitutional format means that if arrangements are found to be no longer suitable they can be changed by the same processes as for any relatively minor piece of legislation. Parliament could alter the composition of the House of Commons or the House of Lords, for example, in much the same way that it could legislate for motorway improvement schemes or bring in a Bill banning hare-coursing. The passage of the Life Peerages Act in 1958 was just such a measure.

Although Britain may be said to lack a formal, written, codified Constitution, constitutional government is well established in this country. This may appear to be something of a paradox, for surely, the rights of the individual cannot be adequately safeguarded in the absence of such a document setting out the limitations on Government? In fact, the strength of British Government has rested to date on the seeming willingness of members of the Government, civil servants and local politicians to abide by the principles of democratic government without the imposition of a formal document. This raises an important point. Constitutionalism is as much psychological as mechanical. The constitutional framework of the USSR illustrates this point.

The Soviet Union has a written Constitution which, on paper, seems to provide for the most democratic system of government in the world. The individual rights of the citizen are safeguarded by an extremely complex set of constitutional controls. The power of Government is confined by a variety of rules and prohibitions. However, the Constitution of the Soviet Union does little to safeguard the rights of the citizen. The absence of a written constitutional document may indicate a mechanical failure in the British system to prevent the illegitimate use of power by the Government, but there is strong psychological support for the ends which constitutional-ism should serve.

The British Constitution will not necessarily remain for all time without a single written codified document. From time to time arguments are put forward in favour of a codified Bill of Rights setting out the limitations on Government in relation to individual liberty. Some commentators have suggested that we are gradually but inevitably abandoning the mutually agreed constitutional procedure which has served us so well for so long. Again, the movement towards devolution which may result in Parliament sharing power with National Assemblies in Scotland and Wales, will inevitably result in the need for a codification of their functions and pow-ers. In the celebrated Dimbleby lecture on television in 1976, Lord Hail-sham argued forcibly for the introduction of a written Constitution "which limits the powers of Parliament and provides a means of enforcing those limitations both by political and by legal means". Only time will tell if this course will be justified by events.

Power, authority, legitimacy

Elected politicians and permanent officials make decisions and carry them out in the name of society. Various means are available to them to ensure that people abide by them.

Power

This is one means by which individuals or groups may be forced to comply with the wishes of the Government. Compliance may be achieved—sometimes inspite of resistance—by the use or threat of physical force and the imposition of strong sanctions. The Government can (and under certain circumstances does) use force to achieve its goals. Indeed, the State is sometimes defined as an important social group with the sole right to use force or violence within a given territory to achieve its ends.

Authority

Power, in the sense just described, is merely one way to achieve compliance with the wishes of the Government. An alternative means of social regulation is authority. Instead of using force or violence people are persuaded that persons "in authority" have the right to make decisions binding upon the community. The advantage of achieving obedience in this way is that the individual does not need to be forced into accepting the decisions of the Government; he will comply of his own accord.

Much is therefore to be gained from basing a system of decision-making and execution on authority rather than coercion. So long as people feel a sense of obligation to a Government they need not be bullied or threatened which can be costly, requiring a militia and sometimes a secret police force. For this reason, even the most dictatorial political system will attempt to use authority as an alternative to force. Authority can be regarded as a particular type of power, based on influence or persuasion. The defining characteristic of authority is that it is based on legitimacy.

Legitimacy

Legitimacy is conferred on Government and administration when the population considers that political and administrative office-holders exercise authority according to accepted cultural values, in a framework of custom, convention, and law. From the moment when legitimacy is conferred upon those in decision-making and decision-executing positions, their actions carry authority.

Legitimacy and authority are of key importance in a democratic political system. The term "democracy" implies the consent of the governed, so Government must be considered legitimate by them. No democracy could last for long if all disputes and issues were resolved by force and violence. "Democracy" suggests the existence of authority and its twin, legitimacy.

Advice and consent

These two words sum up what has been said about democracy so far. Responsibility, representativeness, legitimacy, authority: these principles of democratic government mean that the decision-makers in society will keep in communication with the governed. Elections ensure that the decision-makers are responsible to the electorate for their actions and their decisions: the consent of the governed is essential. Secondly, consultation precedes and, if necessary, follows the making of decisions. In Britain, consultation with "interested" individuals and groups likely to be affected by the decisions of politicians and officials, is a firmly established practice.

British public administration—its surrounding values

"Public" administration in a democratic society must operate within a framework of restraints. The following are some of the most important.

1 *Public administration must operate legally.* Constitutionalism demands that public officials do not act outside the law. Public administration, in fact, works within a strict legal framework and within a set of well-established constitutional practices or conventions. The Courts can decide the legality or illegality of the activities of administrative agencies and will act to prevent abuse of the law.

2 *Public administration must be accountable.* In practice, this means that the appointed official must be subject to the overall political control of the elected representative. A Permanent Secretary of a Government Department, for example, is reponsible to his Minister. The actions of officials are thus subject to political control and direction: officials can be held accountable for their actions by the electorate through their elected representatives.

3 *Public administration must treat the public reasonably.* Public administrators are expected to avoid taking retrospective decisions—decisions, for example, which have the effect of penalising the public for past behaviour. They are also expected to treat individual members of the public fairly without showing special favour to one at the cost of another.

4 *Public administration must be efficient.* It may not be apparent why democracy should require efficiency. Indeed, many people believe that democracy is not a particularly efficient form of government and administration. However, democratic government has occasionally dealt extremely efficiently with major problems and crises; British democratic institutions proved themselves the equal of Nazi Germany during the Second World War. No democratic society could tolerate inefficiency for long for fear that its critics might urge the adoption of more dictatorial methods of running the country.

5 *Public administration must be responsive to public demands.* In other words, it must encourage consultation and, to a degree at least, participation. The Civil Service has been criticised (possibly unjustly) for negligence in this respect.

6 *Public administration must be conducted with a degree of openness.* "Public" administration cannot expect to command the respect of the population if it is carried out behind closed doors. Administration, like justice, must not only be done; it must be seen to be done.

Despite the fact that these values are all important and should be the foundation upon which any democratic system of administration is based, not every administrative act on the part of officials will adhere to them. For instance, there will be occasions when one or more of the values will have to be abandoned in the interest of good administration. The value of openness causes particular problems.

In recent years many people have been in favour of opening up the process of central administration to outside critical review. Supporters of greater openness in government have argued that the time is ripe for amendment of the notorious Section 2 of the Official Secrets Act which forbids civil servants to pass information to outside parties. In the USA, the recently passed Freedom of Information Act has made access to the workings of government easier for the scholar and interested member of the public. In this country, the Government has so far remained hostile to any suggestion that the internal activities of Government Departments should be open to outside scrutiny. While critics of British practice are justified in condemning the sometimes obsessive desire to carry on administration in private, there is little doubt that, for example, in delicate negotiations with a foreign power, confidentiality may be essential for success.

This illustrates the difficulty of pressing principles to their logical conclusion. Excessive legalism would make it impossible for civil servants to take decisions quickly. Again, some of the principles pursued to their logical end are somewhat inconsistent with one another. The need to consult freely before a decision is taken, obviously cannot be pushed to the point where the attempt to involve all interested parties in the decision-making process conflicts with the need to take that decision quickly and efficiently.

Public administration in a democratic society is subject to pressures and constraints which may sometimes conflict. The job of the administrator, in such a situation, is surely to balance the conflicting pressures in the hope of satisfactorily resolving the problem. Herbert Simon, a thoughtful commentator on public administration and the workings of organisations suggested that in this messy world, the administrator cannot spend his time looking for the best possible solution to puzzles—he is often in the position of having to seek the solution which will provide him with the least undesirable outcome.

Suggestions for further reading

S E Finer, *Comparative Government*, Allen Lane: Penguin Press, 1970
Sir I Jennings, *The Law and the Constitution*, ULP, Latest edition
G Marshall and G C Moodie, *Some Problems of the Constitution*, Hutchinson, 1959
S A de Smith, *Constitutional and Administrative Law*, Penguin, 1977

Questions

1   What is meant by "the rule of law"?
2   State the sources of the British Constitution.
3   Why must the study of central government concern itself with "values"?
4   Differentiate between power and authority.

3
Public administration: the institutional setting

Central administration

The preceding chapters have shown that in a democracy public administrators are, or should be, subject to the overall control of politicians. How can we ensure that appointed officials are made properly accountable for their actions? In practice, this is achieved by links established between administrative officials and important political and legal institutions at the centre of our democratic system of government. In addition, officials are influenced by public opinion, the press and organised interest groups. This chapter considers the way in which some of these influences are brought to bear on the administrative system. It begins with an analysis of central administration.

The Government and Cabinet

Without doubt, the most important political/administrative relationship at central government level is that between Ministers and civil servants. Understanding this relationship is crucial to an understanding of the way in which officials are held accountable for their actions. Within the British system of government executive powers—those concerned with policy-making and policy-execution—rest with the Prime Minister and his Ministerial colleagues who make up the "Government".

Within the Government is the Cabinet, a body established by convention and chosen by the Prime Minister. The Cabinet is composed of senior Ministers and is the most important body in the political/administrative system. It has two main functions; firstly, it decides on policy questions and establishes the main aims and priorities of the Government. Secondly, it co-ordinates the work of the permanent Executive—the Civil Service.

The key political offices in the Government are occupied by Ministers. The most important of these is the Prime Minister. Like much else in

British government, the office of Prime Minister developed as a result of convention and constitutional practice rather than by statute. Little more than 200 years old, it is an extremely important position. The Prime Minister is chosen by the Sovereign as the person most likely to be able to form a Government. Usually the choice is an obvious one, based upon the person's command of a party majority in the House of Commons as the result of winning a majority of Parliamentary seats in a general election. In exceptional circumstances where no clear party majority exists the Sovereign may have to make a difficult personal choice thereby risking getting involved in party politics. In a constitutional Monarchy like Britain's, however, it is now well established practice that the Monarch remains aloof from politics.

It was once fashionable to argue that in relation to the other members of a Government, the Prime Minister was "primus inter pares". This implied that he was more or less equal in status with them. Now, however, there has been a re-assessment of his constitutional position. No longer considered merely the "first among equals", he is viewed as having power and prestige akin to that of an American President. His influence rests on his leadership and control of the majority party in the Commons and on his power of "patronage". He may reward members of his party with high Ministerial office; he can choose and dismiss members of the Government; and he can control and direct the deliberations of the Cabinet.

The Prime Minister is at the top of a hierarchy of Ministers. Although, as stated, Ministers hold political office within a Government, distinctions must be made between them. Firstly, while most Ministers preside over Government Departments, not all do. The most important Government Ministers e.g. the Chancellor of the Exchequer, the Home Secretary, the Secretary of State for Education, the Lord Chancellor and so on, are in charge of the most prestigious Government Departments and are assisted by 'junior' Ministers—Parliamentary Secretaries, Parliamentary Under-Secretaries, or Ministers of State. Experience in junior Government posts is generally a requirement for future promotion to full Ministerial rank.

In addition to Departmental Ministers every Government has a number of "Ministers without portfolio". Such Ministers—for example the Chancellor of the Duchy of Lancaster, the Lord Privy Seal and the Paymaster General—are free from Departmental responsibility. They are thus able to perform duties of a general nature; carrying out special tasks for the Prime Minister or playing a valuable co-ordinating role between Departments.

The second important distinction to be made between Ministers is whether or not they hold Cabinet office. As already noted, the Cabinet is at the very pinnacle of the system of government and administration in Britain. Membership of the Cabinet is accordingly highly sought after by Ministers, who will try to convince the Prime Minister that they should be included in it. Claims to inclusion will be varied. Some Ministers may be old, trusted, close political friends of the Prime Minister and may consider that their past contributions to the party should be rewarded. Others may insist that their Departments are carrying out more important work than some.

Such pressures must be considered by the Prime Minister in choosing a Cabinet. He or she will undoubtedly reward some individuals with Cabinet status for services rendered or in recognition of their political importance. However, while seeking to accommodate the claims of Ministers, the Prime Minister will undoubtedly be affected by contrary influences limiting Cabinet size. Cabinets, like all committees, must be kept relatively small if they are to function effectively as decision-making bodies. As a result, some Ministers will be included and some left out.

Some Ministers are almost certain of a place in the Cabinet. The Chancellor of the Exchequer will normally be included, as will the Home Secretary. In addition, Ministers holding certain other important "portfolios" are usually present in a Cabinet—the Ministers of Defence, Education, Foreign Affairs and so on. Other Ministers may be included depending on whether the work of their Departments is deemed to be of particular significance to the main policy aims of the Government at a particular time. Finally, it has become customary to include in the Cabinet certain Ministers without portfolio referred to previously.

Collective Ministerial responsibility

So far as the administrative official is concerned, the most significant feature of the system of Cabinet government is that it is conducted within a framework of important conventions. The first of these is that of collective responsibility. This means that all members of the Government are responsible as a body to the House of Commons for the Government's successes and failures. Collective responsibility implies that all Ministers—not just those in the Cabinet—must defend the Cabinet's actions and refrain from openly criticising it. Two important consequences follow from this. A Government losing the support of the House of Commons—as with the vote of no-confidence passed against James Callaghan's Government in March 1979—must resign as a body. In addition, collective responsibility means that no individual Minister or group of Ministers may dissociate themselves from Cabinet policy while remaining within the Cabinet. If Ministers are in dispute with the Prime Minister or with other Cabinet members and wish to criticise their actions they must resign. Hugh Gaitskell and Harold Wilson are twentieth century examples of Ministers who have taken this course of action.

Individual Ministerial responsibility

The second convention of Cabinet government is that of individual Ministerial responsibility. According to this convention, Ministers are responsible to Parliament as individuals for their personal conduct and, in the case of those presiding over Departments, for the actions of their officials. Ministers are responsible for personal political misbehaviour and may be censured by the House of Commons. In the post-war Labour Government of 1945–51 Hugh Dalton, the Chancellor of the Exchequer, was forced to resign his Cabinet post for revealing the contents of a budget speech to waiting journalists before delivering it to the House of Commons. This was considered an important breach of political etiquette. In 1963 John Profumo, a Cabinet Minister in Harold Macmillan's Conservative Government, was forced to resign for deceiving the House of Commons on a matter concerning his alleged sexual misconduct.

A second aspect of the doctrine of individual Ministerial responsibility is equally significant. Ministers may be held to account for the actions of civil servants in their Departments. Mismanagement of the work of a Department by these officials may lead to the direct questioning of the Minister by Members of Parliament. Thus a Minister may be forced to answer questions in the House on matters arising from seemingly trivial issues. An applicant for social security, for example, may complain to an MP that he has been rudely treated by a civil servant in the local office of the Department of Health and Social Security. If the MP feels that it warrants public attention he may be able to force the Minister to defend and explain the actions of the official in the House. The advantages of such a system of accountability for the citizen are obvious. Firstly, grievances against the abuse or misuse of administrative power can be put right. Secondly, it ensures that civil servants are subject to the discipline of continuous public scrutiny.

Ministerial responsibility has one important advantage for the civil servant. It may protect him from unfair criticism. By tradition, the civil servant is not publicly "named and blamed" for administrative failure; he remains anonymous. The Minister must take ultimate responsibility and will often act as spokesman for his civil servants in the House of Commons. However, a civil servant deemed guilty of causing embarrassment to the Minister through incompetence or indiscretion may be subject to pressures and disciplinary action by superiors within his Department. In return for the protection of anonymity, civil servants are expected to serve the Minister faithfully and offer him impartial advice, whatever Government is in power. In this respect, the doctrine of anonymity has encouraged a strong tradition of political impartiality on the part of British civil servants—unlike some of their counterparts overseas.

The role of Parliament

Examination of the convention of Ministerial responsibility would not be complete without considering the place of Parliament in the political/administrative system. Although the term "Parliament" refers to a combination of the Monarch, House of Lords and House of Commons, it is the role of the latter which is significant in understanding the influence of elected politicians over permanent officials.

As already stated, Ministers may have to answer for the activities of their civil servants in the House of Commons. MPs may question Ministers firstly by means of Question Time. This is a period of one hour during the Parliamentary day when MPs may address questions directly to Ministers on matters for which they are responsible. The threat of a question by an MP to a Minister is not taken lightly within his Department.

Parliamentary scrutiny of Executive activity is achieved secondly by means of the adjournment debate. This is held at the end of each Parliamentary day and before each Parliamentary vacation. It provides an MP with the opportunity to raise issues.

Thirdly, the device of the select committee is widely considered to be the most effective means the House possesses for scrutinising the work of the Government and permanent administration. Select committees, made up of small numbers of MPs are appointed to report to the House on specific matters. Two of the most important of these committees are the Public Accounts Committee and the Expenditure Committee. The first, assisted by the Comptroller and Auditor General, examines the accounts of Government Departments to make sure that expenditure authorised by Parliament has been carried out by Ministers and administrative officials in the way intended. The second committee examines the implications of Ministerial policies and assesses the success of Departments in achieving their objectives. Both provide important checks on bureaucratic mismanagement.

Recently, the ability of Parliament to scrutinise and control the activities of Ministers and officials has been challenged. Several reasons for this failure have been suggested. Firstly, the volume, scope and complexity of Government activity has increased over the years. Increasing pressures and demands from the citizen for better health and social services, improved educational opportunities, guaranteed jobs and so on, has led successive Governments to involve themselves more and more in the economy and to take over responsibilities previously in the hands of private individuals and groups.

Such expansion in the scope of Government activity has been matched by the growing complexity of Government activity. The Government's involvement in high technology industry, for example, has meant that Ministers and civil servants are themselves involved in much more complicated decision-making than was the case a century ago; decisions requiring highly specialised and technical knowledge. To monitor such decision-making effectively the individual Minister requires similar specialist knowledge and information which he often does not have.

The second point is that as Government activities have increased in scope and complexity, the power of the Government—and indirectly the power of the Civil Service—has also increased. The British Constitution is built upon the idea that Parliament (in practice, the House of Commons) is supreme. This supremacy results from Parliament's three traditional powers; the power to legislate or make law, the power to grant or withhold money from the Executive, and the power to debate and criticise Government proposals. In theory, Cabinets and Ministers are vulnerable to the power of the Commons. They must seek its approval if legislation designed to put their policies into effect is to be passed. They must ask Parliament to approve the allocation of money to finance their programmes and they must justify their actions in the face of Parliamentary criticism.

However, the days when the House of Commons might seriously have been said to "control" Governments by voting against their proposals or withholding money from them are long since over. Far from being controlled by the Commons, the Government now effectively controls the House by two important measures. Although Governments depend upon a majority in the House of Commons in order to survive, they can normally rely on majority support through the party system and the threat of Parliamentary dissolution. The first method gives them strong disciplinary powers over individual MPs. If MPs fail to "toe the party line" they may be denied party support—an essential factor in many cases for electoral success. Secondly, a Prime Minister and Cabinet faced with the prospect of defeat in the Commons may threaten to dissolve Parliament and bring about a General Election. This is a constant reminder to MPs that Government defeat in the House may bring about their own defeat in the country. Effective control of a Parliamentary majority gives a Government such power over the proceedings and activities of the House of Commons that critics have pointed to the growing importance of "Executive dominance".

The third point is that whilst the complexity of Government business and the power of the Executive has grown, little has been done to adapt Parliamentary procedures to enable it to keep abreast of these developments.

MPs and commentators on the British system of government have increasingly argued that it is essential to improve the means by which the House of Commons can have more effective oversight over Ministers and permanent officials. There is now widespread agreement that the traditional devices of Question Time and the adjournment debate are no longer an effective means for scrutinising Executive activities.

Many critics have argued that a shift has occurred in the balance of power between the House of Commons, Ministers and civil servants since the end of the Second World War. In an effort to counteract such tendencies various proposals have been put forward for Parliamentary reform. Probably the most important of these was the attempt in the 1960's to strengthen the committee system of the House. During that decade select committees on Science and Technology, Agriculture, Fisheries and Food, and on Education, Scottish Affairs and Overseas Aid were established. The theory behind such a change was that relatively small groups of MPs with a specialised interest in particular areas of Government policy would be able to subject Ministers to closer examination and inquiry than was possible in debates and questions on the floor of the House.

Inspite of such changes, many argue that the committees have only partly increased the ability of MPs to question and criticise Ministers and civil servants. Consequently the imbalance in power between the Executive and the Commons has not been corrected. In November 1977, for example, Neil Kinnoch MP argued in *The Guardian* that the committee system should be further strengthened.

The power of the Civil Service

The growth in power and influence of Governments has already been indicated. While many people criticise the fact that the power of Government Ministers has increased in relation to the Commons, they are even more anxious about the dominating role played in the system of government by civil servants. The pressures and demands of the electorate for the extension of Government activities have not only strengthened the position of the political Executive but have also led to an increase in the power and influence of permanent officials.

Chapter 1 suggested that a common view of politics and administration is that politicians make important policy decisions and that administrative officials then carry them out. It follows that policy-making is generally considered to be a more important activity than policy-implementation. By this argument, Government Ministers make policy and civil servants merely effect it.

There has long been a growing realisation, however, that this distinction between policy-making and administration is too crude. Civil servants are no longer viewed as simply taking orders from politicians and then putting them into practice; it is now widely recognised that the Civil Service itself plays an active role in policy-making. Just as the role of the House of Commons has been weakened in relation to the Minister, so now the role of the Minister is often weakened in relation to his civil servants. The growth in Government and the increasing complexity of Government decision-making have both increased the power of the official over the elected politician.

How has this come about? In the first place, the civil servant occupies a permanent post. Unlike Ministers who are subject to frequent election, civil servants usually remain in post for many years. Such permanence—civil servants cannot easily be dismissed from office—gives them an important advantage over their Ministerial superior. A Minister arriving in a Government Department for the first time may be confronted by a group of top civil servants who have been in post for many years and who have firm ideas about the type of policy which the Minister should pursue and its likelihood of success. While strong-minded Ministers may succeed in getting their way despite Civil Service resistance, more timid ones may not. A Minister determined on a policy radically different from that of his predecessor may be viewed with some alarm by permanent officials. Mrs

Barbara Castle, as Minister of Transport in 1965, saw herself surrounded by "ill-concealed hostility" when she attempted to introduce an integrated transport policy. Permanence also has the advantage that the civil servant can acquire a much greater knowledge of the technical details of policy than a Minister. With the increase in complexity of Government decision-making, policy must be made in areas in which the Minister cannot be expected to have detailed knowledge; he must rely on the advice of his civil servants.

Another factor contributing to increasing Civil Service power is the growth in size of many Government Departments to the point at which Ministers can only consider a small number of key policy issues. They are thus obliged to leave the initiative on many others to civil servants.

One final point worthy of note is the assumption by Ministers and civil servants of some of the important legislative powers of Parliament. Although Parliament is the supreme legislative body in the country, the power to initiate legislation and promote Bills in Parliament now lies largely with Ministers. Once again, however, it is the permanent official who benefits from such a process. With the development of greater complexity in political and administrative matters, Parliament has been forced to agree to the growth of delegated legislation. It can often only afford the time to approve the draft outlines of major pieces of legislation and must leave civil servants to work out the details of that legislation within Government Departments. In this way, civil servants have acquired law-making powers which are increasingly difficult to challenge.

All of these developments suggest that policy-making is not carried on by Ministers in a vacuum. The fact that they must rely on the wisdom and experience of civil servants and that the latter are now armed with formidable powers indicates that they are important partners in the policy-making process. New policies are affected by what has proved to be administratively feasible or difficult in the past. The best judge of whether such policies will be effective or not is usually the official.

Key civil servants have undoubtedly become extremely influential in the policy-making and -executing process in society. Most critics now agree that there has been a shift in the balance of power in the system of government from Parliament to the Executive. Some, like the late Professor John Mackintosh, have gone so far as to insist that the relationships between Parliament and Government should be amended so as to throw much greater public light on the activities of individual civil servants. If policy-makers should be made clearly accountable to the citizen, then the civil servant—active in policy making—should be publicly identified and made directly accountable to Parliament.

This process has, in fact, already begun. Both Ministers and MPs are less willing to allow the civil servant to operate under the cloak of anonymity. Since the Civil Service plays such a central role in the policy-making process, Ministers are more inclined to publicly name and blame individual civil servants when mistakes occur. At the same time, the House of

Commons is keener than ever to question and criticise civil servants on the detailed implications of policy and administration. An important consequence is that the traditional doctrine of individual Ministerial responsibility has been relaxed, civil servants have become more directly accountable to the House and are often called before its select committees to explain and justify their actions. This important change has major constitutional implications.

It has been said that in return for the protection of anonymity, civil servants are expected to be largely impartial—offering to Ministers of all parties the same degree of loyalty and commitment. While the move towards direct accountability for civil servants may have positive benefits, it may also carry disadvantages. The identification of individual civil servants with particular policies, for example, may lead to the politicisation of the administrative system. A new Government succeeding to office might seek to replace particular officials who have been publicly identified as supporting the policies of its predecessor. The advantage of a more "temporary" Civil Service could be that it would be more open and accessible to outside criticism. The costs of this might lie in the development of a "spoils" system, with incoming Ministers rewarding their friends with high administrative office.

The Courts

Examination of the constraints on administrative action at the central government level must include mention of the role of the Courts (the Judiciary). A democratic system of government needs an independent Judiciary which can ensure that the actions of administrative officials conform with the law. The principle of the "rule of law" means that the activities of the Government and its servants must be conducted within a framework of law. The most important function of the Courts is prevention of the abuse of power. When public officials exceed their powers the Courts may declare their actions "ultra vires". The growth of delegated legislation; the passing of important legislative powers from Parliament to the Minister and official was mentioned earlier. It is vitally important in a democracy to ensure that the granting of such powers to administrative officials is not abused. Any attempt on their part to act outside these powers may be declared invalid by the Courts. This is an extremely important safeguard of individual liberty.

The assumption of legislative powers by Ministers and officials has also been accompanied by an increase in their powers of discretion. In the case of the payment of welfare benefits, for example, officials have the power to investigate the circumstances of individual claimants and then decide whether or not to grant them money. Such decisions frequently give rise to dispute between the official and the citizen. An individual aggrieved at a decision not to grant him benefit may appeal to an administrative tribunal which has the power to consider whether the original decision was made impartially, fairly and in full knowledge of the claimant's circumstances. Such tribunals—an increasingly important part of the administrative process—ensure that officials are not judge and jury in their own cause.

Bureaucratic tyranny?

Lord Hewart warned that we are facing the development of a bureaucratic despotism. Support for his view can be found in the frequently expressed conviction that the country is run by "faceless" bureaucrats in charge of an administrative machine which is growing daily more out of control. Reports of the inefficiency of top administrators, coupled with the poor public image of the typical bureaucrat, convinces many people that far from bureaucracy being subject to democratic control, the opposite is true. Bureaucratic power has, indeed, increased in Britain, and weakening of Parliamentary influence is undoubtedly the single most important indicator of this. Yet the suggestion that an "elite" of bureaucrats runs this country in an unrestrained manner is too extreme. Public officials are committed to the values of democracy and one should acknowledge the important role which they have played in restraining and moderating the sometimes ill-thought-out schemes of politicians. Neither should one be complacent, however; the continuing debate about Civil Service power and Parliamentary reform is a necessary one.

While moves may be made to correct the supposed power imbalance between democracy and bureaucracy through such devices as a programme of Parliamentary reform, it is unlikely that change in the political institutions alone will automatically lead to more effective public control. What is needed is a general change of attitude towards Government in society. So long as more and more demands are made upon Government bureaucratic power will remain formidable. Perhaps the real solution to the growth in the numbers and power of public officials lies in limiting the role of Government and curbing the pressures upon it.

Max Weber noted that bureaucracy—a system of permanent officials—is a potential threat to a democratic society. Yet he was also well aware that democracy encourages the development of bureaucracy by stimulating the desires and wants of the population. Public officials are essential in such a system to provide the administrative means by which those demands can be met. Achieving a proper balance between democracy and bureaucracy is one of the core problems of our political/administrative system. While it is necessary to remind ourselves that bureaucracy, unchecked, may lead to tyranny, many positive contributions are made by public officials to the effective working of a democratic society.

Local government

Local government, like central government, must be seen in the context of its political and legal environment. Like central politics and administration, the activities of local government are governed, to a degree, by law and convention. However, it is less easy to be precise about the effect of conventions at local level, owing to the great number of local authorities and to the fact that each is a local political and administrative system in its own right. Local authorities' working arrangements vary considerably over the country. However, they share one problem with central government, namely the problem of the relationship of the permanent paid official to the elected—democratic—member of the system.

The environment of local government is complex. On the one hand, the day to day administration of affairs at local level must be seen in the context of democratic control by the local electorate; local authorities are miniature political systems. On the other hand, they must operate within a framework of restrictions established for them by Parliament and central government.

Local autonomy

Many people argue that local self-government is an essential part of any good democratic system. J S Mill, one of the most important nineteenth century thinkers in this country, argued that local government is educative in that it is a useful training ground in democracy. More recently W J M MacKenzie, accepting this argument, added that the local government—or decentralised administration—method of providing certain services is more effective than attempts to provide them from London or perhaps Edinburgh.

Towns and rural communities require many services, and encouraging local management of many of these services is a convenient and efficient way of ensuring that the needs of the citizen are met. Local authorities are responsive to the needs of a local community in ways which the local offices of a central government Department are not. In brief, there appear to be good democratic arguments for decentralising responsibility for providing important community services to local governments.

Local government is in an ambiguous position in the system of government in Britain. Complete freedom for every local authority to administer services on whatever basis it saw fit would probably result in anarchy. On the other hand, the imposition of total central direction and control would destroy local independence. A balance has to be struck.

Local authorities are allowed a certain independence from central control to enable them to provide services. This allows a high degree of local participation in the decision-making processes. On the other hand, local authorities' legal and political activities are limited by central government.

Control by Parliament

Control by Parliament is an extremely important limitation on local government. Local authorities are bound by Parliamentary statutes and all local authority acts must be approved by Parliament.

Administrative control

In practice, detailed supervision of local authorities is exercised by Government Departments. Local government is thus subjected to important control by the Executive. Certain Government Departments, for example, the Department of the Environment and the Department of Education and Science, are closely involved with the work of local authorities, since important local government functions are bound up with the work of these Departments. A Minister, dissatisfied with the performance of a local authority, may issue a directive compelling it to change course.

Regular inspection is one of the oldest forms of central control over the work of local authorities. Many important services, such as education and the police, are subject to regular inspection. The accounts of local authorities are also subject to detailed examination by District Auditors, whose appointment must be approved by the Government. Local authorities depend upon central government for financial support which provides another means of central government control. The authorities receive grants from central government, and a condition of any grant is that it will be centrally supervised to ensure that the resources are used for the purposes intended.

In addition to inspection and conditions relating to the grant, central government Departments regularly issue a number of circulars which influence the work of local authorities. These may require local authorities to take certain actions. Circular 10/65, for example, required local authorities to prepare reorganisation schemes for secondary comprehensive education.

Judicial control

The most important judicial control over local government is that of ultra vires. Courts can decide whether or not local authorities are complying with the law. The judicial constraint over local authorities, requiring them to act according to the principles of the rule of law is important; no member of a local authority can be judge in his own case. This power has sometimes been used by the Courts to prevent councillors taking decisions which directly benefit them financially. The Courts can also prevent a local authority from taking decisions which are blatantly unfair to certain individuals or groups, such as failing to allow an individual concerned in a disputed planning inquiry to express an opinion.

Local authorities as political systems

Administration within local authorities takes place in a democratic political environment. Just as administration at national level is influenced by a democratic political culture, so local authorities are subjected to local political pressures from ratepayers associations and other local groups. As a foremost commentator, J Stanyer has stated recently that the local government system in Britain is composed of a set of local democratic systems, each with its own political environment. Local authorities are directly elected bodies. Almost everyone over the age of 18 is entitled to vote at a local election. However, local authorities are not only political units, providing an important element in the overall democratic system: they are also administrative units.

Local government must rely on the assistance of paid officials. Once again, as in central government, the question of the relationship of bureaucracy and democracy arises. However, the relationships are not quite the same as at national level. Unlike MPs, local councillors are not full-time politicians. They are amateur, unpaid and part-time.

The elected council meets infrequently, an arrangement which has prevented the establishment of anything like a Cabinet system in all but a few large authorities. The conventions of collective and individual Ministerial responsibility have no direct parallel at local level either. However, it could be argued that the local authority is more directly accountable to its electorate than a Government Department and its civil servants.

The main work of the council is done in committees. These are composed of part-time elected councillors and full-time paid officials. Thus, the councillor and the official work closely in areas of council policy and administration. As at central government level, responsibility for policy and administration is shared. Since the elected member works so closely with the administrative staff, the public is assured of being represented at the centre of the decision-making process. The ease with which individual members of the public can approach councillors and full-time officials indicates how successful the democratic principle can be.

Interest groups in the administrative process

An important feature of a democratic system—and one much envied by people living under more oppressive regimes— is the right of association: the right to band together with people of like mind to attempt to influence Government policy and the administration of the nation's affairs. In any democratic system there are usually groups of people who form themselves into "pressure" or "interest" groups to influence the decision-making process of government. Some critics believe that the existence of these groups goes against the principle of a democratic society, since their purpose is to mould, influence, or alter Government policy in their favour, which may not coincide with the wider interests of the public.

However, the activity of these groups can be seen as contributing to the democratic process. In any event, interest groups are here to stay. The "targets" of their activities will be those centres of power in the decision-making process of government which they hope to "pressurise" into adopting a favoured policy or abandoning an existing one. Some interest groups try to influence the major political parties and the trade union movement goes so far as to sponsor candidates in Parliamentary elections. Other pressure groups seek to influence MPs of any party by—effectively—paying them to put forward their views in Parliament.

The most interesting development in recent years has been the growing number of groups which now operate within Whitehall. The TUC and the CBI not only attempt to exert influence on Ministers, but have also established "good relations" with civil servants. The more Government has intervened in the economy and other sectors of our national life, it seems, the greater is the tendency for groups to attempt to get right inside Government Departments. Indirectly, such a development shows the increasing power of the Civil Service and the relative decline of Parliament in the legislative process.

The Civil Service is an important source of Government legislation. The bureaucracy is a major force behind any legislative proposals, since permanent officials are uniquely placed to be able to see where new legislation is needed to deal with problems evolving over a long period of time. Interest groups have recognised the way in which the power-balance has swung in favour of the public service over the past few years. They are also involved in committees on which permanent officials sit and keep in close touch with key members of Government Departments.

This trend is likely to continue for, just as interest groups need the Civil Service—they need to be able to get civil servants on their side when pressing for particular items of legislation or amendment of existing legislation—so too does the Civil Service need the help of pressure group spokesmen to provide them with help and knowledge. This help is particularly valuable when drafting proposals because this task has been made more complex due to the Government's involvement in areas which have become increasingly technological, sophisticated and involved. The arrival of the "mixed economy" (private and public industry) discussed in Chapter 1 has led to greater Government involvement in public life.

As at central government level, there are likely to be a significant number of pressure groups at local authority level attempting to influence the decision-making process. As local government is so close to its electorate, the immediate impact of the groups is on the authority itself. Ratepayers' groups and groups of local businessmen, such as the Rotary Clubs, the Round Table and the like, are clear examples of local pressure groups.

The following are some examples of the way that the environmental values (see Chapters 2 and 3) have affected the work of public administrators.

Legality

In the opening months of 1975 it became clear that the Government intended to raise the price of a television licence on 1 April. A number of people, seeking to avoid this increase, bought new licences at the old rate before their existing ones had expired. The Home Secretary threatened these people with prosecution under the 1949 Wireless Telegraphy Act, since the BBC stood to lose several million pounds' worth of revenue. In short, the Minister threatened to revoke the second licences of the individuals concerned.

One licence holder appealed against the decision of the Minister and the Court upheld his appeal. It held that while the Minister was within his rights in revoking a licence, he had not acted reasonably and justly. He was making improper use of his discretionary power; he had no authority to demand this money. An important part of the environment is judicial restriction of Executive activities. This is, therefore, an external restriction on the activities of administrative bodies like Government Departments and local authorities. However, there is an important internal set of restraints on Departments and other executive bodies which may be described as quasi-legal.

Two important principles affect administration in the public sector: **equity** and **consistency**. The equity principle holds that citizens in different parts of the country should be treated in the same way unless circumstances suggest that this principle should be relaxed in the interests of all concerned. Thus the Post Office is obliged to provide a telephone service on a universal (countrywide) basis.

While proposals have been made from time to time that people living in different areas should pay different rental charges for their phones, such proposals have been rejected by Governments on the argument that all citizens should be treated alike in this matter. Although the costs of telephone installation vary tremendously—it costs more to bring the telephone to the local community in Ullapool in Wester Ross than in Hampstead—it is nevertheless felt that the extra costs of installation in Ullapool should be spread over the whole system rather than be met by the inhabitants of this small community. Consistency demands that where circumstances merit different treatment from the average, this should accordingly be instituted.

Accountability

This is one of the most important values affecting the administrative system of a democracy. In 1937, a piece of land in Dorset—Crichel Down—was compulsorily purchased by the Air Ministry who wished to use it as a bombing range. In 1949 the land passed into the hands of the Ministry of Agriculture. At this time, various farmers were promised a chance to bid for the tenancy of the land, including Lieutenant-Commander Marten, whose land it was before the compulsory purchase order came into effect. Unsatisfied that his case was being properly considered by Ministry officials, he complained to his MP who put pressure on the Minister, Sir Thomas Dugdale. Eventually, a public enquiry was set up by the Minister, and administrative failure within the Department came to light. Ministry officials—and the Minister—appear to have been remarkably insensitive to Marten's complaints. Eventually, the Minister was forced to resign.

The Crichel Down Case illustrates the importance of the concept of Ministerial responsibility. Although mistakes were made by civil servants, it was the Minister who had to take final responsibility. It should be added that the civil servants in question were disciplined within the Department.

In 1971, the Home Secretary appointed a Tribunal of Inquiry to consider "issues in relation to the circumstances leading up to the cessation of trading by the Vehicle and General Company". The tribunal concluded that there had been negligence within the Insurance and Companies Division of the Department of Trade and Industry, a Department responsible for the supervision and control of companies. The Tribunal specifically criticised Mr Christopher Jardine, an Under-Secretary in the Department, for failing to display "initiative" in dealing with affairs of the company.

The fact that officials were named and blamed in this affair, and that the Departmental Ministers escaped this—they were not forced to resign—has been widely seen as a sign that the doctrine of Ministerial responsibility has been modified in recent years. This indicates that in the realm of public administration, theory and practice may differ. The implications of this have been discussed above.

Reasonableness

A number of agencies "outside" the administrative system keep watch on it to ensure that public officials are acting reasonably and fairly. As in the case of the Vehicle and General affair, they investigate cases of alleged misconduct where the case does not reach a Court of Law; that is, no specific breach of law has occurred. Public inquiries of this type may be set up by Parliament to investigate any matter of public importance.

Recently one of the most interesting developments has been the establishment of the Parliamentary Commissioner for Administration—the "Ombudsman". This office was established in 1967 by an Act of Parliament. The Ombudsman is primarily concerned with acts of "maladministration"—unnecessary delays in decision-making, negligence, bias and the like—and unreasonableness on the part of public officials. From time to time people have criticised the scope of his powers and the fact that complaints by members of the public can only be raised by MPs.

Local government, the National Health Service, hospitals, the nationalised industries and the police were all excluded from the jurisdiction of the PCA by the 1967 Act. However, in 1971 a Health Service Commissioner was appointed. In one respect he has firmer powers than the PCA; he can, for example, investigate cases brought directly to his attention by individual members of the public. Under the Local Government Act of 1974, a Commission for Local Administration was set up to investigate allegations of maladministration in local government.

In 1976 Sir Idwal Pugh, the Health Service Commissioner, strongly criticised a hospital where the husband of a woman who died found her lying on a mattress on the floor of the hospital. This administrative blunder was condemned by the Commissioner as being deplorable: the hospital subsequently apologised to the man involved.

In 1977, Sir Alan Marre, the PCA, criticised the Department of Health and Social Security for not being frank in their replies to MPs about the notorious motorised tricycle which was issued to invalids. The Ombudsman was successful in persuading the Department to release accident statistics for these vehicles which backed up the arguments of the Department's critics that the tricycles were inherently dangerous.

Efficiency

The value of "efficiency" is extremely important in public administration. Efficiency is probably not such a good test of good performance in the public sector as in the private sector; even in the private sector it is not as straightforward as might be imagined. No system of public administration will strive for efficiency at the cost of other values such as compassion, equity and justice. No simple test of efficiency is possible in the public sector for the reasons discussed in Chapter 1. Nevertheless, efficiency is an important means of judging the performance of a Government Department or local authority.

Questions relating to the efficiency of public officials can be raised in select committees of the House of Commons. These select committees, formed to carry out a particular job of investigation, have long been used by the House to question the Executive branch—Government. During the 1960's, great pressure was exerted in Parliament to extend the Select Committee system to enable it to keep a watchful eye on all the central Departments.

Although these "watchdogs without teeth" have been criticised, (Edward du Cann, the Chairman of the important Public Accounts Committee protested that "we are doing a fuddy-duddy job in a jet age"), the committee system can have a desirable effect on civil servants called before it as witnesses. For example, the Select Committee on the Nationalised Industries has, for a number of years, carried out far-ranging investigations into all aspects of the work of the public corporations including questions of staffing, performance and efficiency. All areas of Departmental policy are potentially open to Parliamentary scrutiny. Dialogues between MPs and permanent officials in select committees illustrate the fact that the public expect public officials to operate efficiently.

Responsiveness

It was suggested earlier that Government Departments and local authorities communicate with interested parties before and after decisions are made. It is often mutually beneficial that this process should take place; Government gains expertise and information, and the interest group gains entry to the decision-making process and is thus able to participate directly in the political process.

There are good administrative reasons for involving interest groups in the making and execution of policy, since they can provide the public administrator with much needed expert advice. There are also good political reasons for involving interest groups; a well-known tactic for heading off potential opposition to Government policy is to enlist the opposition's help. If the groups have a hand in the making of policy they may be more reluctant to criticise it.

Again, an interesting source of information for central and local government is the public inquiry system. Public inquiries are a common feature of decision-making processes and are usually set up whenever a decision of an administrative agency is likely to conflict with the private rights of the citizen. An area in which conflicts of this kind are likely is land-use planning. Administrators are bound by the rules of natural justice at such inquiries and are required to give adequate time to all interested parties. There have been cases at local government level where the views of some people have not been adequately represented and the Courts have, on occasion, ruled against public authorities for this failing.

Over the past few years, Government has shown a greater willingness to be more open in its consultative procedures. Since 1967, the practice has grown up of publishing consultative documents for the benefit of outside opinion before the Minister has decided on a course of action. Thus, the publication of "Green Papers" in advance of decisions gives opportunity for early discussion and consultation in a way not previously possible. This raises the last value of "openness".

Openness

The central argument of this chapter has been that the key problem posed by public administration in a democracy is that of controlling the actions of public officials in the interests of the community. This is achieved because of the need for accountability. It is obvious that if accountability is to operate in practice, Government must, to a degree, be open to outside inspection.

The question of "how much openness?", however, reveals the essential dilemma posed by "public" accountability. Governments will obviously want to maintain a policy of secrecy on delicate matters involving national security and the public interest can be served well by discreet public officials. Again, in the field of foreign relations, delicate negotiations could be prejudiced by premature disclosures to the press.

The Official Secrets Act 1911 makes it an offence to pass on secret information: it also makes it an offence to have that information in one's possession after receipt. The Franks Report of 1972 argued that the Act was too restrictive and should be revised. Many people favour its substitution by a Freedom of Information Act modelled on American lines. This would open up the decision-making process in government to outside view on many more issues than at present, while maintaining certain safeguards in relation to defence matters and national security.

Suggestions for further reading

A H Birch, *The British System of Government,* Allen and Unwin, 1973
A H Halsey (ed), *Trends in British Society since 1900,* Macmillan, 1972
W J M MacKenzie and J W Grove, *Central Administration in Britain,* Longman, 1957

Questions

1 What is implied by "open" government?
2 The Crichel Down Case illustrates an important constitutional principle. What is it?
3 What is the role of the Ombudsman?
4 What is an interest group?

4
Organisational structures

Administration and bureaucracy

Chapters 2 and 3 dealt with the environment in which public administration is conducted, and discussed the setting of administration. This chapter examines the nature and shape of the organisations which operate within that setting.

Administration is organisationally based; it is a social activity which requires the co-operation of individuals and groups within a system of mutually shared values and rules, and this is provided within the framework of organisation. Organisations—social institutions deliberately created to achieve certain defined purposes—provide the framework of order within which administrative activities gain coherence, purpose and direction. The nature of those organisations—the way in which they are constructed and run—influences and, in many cases, determines how individual administrators behave.

Before examining the various types of organisations which make up the public sector and considering the nature of their work and how they are organised to conduct it, it should be remembered that the environmental values discussed have a fundamental effect on these organisations. The structure of public organisations—the accepted ways of doing things and carrying on administrative activities—is in important ways shaped and influenced by these environmental restrictions and expectations. In order to demonstrate this point, the values identified in Chapters 2 and 3 will now be examined.

It was suggested that "public" administration is concerned with achieving the purposes of society and with its goals, and that in a democracy public administration is, or should be, controlled and supervised by elected politicians. Administration, then, is conducted within a political framework; public officials are responsible for their actions and may be held accountable for them. As the Crichel Down Case made clear, relatively minor mistakes and indiscretions on the part of officials can have serious political repercussions. Again, impartiality, justice and the requirement to treat individual citizens fairly and equitably mean that public officials must use wisdom, tact and caution in their daily work. They must also be attentive to the principle of consistency. Such values as these undoubtedly influence the thinking and behaviour of civil servants and local government officials; they also affect the organisational setting within which these officials work.

Any examination of the organisational characteristics of public sector bodies must consider the concept of bureaucracy. It is thought that the environmental values of a democracy make bureaucracy inevitable but, far from being wholly negative, bureaucracy can safeguard the positive aspects of democracy: freedom, equality and justice.

This statement may seem somewhat curious. The word "bureaucracy" has come to acquire a negative meaning, and in the minds of some people it has even acquired a sinister aspect. As eminent a public figure as the Duke of Edinburgh recently painted an extremely gloomy picture of British society as one dominated by "bureaucrats". He argued that in the year 2000, life in Britain will be much less tolerable than at present; individual freedom will be eroded by an army of central and local government officials. Government of the people by their elected representatives, by this argument, will be displaced by an establishment of public officials who will be even more difficult to control because they will achieve this powerful position not by force but with the consent of the citizen demanding services and benefits which only the bureaucrats can provide.

Prince Philip was joining those people who, for centuries, have complained that the increasing power of Government in modern society has meant a growth in the numbers of public officials and their detailed involvement in many aspects of our private lives. Dramatic pictures have been painted of faceless bureaucrats, no longer the servants of the public, but their masters.

Arguments about the growing power of public officials have been matched by complaints that "bureaucracy" is inherently and inevitably inefficient. C Northcote Parkinson, in a bitingly witty account of the increase in bureaucratic officials in society, argued that there is an inevitable tendency for the number of such officials to grow, regardless of the amount of work for them to do. Parkinson's "Law"—"work expands so as to fill the time available for its completion"—is often used as a sarcastic criticism of the supposed tendency of civil servants and other officials to create work in order to justify their existence.

In considering such views as those of Prince Philip and Professor Parkinson, an interesting question arises: if bureaucracy is so objectionable because of its non-accountability and inefficiency, why does society continue to tolerate it? Why is it necessary to employ bureaucrats and make use of the organisations ("bureaucracies") in which they work? The answer is that bureaucracy may not necessarily erode individual freedom and produce waste and inefficiency, but on the contrary may be both efficient and promote freedom. This seems to be the dilemma which every modern state must face. People cannot, it seems, do without many of the products of large-scale organisation whether public or private, but these organisations must not be allowed to endanger the public interest.

It is fashionable to deride bureaucracy and central and local government officials as "the bureaucracy". Such negative views of bureaucracy have long been popular, but bureaucratic principles of organisation also have positive merits and can enable Government Departments, local authorities and other public bodies to achieve their goals in accordance with the environmental values outlined.

Students of public administration have for a long time argued that bureaucratic organisations have many distinct advantages over other types of social organisation: for example, they are particularly well suited to handling large-scale tasks, demanding the co-ordination of physical and intellectual effort. There is evidence that the ancient Egyptians used a form of bureaucratic organisation to construct the pyramids—an interesting example of the pyramidal organisation producing the pyramidal physical structure! Another example of early bureaucratic organisation was that used by various Asiatic races to introduce large-scale irrigation schemes.

Chapter 2 referred to the German sociologist Max Weber. A figure of great importance in the development of academic thinking on organisations, Weber identified the main characteristics of the bureaucratic organisation and argued that it was fast becoming the dominant form of organisation in government, industry and in all sectors of society. Any examination of the organisations in the public sector involves an understanding of bureaucracy.

According to Weber, bureaucracy is a very rational form of organisation. What does this mean? Rationality implies that an organisation's structure is based on rules and procedures which are intended to help it achieve its objectives. Such rules provide a system of order within which the work of an organisation can be conducted. Weber, in discussing the growth of bureaucracy in modern society insisted that it was essential if large-scale tasks were to be accomplished. The characteristics which Weber identified as being typical of a bureaucratic organisation will now be considered as well as some of the advantages and disadvantages of such a system.

Weber's view of the main characteristics of a bureaucratic organisation provides a helpful insight into organisational life and the work environment of public officials:

In a bureaucratic organisation:

a)   officials are personally free and subject to authority only so far as their official duties are concerned

b)   officials are organised in a clearly defined hierarchy of offices

c)   there is free selection for the offices

d)   candidates for posts in the bureaucracy are selected on the basis of qualifications

e)   they are paid fixed salaries and have pension rights

f) the job of the office-holder is his sole or main occupation
g) each office has a clearly defined area of competence
h) promotion is by seniority or achievement or a combination of both
i) the official does not own the materials and equipment that he works with
j) he is subject to strict discipline and control

To say that individuals are personally free and subject only to higher authority in their official duties (a) really means that they are not expected to give their whole lives to the organisation; their work and leisure time are separate, for example. Neither do those higher up the organisation control all aspects of the individual's private life.

The second category of Weber's bureaucratic "model" (b) is extremely significant. Most large organisations tend to be structured in a hierarchy. Hierarchy implies that offices and office-holders are so arranged that each post in the organisation is subject to the authority of the one above it. This principle runs through the organisation from the top to the bottom. Government Departments and local authorities as well as other organisations in the public sector are, to an important degree, hierarchically structured.

The notion of free selection for offices (c) means that competition for jobs in the organisation is not restricted by the unfair prohibition of certain candidates. On the contrary, it is assumed that open competition for jobs is more likely to produce the best man or woman for the job than a system which, for example, discriminates against coloured or female applicants. This characteristic of bureaucracy is linked to (d); candidates for posts in the organisation are selected on the assumption that they have demonstrated the necessary competence for the job by, for example, having reached certain educational standards. Candidates thus chosen will not be selected on the whim or fancy of the man at the top of the organisation.

It must be remembered, that appointments to the public service have not always been made so fairly. The novelist Anthony Trollope—himself employed in an important post in the Post Office in the last century—wrote a vivid account of the corrupt methods which were used to help the often dull and dimwitted sons of the leisured classes to obtain posts in the Government service. Until the middle of the nineteenth century, members of the Civil Service were appointed as the result of favouritism and family connection: a system which, according to many critics, resulted in incompetence and the inability to exercise sound judgement.

Consistent with the idea of hierarchy is the view that officials should be rewarded by means of a fixed salary (e)—the idea that officials doing similar work should be rewarded in the same way. The principle (f) that the job of the office-holder should be his sole or main occupation is designed to ensure that the organisation obtains commitment and loyalty from the employee. This is extremely important in the case of public officials for it ensures that no "conflict of interest" arises between the demands of the public office and those of another employer. Strict rules prevent officials from receiving financial and non-financial rewards from outside bodies, thus preventing (or at least making difficult) a wholesale system of corruption.

Each official within the hierarchy has a clearly defined area of competence (g). This ensures that the relationship between the organisation and the office-holder is made standard. It enables both the organisation and the individual to understand the limits and obligations of membership. Thus, the organisation can establish certain claims over its individual members—they will be expected to perform a specified range of duties competently—and the individual member will know exactly what his obligations are.

The stipulation that promotion is achieved by seniority and/or merit (h) makes clear that the individual's career progress in the organisation depends (like his initial recruitment) either upon performance or length of service rather than currying favour with the boss. Promotion procedures within the public service usually aim to prevent unfair promotion.

The official has no personal claim over the property of his office (i), thus ensuring that the property remains under public control. An essential feature of a public organisation is a set of controls to prevent officials from acquiring personal wealth by simply selling or disposing of public assets. The final point is that the official is subject to reasonably strict discipline and control (j). All organisations strive to control the behaviour of the people who work within them. Schools, factories, banks, Government Departments; all attempt to ensure that the expectations of owners, managers and authority-holders regarding the behaviour of their subordinates, are met.

The bureaucratic organisation—one designed and run according to these characteristics—possesses some distinctly advantageous qualities. Firstly, its rules allow it to act with precision—and, in some cases—speed. Secondly, clients of the organisation, whether they are the recipients of welfare benefits, industrialists seeking Government financial aid, or protesters aiming to change Government policy on the siting of a new airport, are dealt with fairly. Just as the rules prevent the organisation showing undue favouritism to certain officials within it, so they prevent unfair advantage being shown to one client rather than another. The organisation "depersonalises" relationships in the interest of efficiency. It eliminates all purely personal and emotional elements from decision-making. Thus, the organisation is well equipped to avoid unfairness, corruption and has an excellent system for achieving political objectives.

The 10 features listed above make for an organisational structure well-suited to serve the values of a democratic system of government. The requirement that officials should be appointed for their competence rather than as the result of favouritism is consistent with the democratic principle of equality. In theory, the organisation could be representative of a broad range of social groups within the country rather than a small, exclusive group. Again, the organisation's commitment to equal treatment (demonstrated by its stress on merit and seniority in the case of promotions for employees and impartiality to its clients) fits well into a democratic system of government.

The constitutional expectations of British society are such that officials at the central and local level are indirectly responsible to the electorate for their actions, and subject to a considerable degree of oversight from elected politicians. Through a hierarchy of offices, the lowliest official in the organisation can be held responsible to the man at the top. The man at the top, in turn, must be prepared to shoulder a degree of responsibility for the mistakes and shortcomings of junior officials.

The bureaucratic organisation—weaknesses?

Bureaucracy has its negative and positive characteristics. However, in seeking to correct a popular negative image of bureaucracy, its weaknesses must not be obscured. While, for example, uniformity of treatment can be seen as a positive virtue, bureaucracy has a less attractive side.

One of the negative characteristics of bureaucracy is over-rigidity: the understandable reluctance of officials to bend rules to deal with special circumstances. Such rigidity can also result from the desire of the official to protect himself from adverse criticism. Taking care in case any action on his part might compromise his political superior, the civil servant may retreat behind a smokescreen of rules. Again, while hierarchical responsibility can benefit the organisation by ensuring that superiors can control their subordinates, the hierarchy can also be used to protect officials at the bottom of the organisation from adverse public criticism. All too often an official pleads that he can take no action on a particular matter without reference to "higher authority".

There are conflicting pressures within an organisation. To ensure speedy decision-making, many large organisations are keen to decentralise i.e. give officials low in the hierarchy adequate power to enable them to take decisions without having constantly to refer to higher authority. However, opposite pressures for centralisation are also a common feature of bureaucratic life. To achieve consistency, organisations may strive to ensure that only a few highly placed decision-makers take key decisions. The extent of centralised and decentralised decision-making varies from organisation to organisation. Public sector organisations as well as their private sector counterparts constantly experience tensions between contrary pressures such as these.

The weaknesses of the bureaucratic organisation can be summed up as follows:

a) Rules aimed at general efficiency may sometimes produce opposite, unintended consequences

b) Impersonal treatment of clients of the bureaucracy may be harmful if it leads to inhumane treatment

c) The individual official may become trapped by rules or may himself use the rules to lower the organisation's responsiveness to the needs of the outside community

d) The rules may prevent, rather than encourage, the organisation to cope adequately with changed circumstances

This last observation has been the take-off point for critics who have argued that the hierarchically structured organisation should be replaced by a different type of organisation constructed on different principles. Such an argument insists that bureaucracy is out of date—it cannot adapt to a changing society, since society (and hence the problems with which public organisations have to cope) is changing at a steadily increasing rate.

What would organisations constructed on different principles be like? It can be argued that they would be like a mirror image of the bureaucratic organisation. They would be "flatter" organisations than their bureaucratic equivalent. If the bureaucratic organisation is represented by a tall, relatively narrow pyramid, the opposite type of organisation would be short with a very broad base.

Advocates of this form of organisation usually argue that in certain circumstances it will prove more adaptable to the needs of the community: it will be able to cope with change more readily. Recent efforts have been made to modify the bureaucratic form of organisation in both central and local government and to take advantage of the contribution of this alternative form.

Since the beginning of the 1970's, deliberate efforts have been made to modify the structure of some Government Departments by introducing flatter structures and encouraging the development of more flexible communications to contribute towards a more efficient organisational structure. In local government, too, efforts have been made since the middle of the 1960's to overcome the fragmented nature of its administrative systems. One of the assumptions of much of this reform programme is that, while the bureaucratic organisation is useful in encouraging high levels of specialisation (thus allowing members of the organisation to concentrate on certain parts of the overall task and become expert in these matters), it spreads responsibility for decision-making in such a way that it becomes blurred: no-one is certain who is responsible for what.

All the organisations in the public sector could be classified according to their structural features; whether they conform to the characteristics of the "bureaucratic" organisation described by Weber or whether they resemble the more flexible "flatter" alternative. In doing this it would be discovered that while the bureaucratic form of organisation has been modified, the principles of bureaucracy have by no means been abandoned. Both central Government Departments and local authorities, for example, have a hierarchy of offices and it is expected that they will appoint people to positions in those hierarchies according to their demonstrated ability. Again, it is expected that members of the public coming into contact with those organisations will be treated fairly and compassionately.

The essential problem for decision-makers in public administrative organisations is deciding how to obtain the maximum benefits from bureaucracy while minimising its negative consequences.

The emergence of "active" Government

The economist Andrew Shonfield, among others, has drawn attention to the phenomenon of "active and ubiquitous Government". He suggests that the extension of Government involvement in most aspects of our daily lives is an extremely important phenomenon in modern society which has affected public administration in organisations in two important ways. Firstly, the size of their task has grown. The number of people employed by central and local government has grown along with public expenditure increases. Secondly, the nature and scope of Government activity has become more complex.

There are many causes of this growth in Government activity. Britain, in common with many other countries in Western Europe and other parts of the world, has experienced a move from an agrarian or rural society to an urban, industrial one. The emergence of a technological society and the constant demands upon Government to regulate the economy to maintain full employment and ensure that the benefits of the society are reasonably shared, has brought politicians, trade unionists, industrialists and others into agreement that a certain degree of Government regulation is inevitable in a democratic society.

Other pressures have also encouraged the development of Government involvement. Britain has experienced two world wars which produced significant social changes and encouraged the view that Governments should take direct action to produce a more egalitarian society: both war periods saw the increasing Government concern with social welfare policies—the introduction of old age pensions and health benefits during the First World War and the construction of a Welfare State during and immediately after the Second World War which sought to provide help for the sick and the aged. Again, demands have been made for many years for the active involvement of the State in providing an educational system to encourage the intellectual development of children from all classes.

The involvement of Government in the economic and social affairs of the nation is, in fact, no new phenomenon. Professor Milton Friedman has recently indicated that the great English lawyer, Dicey, viewed this as a threat to individual liberty at the turn of the century. Other critics have argued that "big" or "active" Government was a central feature of British life much earlier than this. Whatever date is considered the starting point, there is widespread agreement that the powers of Government have grown, accompanied by changes in the nature of Government activity.

In earlier times the role of Government was restricted to that of "night-watchman", namely keeping watch to see that law and order was maintained, both inside the country (by means of a police force) and in external relationships with other countries (by means of the armed services). Government has since entered the field of social legislation—providing high levels of housing, education and welfare. It is now widely engaged in civil and military scientific projects—researching into the peaceful uses of atomic energy and maintaining a nuclear defence capability. In addition, Governments have set themselves the task of maintaining high levels of employment and fighting obvious economic ills like inflation. Two consequences of this process are important in the present context.

Firstly, key public organisations have become larger: the Government Department, arguably the key organisation in central government, has in many cases grown in size. Secondly, just as the tasks of Government have increased, so too have the organisations which make up the public sector. In particular, there has been a growth in special purpose ad hoc bodies which have been set up as separate organisations because, for various reasons, existing organisational arrangements were felt to be inappropriate.

Government participation in "commercial" functions encourages consideration of whether existing bureaucratic forms of administration—predominant in the Government Department—are appropriate for commercial activities or whether these activities might be better performed in a more flexible "flatter" organisational structure.

The question has also arisen of whether good administration is based on standard principles of organisational design. For example, does a "commercial" function, such as that of the Post Office providing telephones to the public, require a different type of organisational structure from the structure needed to administer pensions or welfare benefits successfully. As the Government takes on more and more varied tasks, new and more varied means of accomplishing those tasks must be found.

In recent years organisations of a "mixed" type have appeared on the scene. Mixed or "hybrid" organisations are now a common feature of the organisational landscape of Britain. The growth in their numbers gives some indication of the extent of Government involvement in the economy and the social system. More and more, Government is becoming involved with large, previously private, organisations. Any Government seeking to ensure high and stable levels of employment will naturally seek to influence the investment policies of important firms and industries. Similarly, the firms, too, may come to rely on Government to provide them with much needed sources of finance.

When the Government provides such funds to private companies, it usually seeks some form of influence over the company either by taking a shareholding interest in it, or ensuring that it has representatives on its Board of Directors, or both. These firms are probably best described as quasi-private, meaning that they are not wholly owned and run by private individuals. On the contrary, the extent of public involvement may be high as in the case of Ferranti which, although formally private, attracts vast sums of capital from the Government, and on whose Board representatives of the Government sit.

There are many other organisations which can be described as quasi-public. These organisations conform to the model of the Government Department in some respects: they have a bureaucratic structure, they are run by public servants and they are concerned with more than a simple objective of making profit. Soon after the Second World War, the Labour Government began a policy of taking into public ownership important sectors of the economy. Iron and steel, gas, electricity, the railways: all these basic utilities were felt by the Government to be of such importance that they should be nationalised. The structure and the working of the nationalised industries will be examined in greater detail in Chapter 13. The point here is that they are one of the most important categories of quasi-public bodies in British Government today.

The organisational structure of the nationalised industries is intended to reflect their dual status. On the one hand, they are part of the Government "machine", so they must be responsive to the wishes of the electorate through its political representatives. In other words, they must be responsible to Ministers and Parliament. On the other hand, they are obliged by the statutes which set them up to act in a commercial manner. They are therefore organisations which have public sector characteristics but which are seeking more flexible methods of operating: methods which are more similar, perhaps, to those of the private business firm.

This complicated dual-purpose character has sometimes caused problems of political accountability and control. The question of whether large bureaucratic organisations of this type can truly act in a flexible, commercial manner has not been satisfactorily answered.

Since 1968 when the Fulton Report on the Civil Service appeared, it has become fashionable to argue that existing bureaucratic arrangements within certain Departments could be modified by substituting new, flexible and flatter structures. That Report went so far as to recommend that, if Government Departments were engaged in commercial activities, it might prove necessary to remove them altogether from the bureaucratic organisation of the Department and relocate them in quasi-independent organisations. This kind of recommendation became known as "hiving-off".

The Report also argued that, if full-scale hiving-off was impracticable, every effort should be made to make certain parts of the Departments more flexible by modifying their bureaucratic structure. Although such recommendations have not led to dramatic change in the structure of organisations at the central government level, those changes which have occurred have complicated the structure of government still further.

Bureaucracy and local government

More detailed consideration of local government is undertaken in Chapters 8–10, but no examination of bureaucracy would be complete without looking at some of its characteristics and consequences at the local government level. Local government is made up of a wide variety of different authorities which vary considerably in size, type and in methods of working. Some local authorities are subject to the influence of local political parties, others are not. They all, however, have certain common organisational characteristics.

As with central government officials, local officials are subject to democratic political control. In principle, the elected councillor makes policy and the permanent official establishes and operates the administrative apparatus for putting it into effect. In practice, the local government official shares responsibility for both policy and administration with the councillor. A most important feature of local government is its **committee system**. Local government has many functions and it has to administer a large number of services. Its committees, composed both of elected councillors and permanent officials, are the main workshops of local government. The elected council, which meets infrequently, delegates powers to these committees thus ensuring that the work of the council is carried on in a continuous and efficient way.

The permanent officials of the council are organised within departments on a service basis, for example, the education department, highways department, and so on. These departments are organised on hierarchical lines, similar to central government Departments. And as with central government, the bureaucratic pattern of administration has distinct advantages. Examination of any large local authority, however, reveals its usual weaknesses: diffusion of responsibility and upward referral. Local authorities organised on this basis also tend to suffer from the difficulty of ensuring co-ordinated effort between their various departments. Various efforts in recent years have been directed at preventing this and similar efforts have also been made at central government level.

"Corporate planning"—the attempt to urge local authorities to see themselves not as a collection of widely separate and isolated services but as co-ordinated units has affected recent proposals for local government reform. This idea is also popular at national level. These reform efforts have tried to deal with a common negative result of bureaucracy—the diffusion of responsibility (uncertainty as to where responsibility lies) and fragmentation (the failure of officials in one part of a bureaucratic system to see that they are linked to those in other parts). The reasons for and the consequences of such reform efforts are covered in the later chapters of this book.

Suggestions for further reading

A H Hanson and M Walles, *Governing Britain*, Fontana, 1976
Sir I Jennings, *The Queen's Government*, Pelican, Latest edition

Questions

1 Account for the development of "active Government" in the British
  context.
2 What are the characteristics of a bureaucracy?
3 What are the strengths and weaknesses of the bureaucratic organisation?

5

Central government organisations

Government Departments

Undoubtedly, the key organisation at central level is the Government Department. The official handbook, *Britain 1978*, states:

"Government Departments are the main instruments for giving effect to government policy when Parliament has passed the necessary legislation."

Government Departments are the oldest agencies of central government. In terms of the size of the labour force and the amount of public money which they use annually, the Department is a truly formidable part of Government.

Departments vary considerably in the nature of their work, their size and, to a degree, their shape and structure. What features, if any, do they have in common?

1 Government Departments are subject to political control by Ministers. Although some Departments are headed not by Ministers but by civil servants, e.g. the Inland Revenue, all are subject to Ministerial control.
2 Government Departments are hierarchically organised. Each official has a designated area of responsibility and the offices in the hierarchy are so arranged that a chain of command is established which links top officials—such as the Permanent Secretary—with those at the bottom. In this way, the actions of individual civil servants are subject to overall Parliamentary control.
3 Government Departments tend to be large bodies (there are important exceptions, however). The factor of size is important in encouraging the adoption of bureaucratic procedures. Efficiency demands that duties are clearly allocated and labour divided.
4 The expenditure of Government Departments is subject to the oversight of Parliament. Of particular importance in this connection is the

Public Accounts Committee of the House of Commons which takes a special interest in the expenditure of public monies by the central administration and which can call civil servants before it. It is assisted in its work of investigation by the Comptroller and Auditor General who is an official responsible to the House of Commons and not to the head of the Civil Service. This ensures his independence.

5   Government Departments are staffed by civil servants. This affects the overall shape of the Department. The fact that the Department's hierarchial structure accommodates all the grades within the Civil Service hierarchy means that the number of levels in the hierarchy is inevitably increased. Many critics have suggested that this results in delay and hesitancy. Internal communications must pass through an unnecessarily large number of Departmental filters, so the chances of information being distorted are increased.

6   The work of many important Departments is geographically decentralised. They must operate through local offices because the clientele they are serving is geographically dispersed. The DHSS is a clear case in point. In Departments operating over a wide territorial area, the principles of hierarchy and specialisation are also extended geographically. "Field offices" i.e. offices stationed away from the centre need to be set up to cope with the needs of the clientele with which the Department is concerned and it may be necessary to delegate authority to officials in the provinces. Thus districts, areas or regions (or all three) must be established to carry out the work of the Department.

The exact nature and style of decentralised administration varies from Department to Department. The area organisation of the DHSS, for example, differs considerably from that of the Department of the Environment, and so on. Departments such as the DOE and the DHSS establish "field offices" because they are supervising subordinate agencies such as area health authorities and local councils. Here, they are attempting to provide a supervisory, inspectorial and advisory service which must be conducted on a decentralised basis.

7   Each Government Department performs a wide variety of tasks. For example, the Department of Energy has overall responsibility for ensuring that the energy needs of the country are met: in so doing, it oversees the coal, gas, and electricity industries. In addition, it is concerned with the administration of nuclear power and the oil industries. The Department of Health and Social Security (DHSS) has responsibility for administering the National Health Service (thus involving it with the problems of the sick, elderly and mentally handicapped), providing hospitals and health centres, medical personnel and framing health policy. In addition, it is responsible for paying unemployment benefit, sickness benefit, and retirement and widows pensions. In 1970, the Department of the Environment was created: a vast organisation designed to integrate transportation policy, housing policy, sponsorship of the construction industry and protection of the environment.

8   Smith and Stanyer have shown in *Administering Britain* that the work of Departments is divided up between a number of divisions. **Administrative** divisions prepare legislation, prepare briefs for the Minister to assist him in answering Parliamentary questions, and exercise overall control over the subordinate members of the Department. Their work may also cover policy matters i.e. matters which establish the basic philosophy and principles upon which the work of the organisation will be based.

Executive branches within the Department are concerned with more routine work; record keeping, purchasing equipment, maintaining stores and supplies and the like. The **specialist** divisions provide technical services requiring a degree of vocational training not possessed by the generalist civil servant. The relationship between the generalist and the specialist is examined in Chapter 6.

Each Department has its **common services** divisions. As the name implies, these divisions exist mainly to provide a centralised pool of special skills and services for all the other divisions in the Department. Two of the most important of these are the Finance division and the Establishments division.

The **Finance division,** usually under the control of an Under-Secretary, is responsible to the Permanent Secretary for preparing annual estimates of expenditure for the Department, and for all questions involving finance. It also fulfils the Department's accounting duties. In liaison with the other divisions in the Department, the Finance division uses the annual forecasts of the various divisions' financial needs to prepare estimates of expenditure. It also ensures that money is correctly spent, thus guarding against the improper use of funds.

The **Establishments division** is concerned with the staff position of the Department as a whole. It deals with questions of promotion, disciplinary matters and general questions relating to conditions of service. This division is thus broadly concerned with "organisation and methods" (O & M).

While Government Departments share most of the above features, it would be a mistake to assume that they are all completely alike or that they have the same number of hierarchical layers, the same degree of specialisation or the same degree of separation between specialists and non-specialists. It is sometimes assumed that in the public sector and, indeed, in the private sector, all organisations should be structured in the same way. The assumption is sometimes made that there is "one best way" to organise. According to this argument, it does not matter whether one is running a large Government Department or a small business firm; each will require the same type of administration based on similar principles.

Recent thinking has shown that this view is wrong. Organisations performing tasks which require flexibility and responsiveness may need different organisational structures from organisations which operate in a stable environment and deal with predictable problems. Unfortunately not a great deal is known about the detailed structure and functioning of

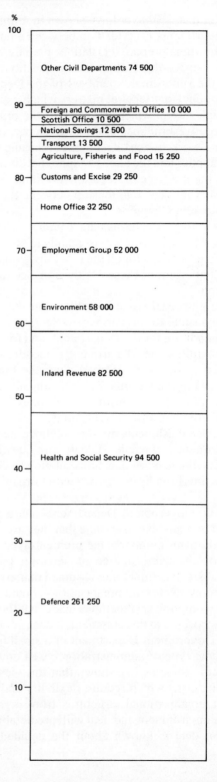

Fig. 2 The Civil Service:
main Departments
(Numbers employed at 1/11/77)
Source: HMSO

Government Departments because civil servants have always been reluctant to give detailed information to outsiders on the running of their Departments. Indeed, the presence of the Official Secrets Act, mentioned in Chapter 2, is a constant reminder that they must be very careful about the information they give to the general public. This makes academic investigation of the subject extremely difficult.

However, enough is known about the running of various Departments to know that the nature of their work is very varied; the Fulton Committee Report in 1968 confirmed this. Some Departments are more heavily engaged in policy work than others; some are more heavily involved in work of a quasi-commercial kind than others; the work of some is routine, the work of others, highly variable.

The variety of Government Departments' work

The present system of Government Departments has developed over a long period; the Post Office and the Treasury, for example, are both extremely old Departments. The origins of the Post Office can be traced back some 300 years, while those of the Treasury are so ancient they have been almost obscured in the mists of time. However, it is interesting to note that much of the present system of Departments has its origins in the last 100 years, for this has been a period of rapid administrative change and development.

Change in the Departmental system has not always proceeded in a continuous and systematic manner. Recent history suggests, in the words of Hanson and Walles, that the Departmental system has not evolved according to a grand plan of design. On the contrary, the system has undergone a "continuous process of creation, fusion, fission and transfer". By this they mean that there has been a certain randomness of development. Some Departments are constructed out of others to meet new needs, and occasionally completely new Departments are created.

Hanson and Walles also suggest that, on occasion, new Departments, like the Department of Economic Affairs, are established to carry out new functions, or parts of a Department are "hived-off" to form another Department, as was the case with the pay and management divisions of the Treasury in 1967. Other Departments, originally separate, may be deliberately joined to form a composite, or single Department. For example, the Air Ministry, Ministry of Defence, the Admiralty and the War Office were merged in 1964 into a new omnibus Ministry of Defence. Sometimes, functions are simply transferred between Departments in the interests of efficiency, or occasionally for political reasons. The overall shape of the Departmental system at any one time is the result of a wide variety of factors.

In order to understand the complexity of the Departmental system and deal with the question of the allocation of functions between the various

Departments, it is necessary to consider the growth of Government. In the early years of the eighteenth century the Government performed three "classic" functions:

a the maintenance of law and order
b the defence of the realm
c the conduct of external relations

Even in Victorian Britain—believed by some to be the high-point of free enterprise—the functions of Government were expanding. Government intervention in factory legislation, health, education and the regulation of private enterprise was becoming commonplace.

By the beginning of the twentieth century, the State acted not only as a controller of the behaviour of individuals and groups, but also provided services desired by the bulk of the population. A Liberal Government, elected in 1905, laid the foundations of the Welfare State by introducing such measures as an Old Age Pension Act in 1908. In 1912 one of the first acts of "nationalisation" took place when the private telephone systems of the country were incorporated into the Departmental system.

Two world wars brought about dramatically increased Government activity in most areas of the national life. During the inter-war period, the country suffered one of the worst periods of adult male unemployment it had ever experienced. This persuaded many politicians and intellectuals that the Government had a major moral responsibility to regulate the economy and manage the demand for goods and services in such a way as to ensure high levels of economic activity and hence, high levels of employment. The doctrines of the economist John Maynard Keynes became extremely popular in Government circles. He insisted that Government spending could stimulate levels of economic demand thus ensuring that people could find work. His influence on Government thinking, slow at first, was of fundamental importance; it provided the foundation for successive Government efforts to become involved in "planning".

During the Second World War, too, Lord Beveridge, the architect of the modern Welfare State, published a report which looked ahead to the time when the State would provide welfare benefits "from the womb to the tomb". This report led post-war Governments to establish comprehensive social security schemes within the country. The National Health Service Act of 1946 established the system of State hospitals and medical practitioner services which are in existence today and the National Assistance Act of 1948 provided a "safety-net" below which individual citizens could not fall into poverty.

Two world wars also established a system of State co-operation with private industry. The Second World War revealed that Britain was better equipped than Adolf Hitler's dictatorship to organise a "total war" economy. Britain's production of aircraft, ships and guns quickly outstripped that of the Nazis. The fact that Government, in co-operation with private industry, could run the economy at high levels of output was remembered by successive Governments after the war.

The post-war Labour Governments, 1945–51, established planning machinery in the form of a Ministry of Economic Affairs aimed at reviving the economy in order to build up the nation again. Various nationalisation statutes took important sectors of the economy—coal, rail, gas, iron and steel into public ownership.

Although subsequent Conservative Governments appeared determined to reverse some of these policies—for example, they returned road transport to private ownership in 1953—Governments of all political persuasions have maintained a high level of State involvement. A recent attempt by a Conservative Government to "reverse engines" and "disengage" the Government from intervention in the private sector of industry (1970–72) lacked success.

During the 1950's the term "Butskellism" was used to refer to the similarities in the approach of R A Butler (a Conservative Chancellor of the Exchequer) and Hugh Gaitskell (his Labour counterpart) to the question of how to run the economy. Both favoured the concept of the "mixed economy"; a combination of State and private enterprise. In effect, both major political parties were committed during this time and in subsequent years to high levels of Government intervention and State involvement. It was a Conservative Government which, in 1962, introduced the National Economic Development Council (NEDC) comprising trade union representatives, spokesmen for the key employers' groups and members of the Government. Its purpose was to encourage joint consultation on the problems of achieving higher rates of growth in the economy and the advantages of planning to achieve this.

Overall, the scope of Government activity has grown over the past 50 years: Government has greatly increased its responsibilities in the fields of housing, education and welfare, for example. In Departmental terms, this has meant that many new functions have been added to the traditional functions of Government.

Changes in scope have accompanied changes in the nature of Government activity. In the last 30 years Britain's overseas commitments have declined. During the Victorian era and the opening years of the twentieth century, Britain was an Imperial and Colonial power. Her extensive commitments overseas were reflected in the importance of Departments like the India Office and the Foreign and Colonial Office. With the loss of Empire (India, for example, achieved independence in 1947), there was a relative decline in the importance of Departments servicing such functions. Ironically, the decline in foreign and colonial responsibilities was not matched by a simultaneous decrease in the number of civil servants or the number of Departments. On the contrary, both have risen over the years. However, this can be explained by the rapid increase in the scope of the domestic functions of Government.

Factors taken into account in the establishment of Departments

How many Departments should there be? What factors affect the setting up of a Department? An analysis of the changing shape of Government since the beginning of the century reveals that two main sets of factors influence decision-makers in dealing with such questions.

Administrative factors

As Government functions have grown in scope and variety during the twentieth century, pressures to expand the number of Departments have increased. As Departments have grown in number so has the Civil Service and the level of public expenditure.

At the beginning of the First World War, the relatively limited involvement of the State in the domestic and economic affairs of the nation was reflected in the relatively small number of Departments (16). Prominent in the list were the Colonial Office, Foreign Office and India Office. The First World War was a period of Departmental innovation: during the war, the Ministry of Labour was created along with the Ministry of Pensions and the Department of Scientific and Industrial Research. The period during and immediately after the war was also a period of considerable administrative change. In 1919 the Ministry of Health was established, thus fulfilling pre-war plans to establish a unified and centralised body for administering health services.

Between the wars there was a period of relative administrative stability. Existing Departments were consolidated rather than any new ones created, although the creation of the Unemployment Assistance Board in 1934 and the re-establishment of the administrative system of Scotland in 1939 into four Departments under the Secretary of State for Scotland were important exceptions. The size of the Civil Service grew considerably during the inter-war period and many Departments set up strong regional and area machinery. Administration was brought closer to the people affected by it.

The Second World War represented a period of considerable administrative innovation. It also marked a definite commitment on the part of Government to extend the social services: in 1943 the Ministry of Town and Country Planning was established and a year later the Ministry of National Insurance was set up to provide comprehensive social security.

The importance of the "domestic" Departments continued to rise after the Second World War. The work of the Board of Trade increased in volume with the ever rising State involvement in business affairs, and the Department of Agriculture, Fisheries and Food expanded as did the social service Departments: the National Assistance Board, the Ministry of Pensions and National Insurance, the Ministry of Health. However, although there have been considerable pressures on Prime Ministers to increase the number of Departments since the Second World War, an opposing pressure has emerged, namely, the pressure to co-ordinate a large number of widely varying Departments to achieve efficient administration.

After 1955, a number of Departmental mergers took place with this object in view. Previously separate Departments were joined, such as the Ministries of Pensions and National Insurance in 1953 and Food and Agriculture in 1955. In 1964, the Ministry of Defence emerged as a result of the amalgamation of the three previously separate Services Departments and part of the old Ministry of Supply. The Foreign and Commonwealth Office emerged out of the old separate Foreign, Commonwealth and Colonial Offices and the Ministry of Overseas Development. In 1968, the Department of Health and Social Security (DHSS) was formed out of the Departments of Health, Pensions and National Insurance. In 1970, the Department of the Environment emerged from the previously separate Ministries of Housing and Local Government, Transport and Public Building and Works. At the same time, the Department of Trade and Industry was formed from an amalgamation of the Board of Trade, Ministry of Technology and Ministry of Power.

By the 1970's there was widespread agreement that the work of Government naturally falls into a few large groups of functions: i.e. overseas/defence, economic/environmental and social services. Experience suggested that it was both practicable and efficient to run much larger Departments than had previously been thought possible. It also appeared that a system of government with a few very large Departments was more effective than one with a larger number of smaller Departments.

Although there have been strong pressures for Departmental amalgamations in recent years, the trend has not been only in the one direction. While the incoming Labour Government in 1974 preserved the Department of the Environment created by the Conservatives before them, it dismantled the Department of Trade and Industry and replaced it with four Departments—Industry, Energy, Consumer Protection, and Trade. Sometimes, the principle of "differentiation" carries more weight than that of "co-ordination".

In 1964, Harold Wilson created the Department of Economic Affairs as a counterweight to the Treasury. It was intended to provide an alternative source of advice about the working of the nation's economy. Similarly, in 1968, the Pay and Management Divisions of the Treasury were "hived-off" to a new Civil Service Department. The purpose of this was to provide a new management style for the Civil Service which was previously under the control of the Treasury. Both are examples of Prime Minister Harold Wilson's alleged fondness for introducing "dynamic tension" into the machinery of Government.

Political factors

Administrative considerations are not the only ones that have to be taken into account in deciding how many Departments there should be. A basic principle of the British Constitution is to ensure that every function of

Government is the responsibility of a Minister accountable to Parliament. Most Prime Ministers have been reluctant to increase the number of Departments since this would lead to an increase in the number of Ministers, each with a claim to a seat in the Cabinet. There are good reasons for a Prime Minister wishing to keep the size of the Cabinet small; large Cabinet meetings are difficult to manage and control and there are undoubted advantages to be gained by having a small well-knit body of key Ministers.

It is surprising that, in view of the great increase in Government activity over the last 50 years, the number of Ministers and the overall size of the Cabinet has remained remarkably small. Inspite of a tremendous increase in Government business since the start of Second World War, the size of the Cabinet has remained fairly constant. In 1938, for example, there were 22 Cabinet members: in 1975, 21. However, a change has taken place in the tasks of the Cabinet between these dates. Of the 22 members in 1938, 8 were concerned with the "traditional" functions of foreign affairs and defence. By 1975, only two members of the Cabinet were directly concerned with foreign affairs. This changing balance reflects the changes which have taken place in Britain's imperial fortunes and the increasing importance of domestic issues.

The need for a manageable Cabinet undoubtedly influences the size of the Departmental system, but there are also contrary political pressures. A Prime Minister facing public criticism or demands that he be seen to be taking action on a particular matter may set up a Department in the interests of "good public relations". A Government attempting to control inflation by pursuing a policy of holding down wage increases may see the need to set up, say, a Department of Consumer Protection to give the appearance of doing something about holding down price increases. Additionally, every Prime Minister is pressured by important politicians in his party anxious for a Cabinet post. As a result, demands are made on him to expand the number of Cabinet posts to find room for the many aspirants to Ministerial status. Even if the Prime Minister creates Ministerial posts without Cabinet rank, pressures to include such Ministers in a Cabinet are enormous. Prime Ministers usually try to form Cabinets representative of the various factions in their own party. Although, therefore, there may be good administrative and political reasons for restricting the size of Cabinets, there may also be conflicting pressures for building large, diverse ones.

The structure of the Departmental system may result as much from convenience as from rational planning. For example, Richard Crossman, an ex-Cabinet Minister, vividly described in his memoirs how Prime Minister Harold Wilson planned to sack from his Cabinet in 1969 four Ministers with whom he was in disagreement. They included James Callaghan, then Home Secretary. Crossman suggests that Wilson said he would cover up this disagreement at Cabinet level by "another big piece of Departmental reconstruction". This, if true, shows that short-term political objectives are sometimes more important than long-term administrative considerations.

What way to organise?

The question has sometimes been asked: how should the functions of modern Government be grouped to ensure that they are well co-ordinated and work efficiently? Modern central administration has developed haphazardly by a process of "fusion, fission and transfer", but there are basically four principles for allocating functions between Departments.

Administration by area suggests that services should be provided by Government on a strictly geographical basis. This means that the country would be divided territorially into a number of units and all services within those areas would be provided by one or a small number of Departments.

Administration by client, the "clientele" principle, implies that particular classes of people such as children, old age pensioners and the sick should be identified. One or a small number of Departments would then provide, across the board, all the services they need.

Administration by service suggests that a particular service should be identified and a Department established to carry it out, for example, Education or Defence.

Administration by technique implies that work would be allocated to a Department on the basis of a special technical skill it possesses, such as data processing.

In 1918, the Haldane Committee argued that there were really only two sensible principles for allocating functions between Departments. They suggested that a choice had to be made between "distribution according to the person or classes to be dealt with (the clientele principle) and distribution according to the service to be provided". They were heavily in favour of the latter on the grounds that to set up Departments dealing with all the needs of children, old age pensioners or any other social group would lead to "Lilliputian" administration—each Department would have to acquire a great variety of skills across such a wide range of functions that inefficiency would result.

However, in spite of such bold attempts to establish the "one best way" of allocating functions to Departments, the structure of contemporary public administration reveals that no single principle has influenced the establishment of all Departments. In some circumstances, administration according to one principle is preferred to another, in other cases the reverse is true. Both the Scottish Office and the Northern Ireland Office are administered according to the area principle and occasionally, important sub-national areas are administered as large provincial Departments for political and administrative reasons.

The Central Office of Information which provides the Government with information and publicity material, and Her Majesty's Stationery Office (HMSO) which acts as a central purchasing organisation supplying other Departments with paper, books and office supplies, are organised on the principle of technique. While many Departments are organised on the service principle (Energy, Health and Social Security, Defence, Education are examples) the clientele principle is not dead. In 1970, two "giant" Departments were created—the Department of Trade and Industry and the Department of the Environment—to co-ordinate the work of several previously separate Departments. They were based on the service principle— Government Departments should be organised by reference to the task to be done or the objective to be attained. The clientele principle was ignored. However, the Ministry of Aviation Supply was not incorporated into the DTI; it was deliberately kept separate to deal with the problems of the aerospace industry—an obvious example of a "clientele" group.

Departments: important differences

Although Departments have one common attribute—their work may be broadly defined as "assisting Ministers to carry out the business of government"—they differ in important ways. In the first place, while Ministers directly head some Departments, they are only indirectly responsible for the work of others. It may be desirable to keep certain Departments, which are doing sensitive work or work of a quasi-commercial character, one stage removed from direct Ministerial and Parliamentary oversight. The Central Office of Information is headed by a civil servant, as is Her Majesty's Stationery Office. Similarly the Boards of Inland Revenue and of Customs and Excise have Permanent Secretaries and not Ministers as Chairmen.

Secondly, while some Departments are comparatively small others are enormous. The Treasury, for instance, comprises some 39 000 civil servants, in contrast to the Department of the Environment which has about 58 000 civil servants.

Large Departments have different organisational problems from smaller ones. The Department of the Environment, for example, must operate with a team of Ministers and a "federal" structure in which each part has a high degree of freedom from another. Size, however, is not necessarily a good indication of importance. The Treasury is probably the key Department in the British system of government and has a crucial co-ordinating role to perform which gives it a pre-eminent position in the Departmental system. Another difference between Departments is that some find it necessary to work through a decentralised system of administration while others do not. Again, some Departments must establish strong links with other decentralised organisations such as local authorities (for example, the Department of the Environment), whilst others can operate without them.

Non-Departmental agencies of administration

The growth in Government involvement and activity is reflected in the growth in numbers and size of Government Departments and in the growing diversity of organisations known as ad hoc agencies. Broadly speaking, these agencies have been established to carry out specific functions for Government, but are not directly answerable to Parliament through a Minister. The reasons for establishing such bodies vary. An independent public body may be established because, although Governments may be interested in developing a particular activity, they may be reluctant to become directly involved in it.

Often Governments establish such semi-independent bodies to take decisions on sensitive issues. For example, the reluctance of Governments to patronise the Arts directly (Governments do not wish to be accused of promoting certain cultural pursuits rather than others) has led to the establishment of the Arts Council, whose members, although appointed by the Government, are not its paid servants.

The growing interdependence between Government and private industry—many business firms now rely heavily on Government contracts—has led to the investment of Government money in their activities. Typically, Governments investing money in such enterprises demand a say in how those businesses are to be run. Rolls Royce and British Leyland (now "BL") are cases in point. Such Government involvement has led many observers to point to the existence of a "contract State": a State in which private enterprise relies more and more on Government sponsorship and financial help. The old distinction between the public sector of the economy and the private sector must be abandoned in favour of a view of the economy as a system in which a large "grey zone" of partly private and partly public organisations has grown. It is sometimes difficult to classify such organisations as either public or private; they are probably best classified as "hybrid" organisations.

These quasi-independent ad hoc bodies (which are dealt with at greater length in Chapter 13) pose questions regarding their independence. Clearly, there is very little point in setting up an agency which is supposed to be free of direct Ministerial control and Parliamentary supervision, only to find that, in practice, it is subject to both. This is the central dilemma of such bodies. They are supposed to be at "arms-length" from Government and yet must rely heavily on public money and public support. Buffers are erected to help them maintain much of their freedom. For example, while certain Ministers are responsible for these bodies in the House of Commons and may be questioned on important matters connected with the work of these bodies, convention insists that the detailed day to day management of many of them is free from direct Ministerial intervention and supervision. As in many things, principle and reality are uneasy bedfellows. MPs have tackled Ministers on the ticklish question of the day to day management of such bodies, and Ministers themselves have interfered when management decisions conflict with Government policy.

The Post Office is a good illustration. Before 1969, the Post Office was a Government Department under the direction of Ministers responsible to the House of Commons. Owing to the commercial nature of its activities—

selling services to the public—successive Governments felt that a Government Department form of organisation was not the most appropriate for the Post Office to conduct its business. It was decided to sever the "Whitehall umbilical" and give it greater independence. The Post Office was given a separate source of funding (a Trading Fund) which allowed it to use its receipts from sales and invest in new equipment and so on. The degree of direct Parliamentary involvement in the running of the new Corporation was deliberately reduced. In fact, the degree of managerial independence which the new Corporation has achieved is a good deal less than many envisaged. It is still subject to Ministers controlling its investment policies and it is not able to introduce commercial pricing. In times of Government restrictions on public expenditure, as in the early 1970's, the actions of Post Office management have been influenced by Government policy and subjected to direct Ministerial control. The question of its independence is therefore highly problematical. Simply setting up a body which is formally described as "independent" is not the same thing as demonstrating that it actually is independent.

The dilemma of the Post Office—trying to act as an independent, commercial organisation, while being prevented by Governments from adopting independent commercial policies—is one that it shares with other nationalised industries (otherwise known as public corporations). These include British Rail, the Gas Corporation, the various Electricity Boards, British Steel and so on.

Since 1945, these public corporations have become an important instrument for the public control of certain basic utility services which have been taken into the central government system. The relationship between Government and the governed has been altered. The citizen is not now simply related to Government as a taxpayer meeting the bill of basic services for the protection of the public and the maintenance of law and order, but he consumes services provided by Government and he demands that these services are run in an efficient, commercial manner.

The nationalised industries show the strengths and weaknesses of the quasi-independent agency. Giving these bodies commercial objectives has also meant giving them considerable powers. It has also involved allowing them some freedom from day to day Parliamentary control. However, the requirement that such bodies operate as Government agencies means that they must be subject to a degree of Ministerial and Parliamentary oversight. This has proved something of a dilemma for these organisations. These questions will be discussed in Chapter 13. The important point here is that the powers of the Boards of public corporations are not clearly defined. The goals of the corporations are sometimes in doubt. Should they pursue an out-and-out profit goal like a commercial company, or should they take into account social obligations to the community, such as fairness? These questions are yet to be resolved.

One final point on these semi-independent agencies of Government: with such a large variety of bodies of this type it is difficult to be specific about their internal organisation. All are, however, likely to display some of the bureaucratic characteristics earlier identified. (See Chapter 4.) For example, the permanent staffs of these bodies will be appointed by merit rather than through favouritism, although not all are civil servants. The larger of these organisations have a clearly defined bureaucratic hierarchy—as in most large organisations.

The Post Office, for instance, has the familiar pyramidal form. This creates another dilemma, however. It has become fashionable to "hive-off" parts of Government Departments, or in some cases entire Departments, to free them from some of the constraints of the Departmental form of organisation. One of the reasons for this is occasionally to reconstruct them with more flexible, "flatter" systems of organisation in the hope that the negative characteristics of bureaucracy—slowness and diffusion of responsibility—will be avoided.

The bureaucratic organisation often makes it difficult to decide who exactly is responsible for taking particular decisions. A constant process of referring responsibility to one's superiors is often noted by writers on bureaucracy. However, the attempt to relocate responsibility by holding particular individuals in the organisation responsible for clearly defined activities has only been partially successful. In the case of the Post Office, well informed members of the organisation continue to insist that the ineffectiveness of bureaucratic hierarchies has only been partially avoided since it became a public corporation.

Decentralisation

Decentralisation means that responsibility for administration is divided geographically between the centre and outlying regions. The growth in Government responsibility for services has made it absolutely essential for responsibility for administration to be divided between London and the provinces. A country in which all administration was concentrated at the centre would probably suffer "apoplexy at the centre and anaemia at the edges"—too much blood in the head, and too little in the feet.

Decentralisation appears necessary in modern conditions for several reasons. Firstly, increased involvement by Government in the domestic affairs of the nation has resulted in the need for a countrywide network of officials to take services to the people: the need is for "local" education, "local" offices of pensions and social insurance, "local" health services, and such personal social services must be provided by taking them to a geographically scattered population. The increase in social legislation throughout the country has been accompanied by a growth of regional and local offices of central government Departments.

Secondly, the value of efficiency, referred to in Chapters 2 and 3, has sometimes encouraged decentralisation. Speedy decision-making requires administrative responsibility to be shouldered at the point where policy will be applied. This may also save expense and unnecessary effort. However, a closer look at decentralisation reveals that it is very complex and takes on a wide variety of forms.

Bureaucratic decentralisation

For many years, many of the central government Departments and semi-independent agencies have established outposts on a regional and local area basis. This pattern of decentralisation—sometimes known as "deconcentration"—was well established before the Second World War. The Post Office has been responsible for maintaining a nationwide system of postal delivery (with the addition in the twentieth century of a nation-wide telecommunications system) for several hundred years. It established a network of local officials—postmasters and latterly telephone managers—to administer its work. Such officials were subject to inspection by travelling officers known as Surveyors whose job it was to maintain standards and report back to Departmental headquarters.

This form of organisation created problems. No important decisions could be taken by area officials without reference to HQ in London, a cumbersome and time consuming business. In 1935, therefore, it was decided to establish strong "intermediate" officials—Regional Directors—whose job would be to co-ordinate the various services and maintain standards as the old Surveyors had done. They would be able to approve decisions taken in the areas without reference to London. Speed in organisational communications was thus ensured.

Many Departments have adopted regional machinery of this type headed by "Regional Directors", "Regional Controllers" or "Regional Officers". The justification for this type of regional and area organisation is that it allows the organisation considerable flexibility; for example, central policy can be modified under special regional and area circumstances. It should therefore lift the burden of policy details from central government and leave it free to consider the "big" questions and decisions. Secondly, decentralised or deconcentrated decision-making allows for quick feed-back from the clients of the organisation.

However, while decentralisation within a bureaucratic organisation has undoubted advantages, it is not without its problems. Conferring powers on local officials increases the possibility that the centre will lose control of important parts of the work of the organisation. In Chapters 2 and 3 on environmental values it was suggested that consistency and political accountability were both important influences on the bureaucratic organisation. Both contribute towards centralisation: the concentration of power at the central headquarters of Departments and semi-independent bodies. In practice, central government organisations are torn between the con-flicting values of achieving flexibility through decentralisation, and accountability and consistency through centralisation. An uneasy compromise must often be struck.

Such tension is indicated by the fashion for establishing regional offices for central government Departments in this century, and the opposing tendency to abandon them and revert to a more centralised pattern. Before, during and immediately after the Second World War, a considerable regional machinery was set up in central government. Many Departments had established regional offices before the War, but to plan the war effort more effectively, 10 Regional Commissioners were established to co-ordinate the regional work of Government Departments. These were disbanded in 1945, but by then the regional principle was well established. Immediately after the War, more Departments set up regional offices watched over by the Treasury, which established a standard system of regions to which all Government Departments had to conform. This was intended to prevent the haphazard development of widely differing regional units.

This high peak of regionalism was followed during the 1950's by a period of disbandment. Regionalism had apparently fallen into disrepute. Commentators have suggested several reasons for this. An important factor appears to have been economy. The setting up of regional units inevitably leads to an increase in the numbers of staff employed by Departments. The Government decided that, in the interests of economy, cuts should be made. It has also been suggested that central government wanted to reassert control over the Departmental organisations. Greater accountability was the object.

At the present time regional machinery is again being developed. This resurgence began during the 1960's and was largely due to the determination of the Labour Government of 1964–70 to establish machinery for regional planning. They established Regional Planning Boards which included the Civil Service representatives of the regional offices of important central government Departments.

Decentralised regional and area offices are an important means of ensuring the flexibility of bureaucracy. However, there is no "best way" of decentralising administration. In practice, organisations must make a compromise, sometimes an uneasy one, between the opposing pressures of deconcentration and centralisation. Decentralisation of national organisations to local units seems consistent with the idea of "accountable management" within Departments and semi-independent agencies.

Political or democratic decentralisation

Bureaucratic decentralisation is a way of sharing administrative responsibility between the centre and the regions. However, responsibility for taking political decisions about the goals of society is also shared between national and local politicians. Although Britain is a unified State—the final political decisions are made by Parliament in Westminster and not divided between competing sovereign bodies—decentralised political decision-making has long been a characteristic feature of British government.

The longest established form of political decentralisation has been in local government. As its name implies, local government is a system of decentralised decision-making in which local authorities are subject to local democratic control in a way that local offices of Government Departments are not. Administrative responsibility for many important services rests with local government: for example, responsibility for administering primary, secondary, and further education, environmental services such as roads and highways, refuse collection, public health inspection and the like. To enable it to carry out these functions, the local council employs large numbers of permanently employed officials subject to the overall control and direction of elected councillors. Amateur, unsalaried council members are subject to popular, elected control, and play an intimate role in the administration of their local services. In addition, local authorities have a degree of financial independence from central government through their power to levy rates.

Various reasons have been put forward for continuing local government in this country and elsewhere:

1   It enables the local citizens to have a degree of democratic control over many important services.

2   It gives scope for democratic participation in the running of local affairs—local electors may vote in the election of local councillors and may stand themselves in council elections.

3   As a result, local government is often felt to play an important educative role in a democratic political system; citizens experience the responsibility of taking decisions and share in local government's successes and failures.

4   Often, experience so gained in local government is an invaluable rehearsal for taking part in national politics. Many MPs and Cabinet Ministers have moved on to Westminster after gaining experience at the local level.

At the time of writing, another form of political decentralisation is capturing the headlines: devolution. **Devolution** refers to the transfer of central government power (legislative—law-making, and executive—policy-making and application) to strong regional or provincial Governments in Scotland and Wales. The establishment of legislative assemblies in Cardiff and Edinburgh and the transfer to them of administrative powers previously exercised by the centralised Westminster Parliament could eventually mark the emergence of an important new phenomenon: strong regional government.

Which form of decentralisation?

As when deciding how best to allocate functions between central government Departments, there is no one best way to decide what administrative functions should be passed over to the local and regional units of Government Departments or democratically elected local authorities.

Deconcentration has certain advantages. Although decision-making powers may be given to local officials of central government, the centre retains a high degree of control over them. Thus, in services which demand a uniform nationwide system of administration, deconcentration is probably the best alternative. Where a high degree of local variation is permitted, and there are arguments for local, popularly elected control, local government may be chosen.

In practice, things are not so simple. Arguments have continually arisen over the post-war years suggesting that central government has tried, by various means, to control the activities of local government in the interests of conformity, to the point where local variation and democratic control have virtually disappeared. This means that local councillors and officials are merely the "agents" of central government. Such arguments, if true, suggest that the differences between deconcentration and democratic decentralisation are fictional. However, such arguments are too simple. There is much evidence that local authorities—particularly large important ones—are successful at resisting and modifying such central government influences.

Suggestions for further reading

J Stanyer and B C Smith, *Administering Britain*, Fontana, 1976
L J Tivey, *Nationalisation in British Industry*, Allen and Unwin, 1966

Questions

1   What features do central government Departments have in common?
2   Decentralisation and deconcentration: what is the difference?
3   Find an example of a quasi-public organisation.
4   What central government Departments deal with a) health? b) housing?

6
The Civil Service

Images and complexity

In the film *The Servant,* Dirk Bogarde played the part of a personal servant who, in a particularly cynical way, eventually usurped the power of his master and effectively reversed their roles. The following comments about civil servants have appeared in books and press comments:

"They have been the target for fairly good-humoured jokes certainly since mid-Victorian days along with seaside landladies, slightly dotty earls and absent-minded professors".... "they have failed in their duty of serving elected politicians" ... "their self-appointed superiority brings them almost immediately up against their obvious and almost complete lack of experience".

These quotations draw attention to four important questions which are raised about public officials: are they too powerful? Do they lack efficiency? How representative are they? Do they have experience of the problems of ordinary people or are they drawn from an exclusive group or class in society which insulates them from the hurly-burly of ordinary life? Before considering any of these questions, the Civil Service structure will need to be examined.

Not everyone shares the negative views presented in the first paragraph. Indeed, many writers and commentators claim that Britain is well served by its public servants. One such is Lord Hailsham who, in an otherwise scathing attack on the institutions of Parliamentary democracy claimed that:

"The Civil Service is, in fact, all that its ardent supporters crack it up to be, like the Brigade of Guards, the Bank of England, the Judiciary, and many other typically British institutions .... any attack on the Civil Service must take account of the immense virtues and integrity of the civil servants .... It is due to them, and not to the system, that British Government has remained reasonably sane, tolerably just, and almost impeccably incorrupt".

This last comment links up with the discussion in the previous chapter.

Many people have a double-sided attitude towards bureaucracy; they criticise it, yet they demand a high level of service from it. Recently, electors in the Strathclyde region in Scotland were asked what they thought about this region as a local government unit. Without exception, they replied that it was large and remote—typical criticisms of big organisations—yet they acknowledged the many advantages it conferred on their daily lives. Attitudes to civil servants and other public officials are very similar. For many people, the words "civil servant" or "local government officer" conjure up an image of a faceless bureaucrat doing little else than push paper around between in-trays and out-trays. They are seen as imposing burdens on the people who really get things done: farmers, industrialists and the like.

On the other hand, people closely familiar with the workings of central and local government state that these public servants are diligent in their work for the community. They often work very long hours and are unstinting in their help to British industry and the commercial community. A recent report in *The Observer* newspaper showed that it was civil servants and not businessmen who had taken initiatives in opening up important new export markets in the Middle East.

The truth about public servants probably lies midway between these two opposing views. Although, as Northcote Parkinson has suggested, there may be a tendency for bureaucrats to increase the amount of work they do in order to justify their existence and keep themselves in employment, the community must share much of the "blame" for the increase in size of the public service over the years by its insistence that Government involve itself more and more in the daily life of the citizen.

The organisations which, together, make up the public sector are extremely varied. There is an important difference between Departmental and non-Departmental organisations at the national level. These must be distinguished from local government organisations, and local government organisations distinguished from others with a distinctive identity of their own, for example, the National Health Service.

This variety in organisations is matched by a similar variety in personnel. Thus there are important differences between the staff of a Government Department and those working for a local council. The essential point is that although the term "public service" can be used to refer collectively to the many millions of people working directly or indirectly for Government—central or local—there is no unified public service in Britain. The different organisations comprising the public sector have their own methods of recruitment and may assess the competence and efficiency of their staff by different methods. The public service is thus highly varied. It includes the staff of the central government Departments, the Civil Service, a diverse group of staff working in the non-Departmental organisations, the local government service and a large varied group of individuals who must be included in the public service but whose status is not so clear-cut as the other groups. In 1977, the figures for personnel in these categories were as follows:

	million
Central government	2
Local government	3
Public corporations	2

The type of work carried out by these groups of staff is very different. The work of many civil servants is administrative while that of others is industrial. Of some 746 000 civil servants employed in 1977, 570 000 were administrative and 176 000 were industrial (those working in factories, stores, dockyards etc.). A relatively small percentage of the non-industrial civil servants are employed in work demanding a professional qualification. This is in marked contrast to the work of local government officials who are required to hold professional qualifications to carry out technical work. A very important distinction can therefore be made between the holders of key posts in central and local government service. In the Civil Service there has been a long tradition of recruiting people for key management posts on the basis of a general, rather than a specialist education. In contrast, the work of local government officers often demands high competence requiring a professional skill.

Other large groups of people could be included in the category "public service", for example, officers and men in the armed forces are servants of the Crown, members of the police force directly serve the community in a public service capacity. There are, in addition, professional groups (such as doctors and teachers) who, while subject to the control of their professional associations, nevertheless receive their salaries from public funds. The overall size of the public service is thus extremely large. This chapter concentrates on the structure and functioning of the Civil Service. While this is only one part of the public service at central government level, it is undoubtedly the most important part.

The importance of personnel in organisations

Any study of public administration must concentrate on the organisations through which it is conducted. This is essential to an understanding of public administration. Public administration is both an activity and a set of important organisations. Considerable attention has been paid recently to the shape and structure of public sector organisations. Many people feel that the bureaucratic organisation requires modification to bring it into line with changing demands, but the individuals who work within those organisations must also be examined. Are they suited to the work which they are required to do? Does their education and training fit and equip them to deal with the conditions of modern government?

Any study of organisations must concern itself with the human element. All too often large organisations are viewed as machines, working independently of their human elements. This is not so. Organisations have rules and regulations but these are interpreted by their members. The attitudes and values of those members are an important influence on the way the organisation works and the methods it adopts to deal with clients and the outside world.

Government Departments are staffed by civil servants: the most important of these take decisions and may be said to play a part in the political process. So powerful are they, that they have occasionally been described as "statesmen in disguise". They are sometimes the equals (or superiors) of Ministers in the amount of power they command. It is essential to understand their backgrounds and resources in order to understand how they can exercise such an important influence.

The Civil Service: origins and structure

In 1931, the Tomlin Report defined civil servants as

"those servants of the Crown, other than political or judicial office-holders, who are employed in a civil capacity and whose remuneration is paid out of money provided by Parliament".

Technically they are servants of the Crown and can be dismissed personally by the Sovereign. In practice, however, day to day control over the Civil Service has resided in the hands of the Treasury for many years. More recently, control of the Service has passed to the Civil Service Department, responsible to the Prime Minister.

In historical terms, the Civil Service is a comparatively recent institution. Before the middle of the nineteenth century, there was no single unified Civil Service in this country. At the end of the eighteenth century, there were under 20 000 civil servants (compared with 746 000 in 1977). These were not recruited through one single agency and set of procedures: on the contrary, they were recruited by individual Departments on the basis of patronage—a system of personal favouritism. The consequence of this was that the sons of the well-to-do and the well-connected obtained positions for which they were often intellectually ill-equipped. Inefficiency and corruption were inevitable.

No common principles of recruitment, control or organisation existed before the middle of the nineteenth century. A growing tide of criticism was directed against corruption in the appointment system. As in the twentieth century, this was a time when Government functions were on the increase: it was therefore vital that the organisation of public administration should be efficient.

The effects of patronage appointments were having a profoundly bad influence on the Civil Service. Often, junior civil servants found their promotion blocked when an "outsider" was brought in to fill a senior vacancy. The Crimean War revealed that there were serious administrative errors in the system for supplying and provisioning the troops—the responsibility of public officials. Such failures drew attention to the effects of favouritism and the appointment of incompetent individuals.

To deal with problems of this type, an inquiry was launched into the structure and running of the Civil Service. In 1853 the Northcote-Trevelyan Report on the Civil Service was published. The Report was the foundation of the modern Civil Service. Northcote and Trevelyan, themselves eminent civil servants, argued that the increase in responsibility of central government made it imperative for the Civil Service to be made more efficient. They acknowledged that its organisation was "far from perfect" and advocated that its structure should be examined and improved. The Service was seen as a relatively closed system to which people tried to gain entry to give them an easier life than they might expect in outside commercial employment. Posts were not filled by people with tested talent, and the consequence was an overall loss of efficiency. Management of the Service was unnecessarily fragmented (each Department laid down its own rules for its employees) and this encouraged widely varying standards and had little regard for finding the best candidates for posts.

The Report established four major principles for recruitment and structure of the Service.

1   Recruitment should be by means of a competitive examination.
2   A clear distinction should be made between individuals suitable for "superior" positions and those who would occupy "lower class appointments".
3   The Service should be unified by setting up a uniform grading and salary structure and establishing the principle that a civil servant could be transferred freely from one Department to another.
4   Promotion should henceforth be awarded for merit rather than automatically by seniority. This principle was an important break with tradition.

The most important result of the Northcote-Trevelyan Report was that the system of patronage and nepotism was completely rejected. The report was responsible for the setting up of a permanent career service based on independent selection by merit. Various writers, both British and foreign, have argued over the years that this innovation was the single most important contribution to the business of government in the nineteenth century.

In 1870, an Order-in-Council put these recommendations into effect. Common recruitment for the whole of the Civil Service was set up by means of an open, competitive examination conducted by an independent Civil Service Commission. Overall control of the Civil Service was placed in the hands of the Treasury which was given the authority to decide how many vacancies there would be each year. In addition to this, two main grades of civil servants were henceforth to be recruited: "intellectuals" and "mechanicals". The work of the Civil Service was to be organised into two main classes.

The advantages of the new system were obvious. The rejection of patronage as a basis for selection ensured that efficiency would be a major concern in recruitment. This recommendation also ensured that the Service would be politically neutral. However, not all the recommendations of the inquiry have resulted in praiseworthy practices and habits of organisation. In particular, the educational thinking behind the reforms has been heavily criticised. T B MaCaulay, the founder of the Indian Civil Service, had argued that it was not so important that a candidate for an administrative position in the public service should have a specialist education as that he had an education at all. In this view, it did not matter whether a candidate had studied Cherokee or Ancient Greek: the fact that he had studied anything to an appropriately high level was what mattered.

This philosophy was based on the belief that civil servants, especially those in the "intellectual" posts in the Service, should be "generalists". This meant that they would be expected to turn their attention to matters in a wide variety of jobs. Civil servants should not be appointed for their expertise in certain technical subjects, but should be chosen for their ability to carry out the widest possible variety of public service functions. This philosophy has influenced appointments to many of the main grades in the Service.

However, the policy has opened up the Civil Service to accusations of amateurism. The accusations have gained importance as the Government has intervened in more and more specialist areas requiring detailed technical and scientific knowledge. A common contemporary criticism of the Service is that the "specialist"—i.e. the man trained in a professional or technical skill—is at a considerable career disadvantage in relation to the "generalist". The specialist suffers in terms of salary expectations and general career prospects, and this is at a time when more and more critics are insisting that the modern Civil Service must rely more and more on technical and professional skills if it is to remain efficient and provide the country with high levels of ability and expertise.

As well as advocating "generalist" qualifications, the reformers aimed to unify the Civil Service and prevent its break-up into many specialised Departments. The "intellectuals", recruited on the assumption that they could with "effortless ease" master the intricacies of foreign affairs and the growing complexity of domestic affairs, were one way of establishing a unified system throughout which individuals could be easily transferred from post to post. This assumption, which is still held in Britain is not followed in many other systems of public administration.

The French Civil Service, for example, has not encouraged the development of a structure heavily in favour of the "generalist". For a variety of historical reasons, the French system has placed great importance on specialist training. Earlier than the British, the French system of government was involved in technical services which inevitably led to high levels of Government intervention in French society. This produced an early awareness of the value of technical specialists, and for many years they have achieved the dominant controlling positions within the French system. The French Civil Service is also much more specialised than the British. French civil servants owe their allegiance to a "corps" into which they are recruited rather than to the Civil Service as a whole. The French have not only gained considerable advantages from specialisation (for example, in the technical excellence of many of their civil servants) but they also seem to have avoided a disintegration of their Service. Whereas, in Britain, the generalist-trained civil servants fill key policy-making and directorial posts, and specialists tend to be "advisers" to superior generalists, the specialist in the French system has an equal opportunity with his generalist-trained counterpart to achieve high office. Some writers hold that the British attitude to a general education (i.e. that it is the best education for administration) has instilled bad habits.

Although the Government has intervened more and more in policy areas requiring technical and scientific skills, sufficient numbers of civil servants with high level technical and specialist skills have not been recruited. This recruitment problem has been further complicated by the fact that "specialist" civil servants are considered to be of second class status. A commonly used phrase is that the specialist civil servant is "on tap but never on top". His skills are grudgingly acknowledged, but he is rarely allowed to hold top posts in the Departments. This situation will now be examined at greater length.

Civil Service class structure

No real understanding of the way the Civil Service works can be gained without considering its class structure. Although efforts have been made since the beginning of the 1970's to improve this structure and abolish certain class divisions, important distinctions are still made between civil servants. Such distinctions have a long history. The Northcote-Trevelyan Report distinguished between higher and lower positions within the Service. There was to be a division between civil servants employing "mechanical" skills, such as simple book-keeping and typing, and those members of the Service needing intellectual and educational skills of the highest order.

In 1920, this division was dropped in favour of a three-fold division of labour which provided the basic structure of the Service for the next 50 years. In that year the Report of the Civil Service Reorganisation Committee was published. It recommended the establishment of three main "general" classes. Firstly, the **Administrative** class would be concerned with formulating policy, with co-ordinating and improving the machinery of government (organisational questions) and with administering and controlling Government Departments. The **Executive** class would undertake

"the critical examination of particular cases of lesser importance not clearly within the scope of approved regulations or general decisions, initial investigations into matters of higher importance, and the immediate direction of small blocks of business".

The **Clerical** class would

"deal with particular cases in accordance with well-defined regulations, instructions, or general practice; prepare material for returns, accounts, and statistics in prescribed forms; undertake simple drafting and precis work and collect material on which judgments can be formed".

Chapter 5 argued that the organisation of Government Departments is "hierarchical": they are organised in a series of layers and may be represented as a pyramid in shape. It was also suggested that the shape of the Departments is linked to the hierarchy of civil servants within them. *Fig. 3* represents the "shape" of the general class structure which arose from the 1920 organisation:

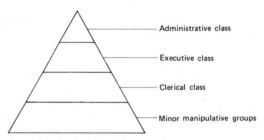

Fig. 3   The pyramidal shape of the general class structure in the Civil Service

Fig. 3 illustrates the fact that the nearer the top of the pyramid, the smaller the class within it. Some would say, in this case, that "small is powerful".

The Administrative class, resident at the top of the pyramid, is extremely small in numbers. In 1968, for example, it had less than 3000 members, but it enjoys a great deal of power through directing and controlling the Civil Service and advising Ministers. The farther away from the top of the pyramid one travels, the larger the classes become in size. In 1968 the Executive class had almost 90 000 members, while the Clerical class comprising both Clerical Officers and Clerical Assistants numbered over 150 000.

Each class is given responsibility according to its importance and status. The nearer the top of the class hierarchy, the greater the responsibilities carried and the more varied and interesting the work. Just as civil servants themselves are arranged in hierarchical form, so are their jobs. The Administrative class civil servant is expected to deal with "strategic" questions involving policy and matters of principle. The farther down the hierarchy, the more obvious it becomes that the officers are dealing with routine matters covered by general rules and regulations.

However, two points should be noted in this connection. Firstly, it is tempting to assume that all Administrative class civil servants deal with broad policy questions during the whole of their working lives. In fact, many Administrative officials spend a lot of time dealing not with important strategic questions, but with formulating the administrative and organisational rules by which these policies will be put into effect. The Administrative class official cannot altogether escape the routine. Secondly, the division of responsibility between these classes has never been absolutely clear cut. For example, officers at the higher levels in the Executive class have engaged in work which is very similar to that performed by members of the Administrative class. The same applies at the boundary between the Clerical and Executive Officer classes; the work of Higher Clerical Officers is often remarkably similar to that of Executive Officers.

Just as the classes within the Civil Service are organised into a hierarchy, so the officers within each class are organised into grades which are similarly arranged. The overall pattern is very complex. *Fig. 4* shows typical patterns of hierarchy within the classes.

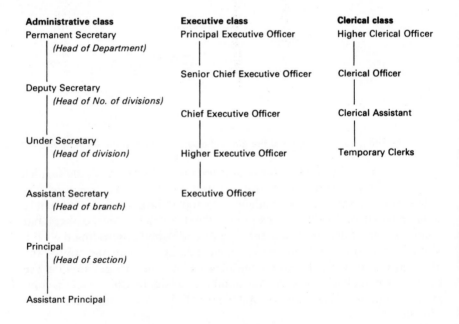

Administrative class
Permanent Secretary
(Head of Department)

Deputy Secretary
(Head of No. of divisions)

Under Secretary
(Head of division)

Assistant Secretary
(Head of branch)

Principal
(Head of section)

Assistant Principal

Executive class
Principal Executive Officer

Senior Chief Executive Officer

Chief Executive Officer

Higher Executive Officer

Executive Officer

Clerical class
Higher Clerical Officer

Clerical Officer

Clerical Assistant

Temporary Clerks

Fig. 4 Patterns of hierarchy within the Civil Service

The grading structure depicted in *Fig. 4* has not remained in exactly that form today. From the beginning of the 1970's, the structure of the grading system has been modified in order to break down barriers between the classes. Some of the grades referred to have disappeared. This will be examined in Chapter 7 when considering recent changes which have taken place in the Service as a result of the Fulton Inquiry in 1968. A knowledge of the structure of the class system as depicted in *Fig. 4* is obviously necessary if the changes are to be understood. Another important point is that although some formal distinctions have been abandoned, very real obstacles still block the easy movement between layers in the hierarchy. Changing the formal pattern of job organisation does not automatically ensure that, in practice, actual change will occur. The Civil Service is still hierarchically based and criticisms persist that the upward movement of bright young men and women is more difficult than it should be.

The following sections examine the method of recruitment and type of work performed by each of the important groups of civil servants.

The Administrative class

Over the last 10 or 15 years, much has been written about the working of the Civil Service. Both criticism and praise have been directed at this branch of the public service and its importance can hardly be doubted. Typically, however, criticism has often been directed not so much at the Service as a whole but at the relatively small group of civil servants who occupy the key posts within it; when a ship goes onto the rocks, it is no good blaming the cabin boy—the captain must take ultimate responsibility. In bureaucratic organisations, overall responsibility increases the further up the hierarchy you proceed. The Administrative class is in a key position of eminence and power within the Civil Service and consequently any faults noticed by the public and critics may rightly be placed at the door of this group.

The importance of the work of the Administrative class civil servant may be measured by examining the responsibilities of its most prestigious members: the Permanent Secretaries. The office of Permanent Secretary is the highest in the Administrative class. The Permanent Secretary heads a Department and is responsible for its overall efficiency and performance. He is also the Accounting Officer of the Department which means that he must ensure that money is spent by the Department only in accordance with the express wishes of the House of Commons. He will be called before the prestigious Public Accounts Committee of the House to answer any criticisms which arise after the Comptroller and Auditor General, an official of the House of Commons, has audited (examined) the Department's finances.

In addition to this responsibility, the Permanent Secretary is directly concerned with the Parliamentary business of the Department. He maintains a close relationship with the Minister and tries to ensure that the Minister is given sufficient information and advice to prevent embarrassment in the House of Commons during Question Time if there is likely to be a detailed examination of the way the Department is functioning. One of the most vital jobs of the Permanent Secretary is to act as a key policy adviser to the Minister: suggesting to him areas where Government legislation is needed, and informing him of the likely administrative consequences of particular legislative proposals by the Government.

In this work, the Permanent Secretary is assisted by subordinate members of the Administrative class. He is assisted by one or more Deputy Secretaries who deputise for him and are in charge of groups of divisions within the Department. Under Secretaries and Assistant Secretaries also perform key functions in the Department. The importance of the work of the Administrative class undoubtedly comes from its duty to advise on policy. Administrative class officers work closely with the political heads of Departments—the Ministers—and their position at the summit of the Department pyramid provides them with important resources (such as power, influence, and prestige) which has long enabled them to influence political decision-making.

These generalist civil servants also have great advantages over other classes and groups within the Civil Service. Their pre-eminent position in relation to specialist civil servants (to be examined below) derives from the fact that certain important functions within the Department have traditionally been performed by Administrative class officials. Thus, finance work and establishments work is under the control of the Administrative class. The Establishments Officer within the Department, usually an Administrative class official of Under Secretary rank, is concerned with important "machinery" questions of staffing and promotion. He is involved in deciding on the appropriate levels of staffing for the Department as a whole and for allocating work to divisions and branches. In most Departments, the Establishments Officer is concerned with questions of "organisation and methods" (O and M). Thus he is responsible for ensuring that the organisation of the Department allows maximum efficiency.

Without doubt Administrative class civil servants have considerable advantages. Firstly, they are uniquely placed to be able to oversee the work of the Departments as a whole. Their virtual monopoly of important functions such as establishments means that they can obtain a great deal of information from their subordinates about the working of the Departments. They are closely in touch with the Ministerial heads of Departments so they have access to important information from above and below. They therefore have an overall view of the work of their Departments.

Secondly, Administrative class civil servants undoubtedly possess formidable educational and intellectual resources. They are judged to be among the ablest people in the community. With such qualities, they can confidently assert themselves over their subordinates and can influence the thinking and behaviour of their political superiors.

Administrative class officers, like all civil servants, have the important advantage of permanent posts. Once a civil servant has passed a probationary period and is considered competent and fit to carry out his work, he is assured of a lifetime of employment unless he is guilty of a serious misdemeanour. Permanence of tenure is an important advantage to civil servants. Ministerial heads of Government Departments are transitory figures. They are aware that they can be replaced following a General Election and that individual Ministers can be replaced or reshuffled by the Prime Minister. Although civil servants can be moved between Departments, the Administrative class is so small that there is an atmosphere of an "esprit de corps" supported by a feeling of in-built excellence. The Administrative class has occasionally been described as a "village community" and such communities can present a united front when challenged from outside.

The work of the Administrative class (sometimes known as the "Higher Civil Service") is of great significance within the system of government. Administrative class officials—selected for their all-round excellence—do possess important skills and carry out much of the most important work of the Civil Service. Although they are recruited on a non-vocational basis (they are not expected to possess high specialist qualifications), Administrative class officials often gain specialist knowledge of particular functions of Government from their experience in Government Departments. This is sometimes forgotten by many critics who crudely describe them as "amateurs".

Many Administrative officers become expert in management. They gain unique financial and budgetary experience and must show considerable skill to be able to analyse the cost of policies for their Ministers. In addition, their work as Accounting Officers for their Departments brings them into close contact with important Parliamentary committees, such as the Public Accounts Committee, through which they acquire important experience of presenting arguments clearly and persuasively. Such skills themselves show a degree of specialist knowledge.

However, it has been fashionable for some time to contrast the work of the Administrative class unfavourably with the Higher Civil Service of other countries. There has long been a feeling that the educational and social characteristics of the British Higher Civil Service, which made it the pride of the world in years gone by, do not fit it for the tasks of modern society. Many argue that officials should be selected for their particular and appropriate specialist skills, such as a lengthy academic training in economics or statistics.

The Higher Civil Service has prided itself on its ability to evaluate the advice of experts in an unbiased way. This suggests that their generalist education allows them to evaluate critically the alternatives suggested by scientists, engineers and the like by assessing the quality of their arguments rather than attempting to understand the details of the proposals. They can thus quickly come to grips with the main points of an argument without becoming bogged down in the details. As the technical details of policy and administration have become more important in government, such claims have been treated with growing scepticism.

Background and recruitment of the Higher Civil Service

There is a famous saying of MaCaulay that "the youth who does best what all the ablest and most ambitious youths about him are trying to do well will generally prove a superior man". The intellectual tradition of the Administrative class can be said to reflect this. The search for excellence has been an important factor in recruiting for the Service. The test of such excellence has long been linked to the intellectual traditions of the most venerable of our educational institutions; Oxford and Cambridge universities (collectively known as "Oxbridge"). The model of intellectual excellence at Oxbridge has traditionally been an education encouraging the development of wide ranging intellectual skills which equip the scholar to take decisions and deal with thorny and difficult problems in any area of work. In the nineteenth century, the idea that such skills could be acquired through studying the literature and works of ancient Classical scholars was common. The "proper study" for the ambitious man of affairs in business and public administration, was the study of humanity itself rather than the detailed technical knowledge within a subject such as engineering.

Many critics of contemporary British society have insisted that although Britain was the cradle of the Industrial Revolution in the eighteenth and early nineteenth centuries, it lost its early advantage over foreign competition through its inability to reward adequately those people who had received an education in the practical sciences. Instead, the leadership of British society passed into the hands of men who did not understand the potential of industrialism. The British practice of appointing men and women to positions of leadership in society without detailed specialist knowledge in important technological areas is not followed by many foreign countries. The Northcote-Trevelyan reformers, however, assumed that an all-round education in Classics was the most appropriate grounding for higher civil servants.

Recruitment to posts in the Civil Service is by two basic methods. **Direct entrance recruitment** is designed to attract people into the Service by means of open competitive examinations. Recruitment to a particular class may also occur as a result of **class-to-class transfer** by means of promotion.

Direct entry recruits into the Administrative class are university graduates who have achieved a high standard of excellence in their final degree examinations. Before the Second World War, candidates for the Administrative class were recruited through a procedure known as Method 1. This involved an examination and an interview. Candidates who had studied Classics at Oxbridge were given preferential treatment in this recruitment system. Every other candidate had to master extra subjects in order to obtain sufficient marks to pass the examination. Unsurprisingly, therefore, Oxford and Cambridge graduates formed a large percentage of successful applicants.

Dissatisfaction with this form of recruitment grew during the Second World War and a new form of testing ability was eventually applied:

Method 2. Like Method 1, the new system aimed to test the candidates' basic intellectual qualities, but, in addition, tests of the candidates' personal qualities such as leadership skills and the ability to communicate (both skills highly prized in administrative jobs) were developed. Psychological testing, used extensively by the War Office to test the character of potential officer recruits to the armed services was adopted. The accepted view that the simple acquisition of a classical education automatically equipped a person for work as a top civil servant was being challenged. Method 2 was introduced partly to widen recruitment to take in graduates from other subjects and backgrounds. Another challenge to accepted ideas came during the Second World War when many people were used as temporary civil servants, many of whom did not have a university degree at all. Their success suggested that the time was ripe for a wider recruitment base.

Eventually the Method 1 form of recruitment was abandoned in favour of Method 2. However, the system of recruitment is still criticised. Reviewing the Method 2 system of admission in 1969, the Davies Committee lamented that candidates from relatively narrow intellectual backgrounds were still being recruited and that the Civil Service was slow to make use of the development of new and exciting subjects in the universities, particularly the social sciences such as economics, political science and sociology, which appeared particularly relevant to the administrative needs of the country. Criticisms of the usefulness or relevance of the traditional areas of study at the universities have always been accompanied by other, linked criticisms. It must be remembered that the entrance requirements of the ancient universities have traditionally favoured those from a privileged social background with a public school education. Many Oxbridge undergraduates have been recruited from Harrow, Eton, Winchester and other major public schools.

In the days before a system of universal secondary education, university study was costly so it was only open to those who could afford it. The major public schools were geared to the production of successful university entrants. Many see such a system as self-perpetuating. The tutors and lecturers of the ancient universities had usually been to public schools themselves and so they naturally favoured public schools applicants. In addition, the entrance qualifications needed for the universities included a competitive examination which stressed the importance of subjects studied at the public school.

Entrance to the Civil Service was similarly biased in favour of the same educational background. Civil servants, themselves educated at public school and one of the ancient universities would, so the argument goes, naturally favour candidates with identical educational and social backgrounds. A familiar criticism is that the elite group of civil servants—the Administrative class—is made up of old public school boys with the appropriate university background.

This is an important criticism. Many commentators believe that the social and educational characteristics of key decision-makers affect the type of decisions they make. Public schoolboys will thus be unfamiliar with the type of social problems to be found in the Gorbals in Glasgow, in Moss-Side in Manchester or Byker in Newcastle. In short, the upper class characteristics of such decision-makers make them unsuited to understand the daily lives of working class members of society, who make up such a large bulk of the population. The civil servant of this sort is out of tune with his environment. This raises questions about the representativeness of key civil servants.

In a democracy, the citizen has a right to expect that those who take decisions in his name will be responsive to his needs, responsible for their actions and representative of their wishes. Although the social and educational characteristics of many top civil servants differ from those of the bulk of the population, they are not necessarily unable to represent the citizen's interests. On the contrary, the high educational ability of this group of civil servants may actually help them to put forward the wishes of the general public with greater skill and expertise.

However, a general non-specialist course in the humanities is not necessarily better than a scientific or technical course of study. While high social and educational characteristics do not prevent anyone from competently supporting and guarding the interests of those less fortunate than themselves, there might be considerable gains from encouraging specialist-trained graduates to apply for posts in the Higher Civil Service.

Inspite of attempts made by the Civil Service Commission to attract graduates from the newer, "red-brick" universities with a wide range of academic experience, the Administrative class of the Civil Service is still believed to be based on the philosophy of all-round competence. Recently the work of the class has been conducted amidst rising criticism. A frequent criticism during the 1960's was that the management of the country's affairs was being conducted by amateurs who were out of touch with the needs of the country.

In 1959 Thomas Balogh, an Oxford economist, accused top civil servants of "amateurism". They were, he insisted, unskilled in management and economics and therefore incapable of taking decisions based on appropriate specialist knowledge. In 1964, a pamphlet produced by the Fabian Society (and said to have been written anonymously by high ranking civil servants) continued this theme. In the mid 1960's Peter Shore, MP, (later to become a Government Minister) produced a book called *Entitled to Know*, in which he argued that the poor quality of advice given to Ministers since the Second World War had been one of the major causes of the poor economic performance of the country.

Following a series of national disappointments in the field of foreign affairs (of which the much criticised Suez affair in 1956 is an example) and domestic policy (typified in the frequent criticisms made, over the years, of Britain's declining economic performance) journalists, academics and other interested political commentators seem to have been infected by a mood of national self-reproach and doubt. It was only natural for critics to try to identify a group which could be held responsible. The Higher Civil Service was uniquely placed to act as a scapegoat. Civil servants were unable to defend themselves against many of these attacks since they were bound by the convention of secrecy and confidentiality. While much of this criticism was probably justified, much of it was clearly misplaced. However, with the election in 1964 of a Labour Government pledged to change and social reform, the stage was set for a deep examination of the working of the Civil Service and in particular its top posts. The effects of this inquiry will be discussed in Chapter 7.

Inspite of this attempt to reform the Civil Service, there are still many critics of its performance. In an article in *The Guardian* in 1977, Lord Crowther-Hunt, a member of the Fulton Committee of Inquiry and a man with experience of Government, argued (and continues to argue) that the educational background of many civil servants—trained in the Oxbridge tradition—is unsuited to meet the demands and deal with the problems of the last quarter of the twentieth century. He argued that the "cult of the generalist" was outdated and a positive danger to a Civil Service trying to be relevant and efficient. The debate between those who argue that the generalist administrator is the best man to fill the top posts of the Civil Service (he has no "biased relevance" to overcome) and those that argue that the specialist should no longer be merely on tap but should be put on top, is likely to continue for some time.

Two important factors moderate such arguments. Figures published by the Civil Service Department reveal that as recently as January 1977 large numbers of candidates have continued to enter the Administrative class from Oxbridge. Of 140 graduate entrants in 1976 to the rank of Administrative trainee (a new grade replacing that of Assistant Principal), 57.9% came from Oxbridge. This appears to support the observation of the Select Committee on Estimates in 1964–65 that Oxbridge graduates were very much more successful even though Oxbridge's share of the total university population of the country was in decline. This drop in the percentage of Oxbridge graduates in the total university population of the country was not matched by any drop in the proportion of candidates entering the Administrative class from these two universities.

One interesting characteristic of Oxbridge graduates should not be overlooked. The social class background of the student at Oxbridge has widened over the years. The public schools now no longer dominate the entrance system of the ancient universities. Candidates from grammar schools and comprehensive schools have increased. The typical progression of candidates for the Administrative class is no longer public school—Oxbridge—public service. Now the typical Oxbridge entrant comes from a broader choice of secondary school. The numbers of Oxbridge candidates who have completed degrees in subjects other than the Classics at these universities is on the increase as well.

While these factors indicate that the recruitment of direct entrants to the

Administrative class is increasing, it is not proceeding as quickly as many might wish. It is true that the percentage of candidates from non-Oxbridge universities has steadily increased since the Second World War, with the development of university education and the dramatic expansion in the number of newer universities.

The basis of recruitment of the Administrative class has also been broadened by the continuing practice of making class-to-class promotions. Not all members of the Administrative class start their careers in the top Civil Service posts by entering directly from university. Almost one half of all people appointed as Administrative class officials are promoted from the ranks of other classes, particularly the Executive class. In recent years, the number of such promotions has shown a dramatic increase. Between 1968 and 1975 there was a six-fold increase in promotions from the Executive to the Administrative class. The educational and social background of Executive Officers is certainly broader than that of many direct entrants to the Administrative grades.

The Executive class

The Executive grades are an invaluable group of people concerned with the day to day running of Government Departments and the transaction of much important business below the level of the Administrative class. The 1920 formula that they undertake the critical examination of particular cases not clearly within the scope of approved regulations or general decisions means, in practice, that members of this class are expected to take decisions and administer important blocks of work with skill and with a fairly high degree of intellectual competence. Although they are not so clearly identified with the work of "policy advice" with which their Administrative counterparts are concerned, they are granted considerable discretion which indicates that the higher ranking members are expected to display initiative and resource skills. In fact, as previously indicated, the highest ranks of the Executive class have traditionally been concerned with work which overlaps with that of the Administrative class. The Executive grades together constitute the major management force of the Civil Service. Their work is similar to that of "middle management" in industry, supervising large groups of clerical staff and running the outlying offices of central Government Departments.

As with the Administrative class, the Executive grades have come in for a certain amount of criticism aimed at their generalist educational background and their consequent lack of specialist training in jobs which increasingly require specialist qualifications. The Executive class, like the Administrative class, appears relatively closed and insulated. Transfer into the class from specialist classes within the Service is relatively difficult and financially unattractive, so the class may be denied the benefit of scientific and technical expertise. If this criticism is justified it indicates that the middle ranks of the Civil Service are inward looking; a failing which is equally important here as at the top.

Although promotions from the ranks of the Executive class into the Administrative class have recently increased dramatically, the relatively disadvantageous promotion prospects of Executive class officials have been criticised. Executive officers are recruited like Administrative officials by means of open competition between direct entrants (the candidates are mostly school leavers with Advanced level certificates) or by internal promotion of members of the Clerical class. Being further from the centres of political decision-making, the Executive class has not attracted the detailed attention from outside reviewers which the Administrative class has had.

The Clerical class

As the name suggests members of the Clerical class carry out book-keeping, the preparation of straightforward statistics and documents, and engage in the simpler correspondence with members of the public. In addition, they may perform minor office functions, such as record-keeping and routine interviewing of applicants for welfare benefits and the like. The Fulton Committee considered that the skills of Clerical personnel were often not fully developed, neither were adequate attempts made to develop their career prospects. The result was that many members of this class felt themselves unnecessarily inferior to the classes above them, and this prevented the development of initiative and pride in their work. Promotion to the ranks of Executive Officer was often unnecessarily difficult leading to resentment and a lowering of morale.

As in the case of the other classes mentioned, recruitment to the class is carried out by the use of two methods. Firstly, direct entry to the class is gained by competition among school leavers with the required GCE passes. The second avenue of entry into the class is by promotion from subordinate grades.

As the numbers of staff in this class indicate, its work is spread extensively throughout the Civil Service. No Government Department can function without using the skills and resources of its clerical personnel. The first contact many members of the public have with the Civil Service is with a member of the Clerical class acting as receptionist in a Government office. This critical point in the relationship between the system and its environment is ironically trusted to a member of the Service in a relatively subordinate position.

The specialist classes

Space prohibits a full-scale examination of the work and characteristics of this large group of personnel. There is a large number of classes in this "specialist" category which includes lawyers, doctors, accountants, statisticians, economists, scientists and engineers. This section examines the relationship between the "specialists" and the "generalists".

Collectively, the specialists can be referred to as the "Professional Civil Service": recruitment to jobs in these classes requires detailed specialist qualifications in a particular area of knowledge. Thus, to be a Medical Officer in the Civil Service it is essential that the candidate possess the appropriate professional qualification: the same applies to the other groups in this category.

The distinction made between generalist and specialist administrators is sometimes misleading—it is often assumed that this is an absolutely clear-cut distinction. However, the so-called generalist may become expert in one or more aspects of the work of the Service; this, in fact, makes him a specialist. Nevertheless, there is a clear-cut distinction in Civil Service practice between a generalist and a specialist education: this distinction also exists at school level.

The structure of the specialist classes closely follows that of the generalists. Two of the most important groups of specialist civil servants—in terms of numbers employed and the work carried out—are the Scientific Civil Service and the Works Group. The first is organised into a three part structure, corresponding to the Administrative, Executive, and Clerical classes in the general ranks. Since 1945 the Scientific classes have been organised into the Scientific Officer class, Experimental Officer class and Scientific Assistant class. Within these classes there is a similar grading arrangement to that in the generalist classes. The Scientific Officer class is selected from graduates in science, engineering or mathematics, the Experimental Officer Class from candidates with Advanced GCE passes and the Scientific Assistant class from candidates with GCE "O" level passes.

The Works Group of the Civil Service is composed primarily of engineers, although included in it are architects, maintenance surveyors, quantity surveyors and land officers. The principles of hierarchy and grade are evident in this group too.

The Administrative class of the Service is given responsibility for some of the most important functions: advising Ministers, formulating administrative policy, controlling the organisation of the Departments and exerting financial control. This responsibility is reflected in the differences in pay and status between the non-vocational generalists and the vocationally-trained specialists. Over the period of his career, the specialist will earn less than his generalist counterpart and will have worse promotion prospects. Coupled with this is the feeling of being inferior to the non-specialist. In general, the work of the various specialist branches of the Service is under the ultimate financial and administrative control of the generalists. Where such work involves liaison with other Departments or has important Parliamentary and legislative implications, the overall control of the work will be entrusted to members of the generalist classes.

In many areas of the Civil Service, members of the specialist classes are employed entirely on professional and technical work, for example, in research establishments. In these specialised organisational units, the work is under the direction of senior scientists or engineers. However, in many areas the formulation and development of policy and the management of operations call for both specialist and administrative expertise. It is in these situations that general practice has been for overall responsibility for policy and management to be in the hands of administrative personnel. This assumption—that the non-specialist or lay administrator is best qualified to take an overall view of the work of the organisation—is not held in other countries. In this practice, the British Civil Service is the odd man out. In other countries the assumption is that administration in such technical and scientific areas can more appropriately be placed in the hands of trained specialists rather than "amateur" officials.

The organisation of the British Civil Service is based on a separation of both persons and functions into generalists and specialists. The British Civil Service distinguishes between those who administer and those who advise. The central issue in this situation is whether the responsibilities of professionals could be extended so that they have full control of the administrative and clerical work upon which they are engaged.

Moves are being made to give specialists a greater say in such questions as the formulation of policy—traditionally the responsibility of the generalist. In some Departments there has been a move away from the traditional structure whereby specialists and generalists have been organised into either **separate hierarchies**—where policy is determined by the generalists and executed by the specialists—or into **parallel hierarchies** in which each class has its own hierarchy but is co-ordinated by generalists at the head of the Department. The Department of Education and Science is one example of a trend towards **joint hierarchies**, in which the professional and administrative aspects of the work are so closely integrated that administrators and professionals must work in the same division or unit of the organisation. The importance of this type of organisational arrangement is that there is no rigid definition of function, and senior professionals participate on equal terms with their administrative counterparts in formulating policy.

Naturally, specialist officers are dissatisfied with many aspects of their relationship with their generalist counterparts. Their professional association, the Institute of Professional Civil Servants, made clear in its evidence to the Fulton Committee that many of them do not agree with the logic that the generalist administrator is best placed to take key policy decisions because he will not give undue weight to technical considerations. Specialist officers do not share the Northcote-Trevelyan belief that generalists are superior in administration to those with a specialist background. Many have put forward a case for the specialists in recent years, arguing that administrators, unfamiliar with any technical and specialist training, may fail to give proper attention to the many technical and specialist aspects of public policy. More and more informed observers of the British system of government and administration are questioning the fact that administration and specialist functions are kept separate, and point to many industrial and foreign situations where no distinction is made and where overall efficiency seems to have been increased.

The question remains: does the present system of dividing responsibility and personnel in this way enable the British Civil Service to cope effectively with its changing role in a complex technological society?

Suggestions for further reading

A H Hanson and M Walles, *Governing Britain,* Fontana, 1976
F Stacey, *British Government: 1966–75,* OUP, 1975
J Stanyer and B C Smith, *Administering Britain,* Fontana, 1976

Questions

1   What principles did the Northcote-Trevelyan Report establish for the recruitment and structure of the British Civil Service?
2   Outline the class structure of the Civil Service.

7
The Civil Service: recent changes

Contemporary developments

The British system of public administration has been faced with the challenge of change throughout the twentieth century. The move from a "limited" view of Government to an "interventionist" one has been an important development. Government has involved itself more and more in activities which are commercial, social and economic: it is no longer restricted to maintaining law and order and defence, although these are still supremely important.

These changes have greatly affected the public service of the country. The Civil Service, in common with other parts of the public service, has acquired responsibility for administration in areas demanding high levels of management expertise. The public sector, as suggested in Chapter 1, is performing functions which were traditionally carried out by private industry. The Civil Service now performs management tasks similar to those in private business.

Many critics have suggested in recent years that the standards used to assess private management should be applied to the work of civil servants. Naturally, differences between "private" and "public" organisations have not been ignored. For example, the need to ensure that the Civil Service remains accountable to the political office-holders is recognised as being an important restraint on the use of many practices greatly favoured in the private sector. Nevertheless, many areas of Civil Service work could greatly benefit from various practices and techniques used in private industry.

This chapter considers important areas of concern which surround the work of the contemporary Civil Service, and examines attempts which have been made to improve it and render it more capable of dealing with contemporary problems. Firstly, concern has been expressed for many years that the Civil Service has increased in power in relation to the political—that is the elected—members of the system of government.

Chapter 3 highlighted an important environmental factor: that of ensuring that the Civil Service remains properly accountable for its actions. This is the "bureaucracy-democracy" problem.

The old question of the place of the Civil Service in a democratic system of government continues to excite the interest of observers. In a recent article in *The Guardian*, Lord Crowther-Hunt argued that the work of Government is now so immense and the Ministers have such a wide range of responsibilities, that they hardly have time to take well thought-out decisions on the major issues of the day. Parliament, too, has failed to adapt itself to deal with the great expansion of Government responsibilities, and finds it increasingly difficult to scrutinise Government policies and the internal workings of the Civil Service. The inevitable tendency is for the power of the permanent Civil Service to increase, in such circumstances, to fill the vacuum left by the politicians.

Pressure on top politicians has been accompanied by an increase in power of the Civil Service. The continuing tendency to move Ministers around between Departments with great frequency has weakened their ability to control their Departments. They do not have long enough in particular Departments to be able to challenge the views of their permanent staff. Many important decisions on the implications of policies are in fact not taken by Ministers at all, but are worked out in inter-Departmental committees of civil servants. Denied the means to build up expertise in the way that civil servants can, the Minister can only sheepishly approve these decisions taken in his name after they have been made. This denies him the opportunity to contribute effectively to discussions about policy-making until it is too late for him to exercise any real influence. Furthermore, the Civil Service is skillful at ignoring or overturning decisions which it does not like. This is particularly evident in the case of recent proposals for reforming the structure of the Civil Service.

Secondly, as the Civil Service has increased in power, important changes have developed in the constitutional conventions surrounding its work. The assumption that the civil servant should remain anonymous while the Minister assumes public responsibility for his actions is in decline. The Vehicle and General Case, cited in Chapter 3, showed that in specific cases, individual civil servants have been singled out for criticism and publicly named. On other occasions, the actions of public officials have been praised, and the individuals named.

The "visibility" of civil servants has also been revealed through the practice of Parliamentary committees calling individual civil servants before them to account for policies and administrative actions taken in their Departments in the name of the Minister concerned. It is probably too early to speculate on the implications of such changes, but there is a danger that the extension of such practices might change basic constitutional relationships established over many years.

The doctrine of Ministerial accountability is also in decline. If that indicates the complete loss of anonymity for the public official, there is proper cause for concern that the Civil Service will no longer be considered impartial. Ministers may cease to trust specific individuals on the grounds that they have been identified with the policies of their political predecessors and will thus be hostile to those of an incoming Government.

Hopefully, the development of a fully "politicised" Civil Service is a thing of the far-distant future, but one day we may be faced with a situation similar to that in America where large numbers of key civil servants lose office with the arrival of a new Government. Anonymity ensures a high degree of political impartiality on the part of the Civil Service. This has meant in the past that Governments with different political beliefs can expect efficient and loyal service from the Civil Service.

The other major change which has taken place in recent years is the gradual development of temporary appointments to the Service. This is an important phenomenon and is considered to bestow certain advantages. Firstly, it is argued that "temporary officials" may bring with them into the Government service, qualities and skills which are supposedly lacking amongst the ranks of permanent officials. Many people have criticised the educational background of civil servants for failing to equip them with the kind of technological, commercial and economic experience and skill needed in a modern system of government. Edward Heath, newly elected Prime Minister in 1970, brought businessmen into the Civil Service for precisely this reason. The lack of "managerial skills" in the Civil Service was singled out in 1968 by the Fulton Report as one of its major weaknesses. Under the Labour Governments of 1964–70, "specialist" skills in economics and technology were recognised as important, and this was made clear by Prime Minister Harold Wilson's decision to increase the number of temporary special "advisers" in such Departments as Economic Affairs and the Ministry of Technology.

The second major reason for increasing the number of temporary appointments in the Civil Service is to use them to offset the power of the permanent officials. Following the return to power of a Labour Government in 1974, Harold Wilson, Prime Minister at the time, encouraged the appointment of "temporary special advisers" to help Ministers formulate and develop political programmes affecting the work of their Departments. Mrs Marcia Williams, now Lady Faulkender, has written in her book *Inside Number Ten* of the deep suspicions which lurked in the minds of many members of the Labour party that the Civil Service was traditionally more hostile to the policies of a Labour Government than a Conservative one. She insists that during the lifetime of the Labour Government 1966–70, many influential people in the Labour party and Labour Government believed that many of the reforms which the Government had wanted to bring into effect had been blocked by top civil servants who were hostile to many of the changes proposed.

The appointment of about 40 temporary special advisers in 1974 can be seen as an attempt to provide Ministers in the incoming Government with a set of alternative ideas, which could be used to counteract those of the Civil

Service. Such a policy—of recruiting temporary advisers to offer policy advice—marks a move towards establishing "ministerial cabinets", which form an important element in foreign systems of government, for example the French. They have not traditionally figured so prominently in Britain and, like all things new, have been challenged and regarded with suspicion. Top civil servants have been uneasy about such appointments and have tried with considerable success, to prevent them exercising any real power within the Departments. The effectiveness of many of these policy advisers has suffered as a result.

The Fulton Report

The above example of the Civil Service blocking, or making difficult changes proposed by Governments to produce new working patterns illustrates an important fact of organisational life: that organisations are not simply machines—they are made up of individuals with feelings, ideas and attitudes. The study of organisations must not only take into account the structure and rules of those organisations, but must, in addition, concern itself with the attitudes and behaviour of individuals and groups within the organisation.

Consideration of the human relations element within organisations shows that if individuals feel threatened by proposals to change the organisation, they will be hostile to the proposals and will actively conspire against them. There is evidence from all sorts of organisations that change can be very unsettling for many people. Strikes and industrial disputes often appear to be caused by the reluctance of workers—and management—to accept changes in working practices which they see as threatening their livelihood or causing them upset. *The Sunday Times* newspaper's typesetters are an example of a group of workers profoundly disturbed by changes in the industry.

In 1966, a Committee of Inquiry was appointed under Lord Fulton to "examine the structure, recruitment and management, including training, of the Home Civil Service, and to make recommendations". The barrage of criticism to which the Civil Service had been subjected since the middle of the 1950's had had its effect—the Government of the day decided that the time was ripe for an examination of the system. It was probably the most thorough-going inquiry into the Service since Northcote-Trevelyan. The Fulton Committee marks a major landmark in the development of public administration in Britain.

There are some obvious similarities between Northcote-Trevelyan and Fulton:

1 Both inquiries were considered necessary as a result of changes which had taken place in the tasks of Government.

2 Both followed a considerable body of criticism that the Civil Service was unsuited to its task.

3   Both were mid-century documents, and the two centuries in question—the nineteenth and the twentieth—were periods during which the nature and scope of Government activity were changing.

4   Both were aimed at making the Civil Service more efficient and capable of dealing with the changing tasks presented to it.

5   Both called into question established practice.

An intelligent observer transported from 1853 to 1968 might be forgiven for thinking that little had changed. Many of the criticisms of Fulton mirror those of Northcote-Trevelyan over a century earlier and, indeed, the Committee notoriously observed that the Civil Service was still the product of the nineteenth century—still very much the product of Northcote-Trevelyan. This view can be challenged, however.

The Fulton Report followed a fairly well-developed line of criticism on the Service. This is hardly surprising considering that it was set up in response to criticisms that the Service was amateurish and out of touch with contemporary reality. The Fulton Committee made three major criticisms:

1   Civil servants often **lacked relevant skills**. They had no professional training to equip them to carry out the tasks of modern government.

2   The **cult of the amateur** was still much praised in the Service. There was still the feeling that the "all-rounder" or generalist was still the best man to carry out the tasks of public administration.

3   There was a **lack of adequate training** of civil servants once they were recruited into the Service and too little attention was paid to their career development. In the event, this meant that both the individual and the organisation suffered. Too much reliance was placed on seniority rather than on demonstrated ability so that overall, the structure of the Service and the training of its personnel were out of keeping with modern conditions.

In summary, the following criticisms of the Civil Service were made in the Committee Report. The Service was still based on the philosophy of the generalist, and the system of classes hindered its work by artificially dividing up the work of the Service and preventing the easy movement of staff. In addition, too few civil servants possessed managerial skills and they were inadequately utilised (a typical criticism was that they were moved around between jobs far too frequently thus preventing them gaining detailed expertise in particular areas). As a whole, the Civil Service was too cut off from the outside community: its work would benefit from the encouragement of more temporary appointments to bring in outside talent.

The recommendations of the Committee Report were an attempt to counteract these negative features. In order to understand its proposals the nature of bureaucratic organisations must be borne in mind.

In many ways, the criticisms of the Fulton Committee are criticisms of the negative aspects of the bureaucratic organisation. One lesson of Fulton is that under certain circumstances the strengths of bureaucracy are outweighed by its disadvantages. The advantages of hierarchy, for example, encouraging a proper specialisation of tasks and allocation of responsibilities, were seen as being counteracted by certain important disadvantages. The class structure of the Service was another example of disadvantages outweighing advantages. The existing class structure caused diffusion of responsibility and the unnecessary upward referral of decisions which should have been taken much lower down the hierarchy.

The Committee also argued that much of the work of modern Government demanded speedy decisions and a "management" approach to its tasks. Neither quality was typical of a bureaucracy or of civil servants. The Committee's proposals for flexible use of outside staff and an end to much unnecessary secrecy in central administration was another challenge to the accepted practices of a large public bureaucracy.

During the 1960's, academic research into the working of organisations became fashionable. More and more university-trained academics became interested in the ways in which organisations functioned to provide the goods and services of an advanced society. An early result of such research was a challenge to the conventional belief that, to run an organisation effectively, all that was required was a set of simple skills which could be used in all organisations and would guarantee managerial success. Many writers suggested instead that the working of organisations could be affected by the type of product they were producing, the nature of the work force and the amount of "environmental" change they faced. In effect, organisations facing a shift in demand for their products and having to cope with rapidly changing technological and social conditions would need to be organised on a more flexible basis than organisations coping with the same task year in and year out.

In many respects, the Fulton Committee contributed to a developing debate on the role and effectiveness of the Civil Service and the organisations of central government. It drew attention to the fact that the bureaucratic organisations of Government were proving themselves inadequate in dealing with the pressures of a changing environment and the consequent changing set of tasks which this brought. Their recommendations certainly attempted to remedy this situation.

Firstly, the Committee advocated a radically altered class structure. This recommendation had serious implications since the class structure of the Civil Service (the hierarchy) was a basic part of bureaucratic organisations. The Committee's aim was a classless Civil Service, with a pay structure closely related to the type of work carried out by each officer. Henceforth, jobs within the Civil Service should be graded and paid strictly according to the job carried out. The previous class structure, they insisted, was in many cases the result of historical accident. Over a thousand separate classes existed in the Civil Service and the differences between them were often artificial. In addition, they restricted mobility and initiative. The Committee also insisted that the specialist groups within the

Service should be given more responsibility to suit their undoubted ability and professional skills. The system should be made more flexible by encouraging the importation of outside talent and the opening up of the Civil Service to outsiders on short-term appointments.

Another common disadvantage of large bureaucratic organisations is the tendency to fragmentation, already mentioned. The Committee argued that top level management of the Civil Service should be taken away from the Treasury (the central finance Ministry) and placed under a new Department to be called the Civil Service Department. This Department would be in charge of overall recruitment to the Service, and ensure that all the Departments were providing adequate training facilities for their staff and that each was dealing properly with questions of internal efficiency. The intention was that one central Ministry should co-ordinate the functions of central management of the Civil Service.

Other recommendations of the Committee were equally important. One of these has created considerable interest since it suggests that important parts of central government work may be suitable for a different style of management—accountable management—than that exercised in the traditional Government Department. "Accountable and efficient management" meant for Fulton that individual civil servants should be held directly accountable for the performance of the work for which they were directly responsible.

One consequence of this recommendation was that it was necessary to identify those parts of an organisation to which costs could be allocated and to which standards of achievement could be applied. In those parts of Departments where this was possible, the Committee recommended the establishment of "budget" centres. Where costs and benefits could not be so easily measured, but where it still made sense to talk about holding members of the Department responsible for results, they recommended the establishment of "responsibility centres". A recommendation linked to this was that accountable management could be best introduced when the activities in question were taken out of the hands of Departments altogether and placed in a semi-autonomous agency. (Chapter 5 argued that such agencies are, to a significant degree, free of political control).

Fulton also saw a weakness in the traditional management structure of many Departments. The fact that top civil servants in these Departments were concentrating on matters of day to day concern, meant that too little attention was given to planning for the future. The question of planning—making intelligent forecasts about the demands on the organisation and the likely performance of the members of the organisation in meeting those demands—is essential in any management situation. The Committee argued that planning matters should be separated from those of day to day management and made the responsibility of a Senior Policy Adviser who would operate at the same level as the Permanent Secretary and work informally with him.

Fulton: an evaluation

The Fulton Report was a document of its time: its recommendations and the deliberations of the Committee which produced it were permeated by the management ideas of the 1960's. A commonly expressed view during this decade was that the "bureaucratic" organisation was no longer an appropriate organisational design. Flexible organisation was needed in order to cope with the problems of a changing society: this applied to the organisations of Government as well as to those in the private sector. A popular view that British society was somehow unsympathetic to the trained professional and preferred the "gentleman amateur" is evident in the Report.

Fulton's recommendations for better training and career management of civil servants and for improving the planning capability of Departments echoed a concern expressed more widely in industry, and the recommendation for "accountable management" was consistent with a popular theme that responsibility should be decentralised in large organisations and given to those relatively low down the hierarchy. Accountable management was also consistent with the writing of many management theorists of the time who were insisting that the best way to motivate people and make them perform to the best of their ability was to increase the amount of responsibility that they carried.

Fulton was a necessary document: the time was ripe for examining the working and performance of the British Civil Service to see whether it was effective. However, the Report has been criticised on a number of scores. Many critics hold that the Report was not entirely fair in its criticism of the structure of the Civil Service. In one notorious passage, the Report criticised the Civil Service for failing to respond to change. As has been seen, change is a factor which has affected British government throughout the twentieth century. In addition, the civil servants which the Report chose to criticise were the same civil servants who had set up a host of new Departments and who had successfully administered new Government policies and programmes since the Second World War.

Another criticism is that the Committee's terms of reference were so restricted that it could not properly investigate the real problems of twentieth century government. For instance, the Committee was prevented by those terms of reference from considering the relations between the Civil Service and Parliament and from examining the role of the Minister in relation to his civil servants. This is significant since the Committee's recommendations on, for example, the introduction of "accountable units" involved it unavoidably in such questions. The proposal to decentralise authority to low level officials—necessary in any "accountable management" system—is not consistent with the doctrine of individual Ministerial responsibility which involves centralising decision-making at the top of the Department.

These shortcomings cast doubts about whether the recommendations of the Committee, that the best practices of outside management should be introduced into the Civil Service, are really feasible. Can "efficiency" and "accountability" be reconciled in the way that Fulton thought possible? Is the decentralisation of decision-making feasible if decisions must be taken with a high degree of consistency and subject to the overriding authority of Parliament?

Fulton was also criticised for the inconsistency of some of its recommendations. For example, the principle of "accountable management" —making individual civil servants responsible for achieving efficiency in clearly defined areas of work—only makes sense if they are given full control over staff and resources. Yet Fulton proposed that the overall control of staff and their training, promotion and salary prospects should remain the responsibility of the Civil Service Department rather than be decentralised in this way. Thus the individual in charge of an area of work could not decide how many staff to employ on a particular job, nor could he decide to award junior officials greater salary increases than others if they had displayed greater initiative as was the case in private industry.

In other words, the reforms proposed by the Committee, although based on the best practice in private industry, would have to be amended if applied in central government. The environment of the public sector with its values of consistency, accountability and so on has caused many of the proposals to be modified.

Fulton: ten years on

One thing is certain: many of the criticisms of the Civil Service which led to the establishment of the Committee are still in evidence today. A decade after the Report, the Civil Service was still not geared to produce maximum efficiency and the best results. In May 1978 Leslie Chapman, an ex-civil servant of high rank in the Department of the Environment, published a book entitled *Your Disobedient Servant* in which he condemned the Civil Service for its inefficiency and management failure. In particular, he singled out the Higher Civil Service which, he argued, was resistant to change and had blocked those reforms proposed by Fulton with which it did not agree or which were seen as threatening its power base within the system of government. He quoted the reported words of Mrs Barbara Castle, an ex-Cabinet Minister, that the Civil Service was typified by deep seated lethargy—an inbuilt resistance to change.

According to Chapman, many of the radical changes in the working of the Service proposed by Fulton have failed to materialise. The recommendation that accountable management should be introduced was a failure: indeed, it is in the Property Services Agency in which Chapman worked, one of the much vaunted, hived-off agencies in which accountable management is supposed to be such a success, that many failures of administration are to be found. In Chapman's opinion, the Civil Service has been unable to shake off the negative consequences of its bureaucratic structure and adopt up-to-date business methods in striving for efficiency.

Against a background of criticism that changes have either not taken place, or have taken place too slowly since the Fulton Report, some things appear to have altered. In 1968 the Civil Service Department, a Fulton recommendation, came into being to bring about a closer, more coherent relationship between recruitment, training and all other aspects of Civil Service management. Since Fulton, the training of civil servants at all levels has been improved, and a Civil Service College has been established for this purpose. More attention has been given to providing the general class civil servants with specialist training in subjects related to their work—for example statistics and economics. Conversely, specialist civil servants are being trained in general administration in the expectation that more of them will transfer to posts in the general classes.

One of the most important changes which has taken place—at least on paper—is the breakdown of the existing class divisions in the service and their amalgamation into "occupational groups". Theoretically, this should allow better career prospects for those lower down the old hierarchies. In January 1971, the general classes—Administrative, Executive and Clerical—were amalgamated to form the Administration group. In September of that year, the scientific classes were merged to form the Science group, while in 1972 the Professional and Technology group was formed from the old Works classes. *Fig. 5* shows the occupational structure which has replaced the old general Administrative class structure outlined on

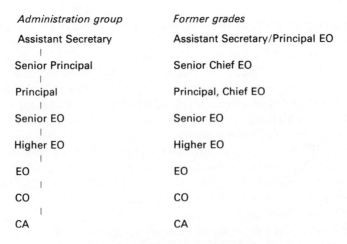

Administration group	Former grades
Assistant Secretary	Assistant Secretary/Principal EO
Senior Principal	Senior Chief EO
Principal	Principal, Chief EO
Senior EO	Senior EO
Higher EO	Higher EO
EO	EO
CO	CO
CA	CA

Fig. 5 New grading structure

Note: The new Administration group structure has in principle merged the previously separate Administrative, Executive and Clerical grades. It has also abolished the previous overlap between grades by merging such grades as Principal EO and Assistant Secretary.

page 84. In theory easier upward mobility should result. Similarly, the old divisions between specialist and generalist grades have been modified. It is now more common for the two sets of officials to work together in project groups than in completely separate hierarchies. In principle this should allow more flexible and fairer location of professional staff.

Disappointments

In September 1977, the Eleventh Report of the House of Commons' Expenditure Committee was published, following a lengthy investigation into the working of the Civil Service. An examination of the Report and the evidence presented to the Committee illustrates the point that the period since Fulton has not been one of great revolutionary change. Lord Crowther-Hunt believes that civil servants have put into effect those parts of the Report which they considered did not threaten them in any way, and avoided, ignored or actively conspired against those proposals which they thought would weaken their position. This may be an unfairly sweeping condemnation of the Civil Service, but many critics, including members of the Expenditure Committee, share this view.

Some of the Fulton Report's recommendations do, indeed, appear not to have been implemented; for example, the recommendation that Senior Policy Advisors be appointed to improve top level planning in Departments. Permanent Secretaries expressed hostility to such appointments on the grounds that responsibility for planning should not be separated from the day to day running of the Departments—both should be the responsibility of the Permanent Secretary.

Some recommendations have proved difficult to implement in practice. The Expenditure Committee Report argued that the proposal to "hive-off" parts of Departments and relocate them in separate, semi-autonomous agencies is fraught with difficulties. It has proved difficult to identify wholly commercial activities which might be taken out of the scope of Departments and placed under the management of non-Civil Service personnel. The Report argues that the principle of "hiving-off" conflicts with the environmental value that Government functions should be accountable to Parliament and subject to Ministerial control. Progress in appointing more lawyers, accountants and other specialists to the Service with managerial qualifications has been painfully slow. In 1975, the Heaton Williams inquiry into Civil Service training revealed substantial and worrying variations in the quality and quantity of training provided by individual Departments, a point made in the Expenditure Committee Report.

Again, some of the Fulton Committee's recommendations have been criticised for being ill-considered. Fulton had recommended the establishment of a Civil Service Department to take over the pay and management responsibilities of the Treasury with a view to improving the quality of training in the Service and the efficiency of its operations. Both training and efficiency have been heavily criticised by the recent Expenditure Committee inquiry. This led to the recommendation that the responsibilities of the new Department should be transferred back to the Treasury and that the work of the Civil Service College, established in 1970, would probably be better performed by outside educational establishments. Finally, some of Fulton's recommendations which have been put into effect, have been watered down in practice. The decision to amalgamate the old class structure into a unified system has been criticised on the grounds that many classes are still in existence and prevent the easy movement of staff and maximum efficiency. Inspite of the alleged attempt to improve the promotion prospects of junior staff and specialists, old biases in favour of the Oxbridge-educated generalist remain.

Conclusions

Change in any large-scale organisation is inevitably hesitant and piecemeal rather than swift and all-encompassing. The foregoing observations should convey the flavour of much of the debate which still surrounds the Civil Service. It is too easy to criticise it for failing to keep up with the pressures of twentieth century life and some criticisms have been overstated. One such example is that of Brian Sedgemore, MP, who submitted a report to the Expenditure Committee in which he argued that the Civil Service remained too powerful and not sufficiently accountable for its actions to the elected politician. However, as Lord Hailsham has said, and as the majority of members of the Committee agreed, civil servants can often prevent over hasty action by the Minister. Neither are they immune from outside criticism. Chapman's book is a timely reminder that some reforms are needed and must be attempted. It is interesting to note that at the time when the Civil Service has been criticised on the grounds that its all round amateur status is out-of-date, the Australian Civil Service is trying to get away from a concept of the civil servant as a professional, and is arguing that the British public official has many merits, including the ability to take an overall view of important problems.

   The lesson from this appears to be that "generalists" are not wholly bad nor "professionals" wholly good. Change and reform may have negative as well as positive consequences. Improvements can undoubtedly be made in the structure and working of the Civil Service, but one should not forget the very real contribution made by the Civil Service in the face of many difficulties over the years. A bureaucracy and the bureaucrats who staff it can have negative effects on a society, but they can also bestow considerable advantages. The debate about the Civil Service will continue but its inevitability assures it of a place in any democratic system of government.

Suggestions for further reading

The Civil Service Vol 1, Report of the Fulton Committee, HMSO, 1968
D Keeling, *Management in Government*, Allen and Unwin, 1972

Questions

1   What principles did the Fulton Report establish for the operation of the Civil Service?
2   What did the Fulton Committee mean by "accountable and efficient management"?
3   What comparisons can be made between the Northcote-Trevelyan Committee and the Fulton Committee?
4   Should civil servants take an active hand in the making of the nation's policy?
5   What are "temporary" civil servants?

8
The structure of local administration

Unity and diversity

The United Kingdom is mainly a political idea; for practical purposes of administration it must be modified to cater for the special needs of different parts of the kingdom. Both things are important—political unity and administrative variety—and neither can be discounted for they go together and each must make allowances for the other. The local government system tries to combine these two goals of unity and diversity.

In England and Wales, the 53 counties and 369 district authorities which are the main administrative units of local government are at present involved in current expenditures as shown in *Fig. 6*.

Service	£ million
Education	4 404
Personal social services	754
Police	661
Fire	165
Parks	264
Highways	762
Environment health	104
Planning	172
Housing	2 033
Refuse collection	230
Libraries and Galleries	139
Other	2 566
	12 254

Fig. 6 Expenditure on local services *(Annual Abstract of Statistics, 1977)*

These local authorities, while they range in size in terms of population from less than 100 000 to nearly 3 million, all have two essential characteristics, namely, that they are independent, self-governing organisations with locally elected councils, and secondly that they have the power to finance their activities by levying rates. Each in its way is a Government within a Government, deriving its powers from Parliament.

The new local government structure was brought into being in 1974 following a review of the existing system. The review had taken 15 years to complete and culminated in the Local Government Act 1972. That Act altered boundaries, changed structures, reallocated functions and, in general, introduced reforms which are still being introduced in some areas.

Apart from London (which, as the capital, has always presented particular problems of government calling for special solutions) England and Wales were divided up into county and district authorities, the counties providing large services such as strategic planning and police and the districts providing those services which, like housing and refuse collection, were more local in nature. Six[1] of the counties—those in heavily populated conurbations—became known as "metropolitan" counties. The districts within them, being large and having adequate resources, were given additional responsibility for some of the larger services. This primary system of metropolitan and non-metropolitan counties and districts was supported at a more local level by parish councils and community councils. Each had certain limited powers together with the special advantage of providing forums through which local people could voice their views and opinions.

The Local Government Boundaries Commission, a permanent body which was set up under the Act, now has responsibility for keeping all these local areas and boundaries under review and ensuring that the geographical divisions reflect the changing pattern of social and economic needs. The artificial separation between urban communities and their surrounding rural areas, for which the previous system was criticised, no longer exists; the balance between town and country has finally been recognised as an important factor in constructive planning.

However, despite the considerable efforts to simplify and unify the system, certain areas of the country stubbornly refuse to conform for various reasons. London, for example, is and will always be a special case where the problem is to devise an administrative structure which will meet the needs of some 8 million people for services covering everything from refuse disposal to fast public transport. The solution was found in the London Government Act 1963 which set a boundary to the London area and gave responsibility for its local services to the Greater London Council, to 32 London boroughs with populations varying between 150 000 and 325 000, and to the City of London Council.

Thus, some services are the sole responsibility of the Greater London Council while others have been given to the boroughs. Some services are shared under special arrangements, such as those which apply in the huge

1 Greater Manchester, Merseyside, South Yorkshire, Tyne and Wear, West Midlands and West Yorkshire.

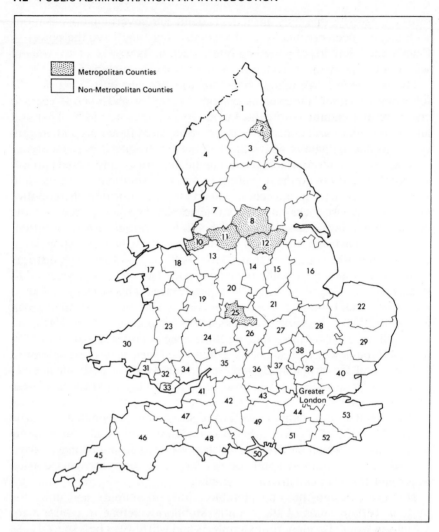

Fig. 7 English and Welsh areas. Counties: 1 Northumberland, 2 Tyne and Wear, 3 Durham, 4 Cumbria, 5 Cleveland, 6 North Yorkshire, 7 Lancashire, 8 West Yorkshire, 9 Humberside, 10 Merseyside, 11 Greater Manchester, 12 South Yorkshire, 13 Cheshire, 14 Derbyshire, 15 Nottinghamshire, 16 Lincolnshire, 17 Gwynedd, 18 Clwyd, 19 Salop, 20 Staffordshire, 21 Leicestershire, 22 Norfolk, 23 Powys, 24 Hereford and Worcester, 25 West Midlands, 26 Warwickshire, 27 Northamptonshire, 28 Cambridgeshire, 29 Suffolk, 30 Dyfed, 31 West Glamorgan, 32 Mid Glamorgan, 33 South Glamorgan, 34 Gwent, 35 Gloucestershire, 36 Oxfordshire, 37 Buckinghamshire, 38 Bedfordshire, 39 Hertfordshire, 40 Essex, 41 Avon, 42 Wiltshire, 43 Berkshire, 44 Surrey, 45 Cornwall, 46 Devon, 47 Somerset, 48 Dorset, 49 Hampshire, 50 Isle of Wight, 51 West Sussex, 52 East Sussex, 53 Kent

Inner London Education Authority, while others are the sole responsibility of special ad hoc agencies such as the Port of London Authority or the Metropolitan Police (which for reasons of state security answers directly to the Home Secretary).

The ancient nucleus of the "City" in the city of London, which is the commercial and financial centre of Britain, is even more of a special case. It has its own electoral structure and its associations with the traditional livery companies and guilds. Though tiny by comparison with any other authority, it is of immense importance and its permanent population of just a few thousand daily swells to about one million as people arrive for work. From a power base founded on expertise, tradition and ceremonial, it retains the character of a separate local authority complete with its own Lord Mayor and its own administrative forms.

Outside the capital other areas differ from the pattern. Local administration in Scotland is carried on by 9 regional authorities divided into 53 districts, together with 3 "all purpose" island authorities for Orkney, Shetland and the Western Isles. However, local government provides the same basic services in Scotland as in other parts of the country.

For many years Scotland has been responsible for much of its own governance. It has its own law and education systems and social work service, its own Law Courts and its own central Departments of Government, located at St. Andrew's House in Edinburgh. The reasons for such differences are partly historical and partly a reflection of the particular needs of a part of the country which has always had to deal with problems of distance, remoteness and sparsity of population. The result is a system of regional and local government which is unique and different in many ways from the system south of the Border.

Another part of the United Kingdom—Northern Ireland—also has its own special problems which have led to yet another variation in the pattern of local government. Northern Ireland has looked after its own domestic affairs for many years. Under the Government of Northern Ireland Act 1920, the province was given its own Legislature and Executive to deal with transferred functions such as the police service, subject to the supreme authority of the United Kingdom Parliament. This arrangement remained in force until 1972 when, because of political instability, the direct rule of the United Kingdom Parliament was introduced with executive powers exercised by a Secretary for Northern Ireland.

As matters are at present, inspite of various efforts towards partnership, participation and power-sharing, Northern Ireland continues to be governed by direct rule as provided under the Northern Ireland Act 1974. In practice, the Department of the Environment, which has central responsibility for local government, is concerned with administering major services like water supply and roads while environmental services are administered by 26 district councils. Other devolved services such as education and the personal social services are provided by area boards and local offices directly responsible to central government Departments in Whitehall.

Fig. 8 Scottish areas

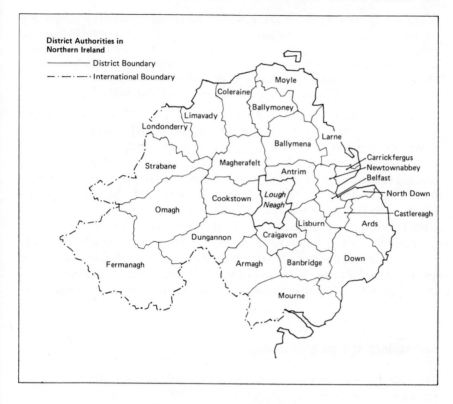

Fig. 9   Northern Ireland areas

An arrangement like this which departs from the standard pattern is temporary and represent an adjustment to a situation which is fluid and changing. The underlying aim is "good rule and government" and how this is achieved must ultimately depend on each individual situation. An area like the Falls in Northern Ireland, a crofting community in the Highlands of Scotland, the Potteries in Staffordshire and the London Borough of Hackney all have a common heritage but they are very different places. It would be convenient to have an administrative system which applied to all parts of the United Kingdom, but it would not be a practical solution; needs vary over the country and compromises and adjustments are called for. In making these adjustments local government has a complex task to perform.

The task is to provide government on a local basis throughout the country. Local government in the sense that we know it to-day is primarily a creation of the nineteenth century. Sidney and Beatrice Webb, who were observers of the emergence of English local government, wrote of:

" . . . the gradual supersession of feudal institutions based on mutual obligations of lord and tenant and of the new mutualities of chartered corporations and guilds, of craftsmen and merchants, all alike holding allegiance to the king, by a new species of authority arising directly out of the needs of this or that section of the community: such as the need for land drainage, town sewers, highways, street lighting and policing, for the regulation of markets and last but not least for the better relief of destitution and the suppression of vagrancy . . . It was this slow but fundamental change that was brought to a climax by the Reform Parliament in the Poor Law Amendment Act 1834 and the Municipal Corporation Act 1835.''[2]

The Municipal Corporation Act established a reformed system of local government in most of the boroughs and with the expansion of services during the next 50 years, the Local Government Act 1888 set up county councils and county boroughs. A further Local Government Act 1894 created urban and rural district councils and parish councils and meetings for the rural districts. This basic pattern lasted for the next 70 years. Certain services were taken over, others were handed back, boundaries were extended, amalgamations took place and everywhere improvements in administrative practice were made, but essentially the administrative arrangements of the late nineteenth century remained unchanged. By the 1950's, questions were being raised as to whether these arrangements were still adequate for a country on the threshold of a new and technological age.

Councillors and committees

The object of the major restructuring of local government which took place throughout the United Kingdom in the early 1970's was mainly an attempt to modernise and to make the system more responsive to the pressures for change which were then making themselves felt in Britain. The Civil Service was in the process of being re-modelled along the lines proposed by the Fulton Committee and the National Health Service was also being reorganised. Local government was being required, as the Wheatley Commission stated at the time,

"to play a more important, responsible and positive part in the running of the country—to bring the reality of government nearer to the people. It should be equipped to provide services in the most satisfactory manner, particularly from the point of view of the people receiving the services, and power should be exercised through the elected representatives of the people who are accountable to the public for their actions".

Most important of all perhaps, in view of the traditional apathy of people towards community affairs, local government "should bring the people into the process of reaching decisions as much as possible and enable these decisions to be intelligible to the people".

With such aims in view, the reform of local government introduced new styles of corporate management. The system was based on councils composed of unpaid elected members. Councillors are normally elected for a

2   S and B Webb, *English Local Government, Vol 4*, 1922.

four year term of office as a result of votes cast at a local election. Councils elect their own Chairman each year, and in the boroughs and cities this Chairman is usually referred to as the Mayor. Unless a candidate is standing for election to the council as an independent person or as the nominee of some local organisation he usually represents one of the main political parties. Most local councils are consequently run on a party basis.

Since party support will be necessary to secure nomination at the next election, councillors will have to follow the line taken by their party concerning policy decisions. In this way they are at least to some extent accountable to those people who voted them into office. With certain exceptions, which are set out in the Local Government Act 1972, any British subject who is over 21 and a local government elector is entitled to stand for council and, if successful, to be elected as a member. It is a disqualification to hold any paid office of the local authority or to have been convicted of a criminal offence within the last five years or to have been adjudged bankrupt.

The work of governing at local level is divided up over a number of committees of council, some of which are concerned with providing public services, while others are more particularly involved in finding the resources needed to finance this. Thus, the Education Committee is concerned at local level with formulating education policy and developing an education programme. It lays down operational guidelines for the schools and colleges in its area and allocates teaching and other staff as well as providing advisory support services. By contrast, the Finance Committee receives and allocates finance and sees that a proper accounting of its stewardship is given to the ratepayers.

Each local council has great freedom to make its own arrangements for forming and executing policy through its structure of committees and departments, so there is no real uniformity of practice. In some cases, each separate service has its own committee and its own department to run it; in others a few large departments each bring together the work of several related services with common policies and programmes. Other authorities use "programme area" teams drawn from different departments in an effort to provide a more integrated service. There is room for considerable variation in approach, though the recent trend has been towards fewer committees and closer co-ordination of the work of members and officials.

A fairly typical structure would include, apart from the council itself, a Policy Committee composed of certain members, a management team made up of the main chief officers led by a Chief Executive, and departments under their Directors concerned with the major services. The Policy Committee, a key committee in most authorities, gives detailed and specialised consideration to major policy and makes proposals which will eventually go before the council for approval. From these, a master plan will be drawn up and all other plans will depend upon it.

Committees are where the real work of local government is done. Their decisions are formalised at subsequent meetings of the full council. Local

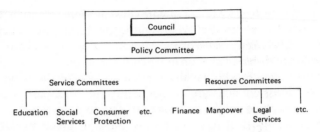

Fig. 10 The structure of local government

authorities appoint committees to carry out business and allocate councillors to serve on them, sometimes co-opting members from outside whose advice is considered useful.

Committees take a number of different forms: some are standing committees set up on a permanent basis such as a Housing Committee, others may be created for a particular purpose and are sometimes known as special or ad hoc committees. In certain cases, for example for education purposes, a local authority is required by law to appoint a committee and these are referred to as statutory committees. Others may be joint committees set up by any two or more local authorities and with such powers as the joint authorities may entrust to them. All such committees, and any subcommittees they may divide into for special purposes, work under their Chairman. They conduct their meetings, keeping minutes of the proceedings, according to procedural rules and standing orders of council which may stipulate such matters as the order of business, the place of meeting and the number of members required to make up a quorum.

This structure of council and committees made up of elected representatives charged with the task of conducting local affairs, is matched by a staff of Chief Officers and officials appointed and paid by the council and providing the wide range of professional, advisory and other services which is nowadays required by any local authority. By any standards, the many activities carried on by even a small authority to-day could be described as "big business", demanding administrative skills of a high order as well as the spending of very large sums of money. It is perhaps through its financial concerns that the work and nature of local government is best understood.

Finance

Examination of the figures in *Fig. 6* on page 110 suggests firstly, that these are massive and increasing commitments calling for continuous financing, and secondly, that the services listed are important because they cover so many aspects of national life. Concerning the first point, if one ignores the by no means unimportant contribution of fees, rents, and other miscellaneous items of income, the local authorities find the money from two sources, that is, from levying local rates and from grants paid by the State out of national taxation. Of these, the grant contribution from central government has become the most important element in recent years.

At first, this arrangement came about by convenience. The early nineteenth century councils and ad hoc authorities had been able to raise money as of right by levying a rate to cover the cost of the few public services then being provided. It had seemed to be a good administrative arrangement, since the services were of a local nature for local people—the making of streets, the clearing of refuse, the maintenance of a police force. The traditional method of raising money by levying local rates based on the "real rent of all local heritable subjects"[3] seemed the most effective and indeed, the only way available.

As time went on certain of the new services being provided were no longer entirely local by nature, but were of national importance. It therefore became necessary to distinguish between those services in which the local authorities should take a particular interest, such as the provision of parks, and those like the police in which the State had a general interest crossing all local boundaries. A local population benefitted from its police force, it was true, but the preservation of law and order and the protection of public property was undoubtedly a State concern; one of the "duties of the Sovereign", as Adam Smith, the economist, had classified it in *The Wealth of Nations* as far back as 1776. Furthermore, it was clearly desirable to achieve a uniform standard of service everywhere, so that law and order was no worse in one area than another. In this way an uneasy and continuing partnership grew up between central and local government in financing the developing services.

Nowadays the central and local shares of the cost of services are negotiated each year by the Government and the local authority associations.[4] Local authorities receive what is known as a "rate support grant" towards their total expenditure while, in addition, the Government pays money towards the cost of certain specific functions like the police or housing, over which they wish to retain a special degree of control.

Rate support grants are calculated according to a formula which has been refined over the years and which tries to ensure that those councils whose needs are greatest receive the most financial assistance. The formula which is used at present to distribute the very large sums involved is calculated each year in three parts (see *Fig. 11*). It contains a "needs" element which favours authorities with a high level of spending, a "resources" element to supplement the rate income of councils whose rateable value is below an agreed standard and a "domestic" element which subsidises domestic ratepayers.

The formula is complicated and its terms can be varied, if required, to take account of additional factors such as sparsity, remoteness, population

3 Report of the Royal Commission on Municipal Reform, 1835.
4 That is: the Association of County Councils, the Association of District Councils and the Association of Metropolitan Authorities.

components and so on. Individual cash limits are placed on items which qualify for rate support grant. These cash limits are notified to local authorities in annual guidelines which leave councils free to decide how to spend the money within the limits set.

STRATFORD-ON-AVON DISTRICT COUNCIL

This Statement Forms Part of The Rate Demand Note

PARTICULARS OF ITEMS—YEAR ENDING 31st MARCH, 1978

The following statement shows how the rate in the pound is made up. It sets out in relation to the District Council and the Warwickshire County Council and in terms of the rate in the pound the expenses, after deducting fees, rents, recoupments etc. of the services and the amounts of government grants and other monies receivable.

Service Administered	By County Council p	By District Council p	Total General Rate p
Housing Revenue		11.83	11.83
Other Housing Services		2.95	2.95
Public Health		5.55	5.55
Education	71.00		71.00
Social Services	7.80		7.80
Police	8.60		8.60
Fire Service	2.50		2.50
Highways and Transportation	9.10	0.12	9.22
Other Services	5.30	5.01	10.31
Additional Expenses—Pay and Price Increases etc.	6.40		6.40
	110.70	25.46	136.16
Deduct in respect of—			
Housing Subsidies		11.83	11.83
Government Grants for Specific Services	9.40	1.25	10.65
L.G. Act 1974—			
R.S.G.—Needs Element	37.20		37.20
Appropriation from Balances	1.40	—	1.40
	62.70	12.38	75.08
Estimated Product of a Penny Rate	£788 707	£162 797	
Local Deficiency in Rateable Value		£3 565 559	

Fig. 11 Local rates

All local authorities annually charge their local ratepayers rates which are assessed on the basis of rateable values impartially fixed from time to time by the Board of Inland Revenue, or in Scotland by regional assessors.

Rateable value is the approximate rental value of local properties and it is a local council's main source of revenue apart from Government contributions. The rating authority keeps a record of all occupiers of local property showing the rateable value of the property. It then multiplies each rateable value on the roll by a rate poundage[5] which the council has calculated and fixed so as to cover its estimated costs for the forthcoming financial year. Demand notes are then issued to ratepayers and the rates are collected accordingly. Each year, district councils and the borough councils in London levy and collect the rates in this way, while the expenditures of county councils and the Greater London Council are recovered by contributions from these districts and London boroughs.

Local government current finance—the method of paying for regularly recurring expenditure—thus centres round the rates and the Government grant. Since the Government grant plays such an important part, the Government has a ready-made measure of control over local expenditure. It can and does impose cash limits on grant assistance, and it can and does encourage spending in particular directions by offering specific subsidies.

Apart from **revenue expenditure,** in which all authorities are involved on a day to day basis and which they pay for from rates, grants, rents and other charges, all local councils incur **capital expenditure** on building new schools, constructing highways, and acquiring other permanent assets. The money to pay for this comes from a variety of sources. Capital grants may be obtained from central government, repayable stock may be issued to the public in return for subscribed money or mortgages may be offered to private lenders. The authority may also borrow in any appropriate capital market in Britain or Europe or from the Public Works Loan Board which is a Government-sponsored agency of long-standing. Much of the work of the Finance Department of any local council is taken up in arranging and servicing temporary borrowing and medium- and longer-term loans and in using the money for purposes authorised by the council.

Where capital expenditure is concerned, there are limits on what a council may borrow, and loan permissions or sanctions must be obtained from central government. For certain types of capital expenditure, loan sanctions would be sought from the Government Departments concerned, while in other cases, an annual block loan sanction is given within which authorities are free to plan their own spending. The Government's ability to supervise local government capital investment in this way is a powerful instrument of Treasury control.

Numerous other controls over local finances are, of course, available, most of them well developed. Some are internal, others external. All local authorities, for example, control their own financial affairs through their finance committees and accounting procedures, including submitting their annual accounts for audit or examination by district auditors or approved private auditors. In Scotland there is an independent Commission for Local Authority Accounts responsible to the Secretary of State for Scotland.

---

5   e.g. with an estimated expenditure of £5 000 000, and the revenue received from a penny rate £100 000, the "rate poundage" would be

$$\frac{5\ 000\ 000}{100\ 000} = 50p$$

Every public body is, in addition, subject at all times to external control through publicity. Everything municipal is done in the limelight of public interest: it may be reported in the press, it may be discussed on television or even be raised as a Parliamentary question in the House of Commons. All these are very powerful democratic controls which public administrators in local government are aware of.

Following the example of the Parliamentary Commissioner for Administration—the Ombudsman, first introduced by Parliament in 1967—Statutory Commissioners of Local Administration were also set up for England and Wales by the Local Government Act 1974, including a Commissioner for Scotland. Through these agencies, complaints and allegations of maladministration made by members of the public may be investigated. Thus, in both its financial administration and its conduct of affairs in general, a local council is accountable in the fullest sense of the word to its own ratepayers and to Parliament.

The financing arrangements of local government are undoubtedly complicated, and from time to time the view has been expressed that they should be simplified. In particular, various commentators have suggested that the rating system should be abolished since it is no longer soundly based. They feel that some form of local income tax would be fairer than rates based on notional rental values which tend to be "regressive" and not properly related to ability to pay.

In 1974 a Committee of Inquiry was appointed, with Sir Frank Layfield as Chairman, to review the whole system of local government finance in England, Scotland and Wales. The Layfield Committee reported in May 1976 and the Green Paper which followed proposed that grants, rates and charges should continue as the three main sources of finance for local government. The Government view was "that the abolition of rates would impose unacceptable burdens on national taxation".

There are other arguments for leaving financing arrangements broadly as they are at present, the most significant being the need to preserve the power of the local government system as a whole. Without control over their own finances their standing as independent local units would quickly crumble and there is a political need to hold on to this kind of independence. This was a powerful consideration in the minds of central government administrators.

Functions

Local government services have arisen out of social policies—many of them with "control" as their main concern—which have been pursued in some cases for at least a century. Right up until the 1850's, indeed, public order was the main concern of local authorities in England together with a rudimentary Poor Law which was Dickensian in its application.

Function	Metro-politan County	Metro-politan District	Non-Metropol-itan County	Non-Metropol-itan District	Greater London Council	London Borough
Arts and recreation	X	X	X	X	X	X
Cemeteries and crematoria		X		X		X
Consumer protection	X		X			X
Education		X	X			X
Environmental health		X		X		X
Refuse disposal	X		X		X	
Fire service	X		X		X	
Footpaths:						
Creation	X	X	X	X		X
Maintenance	X		X			X
Protection	X	X	X	X		X
Signposting	X		X			X
Surveys	X		X			X
Housing		X		X	X	X
Markets and fairs		X		X		X
Planning:						
Local plans		X		X		X
Structure plans	X		X		X	
National Parks	X		X			
Derelict land	X	X	X	X	X	X
Conservation area	X	X	X	X	X	X
Police	X		X			
Rate collection		X		X		X
Social services		X	X			X
Highways	X		X		X	X
Lighting:						
Footway	X	X	X	X	X	X
Highway	X		X		X	X
Public transport	X		X		X	
Road safety	X		X		X	
Traffic regulation	X		X		X	
Transportation planning	X		X		X	

Fig. 12 Principal functions of local authorities in England and Wales

(Adapted from: *Local Government in England and Wales,* Department of the Environment, HMSO, 1974)

Changes in the structure of society were brought about by the Industrial Revolution and a great burden was imposed on localities by the ever-present nineteenth century threat of cholera and ill-health. These factors led to the gradual development of a centrally-controlled system of services provided by local government. These services are nowadays classified into three groups, namely environmental, protective and personal services.

Education, a personal service, is considered by far the most expensive and far-reaching; it is experienced at first hand by everyone in the country and everyone is greatly affected by the way it is organised. Other services like police and highways, though less apparent, are equally important. Indeed, services like these are taken very much for granted in Britain in the latter part of the twentieth century, but civilised life would deteriorate very quickly without them.

Housing has been a point of heated political discussion for years, since one of the human rights upheld in this country is the right to shelter. Homelessness is thus a constant and pressing concern of all public authorities. Even a relatively minor service like weights and measures, which is administered nowadays as part of consumer protection by counties and London boroughs, has a very long history which goes back at least as far as the Middle Ages and is allied to the idea of public order and control.

Local councils are obliged, and in other cases, allowed to provide such services for the benefits of their ratepayers. In each case the services are of a community nature, beyond the resources or powers of individuals or firms to provide for themselves. The term "common good" perhaps most aptly describes what they are about. An authority may also acquire additional powers by making byelaws or an order to compulsorily purchase land; statutory approval would be needed in both cases. An authority may even promote a Private Bill in Parliament to obtain Local Act powers to do certain things.

Each of the functions listed at the beginning of this chapter is technical, specialised and requires trained work forces of thousands of employees to carry it out. Between them, all local authorities currently employ nearly three million people, and these range from Chief Fire Officers to dust collectors, all of whom are daily involved in providing, in accordance with the law, an essential service for those who live within their boundaries.

It goes deeper than this, however. There is more to effective local government than a routine compliance with the legislation; a provision of education and housing and environmental health services which merely follows bureaucratic guidelines issued by Government Departments would fall short of the true requirements of the situation. Every local area has its own special difficulties to contend with: problems of slums and deprivation, racial integration, unrest, unemployment and lack of outlets and opportunities. Every area faces the enormous challenge of change and adaptation and renewal in towns and cities.

Central—local relations

The key principles underlying the local government system are the sovereignty of Parliament and the importance of local democracy. These two principles, taken together, lay the foundation for central control of local administration. Local councils are independent; they are locally elected and have very wide powers and duties, yet these powers and duties have been carefully conferred upon them by Act of Parliament and local councils can do nothing which is not authorised by Parliament itself.

It is true that central government will try not to interfere in local concerns and will endeavour to keep its control over local affairs as minimal as possible, but a degree of control must remain in the interests of national uniformity. It is important that standards in education, in police protection, in matters concerning the welfare of children and so on should be set at an equally high level everywhere, and since such services are, to a large extent, paid for out of national taxes which are uniformly assessed, it follows that these services must be uniformly good throughout the country.

For such reasons there is a continuing relationship between central and local government which shows itself in a variety of ways. Thus, a continuous process of consultation and collaboration takes place between civil servants and their counterparts in local government which may, for example, involve discussion of Government White Papers, the exchange of information and the publication of guidelines. Local authority representatives may co-operate with civil servants on working parties, while civil servants explain Government thinking on different topics and try to gain acceptance for an official point of view. There are close contacts at all levels similar to that of a partnership where the Government plays the role of the dominant partner.

There are many occasions when local authorities must obtain approval from central government for certain actions. Some of these have been mentioned in connection with finance, but others include the approval of compulsory purchase orders, of administrative schemes and byelaws, and of the appointment and dismissal of certain chief officers. Similarly, central Departments may have powers of inspection when reporting on local levels of efficiency, and over the years, Inspectors of Schools, of the Police Constabularies or of the Fire Brigades have contributed to the raising of standards in these services.

The central-local relationship is founded on these arrangements and understandings, and control is a fundamental part of the process. As Garner[6] says:

"the ubiquitousness of the controls that may be exercised by the organs of the central government over the manner in which a local authority exercises its

6   J F Garner, *Administrative Law*, Butterworths, 1963.

administrative discretions makes a local authority appear (and feel) at times to be a mere Department of the central government".

Yet it is not a mere Department, but an independent body exercising powers conferred on it by statute in its own right.

Instead of arranging matters so that State and semi-State services are administered locally by the local authorities, it might be more efficient to relieve the local authorities of this work and make it wholly a State responsibility administered by Government officials. In this way a financial relationship between central and local government would no longer be necessary, for finance would be provided out of national taxes. The complicated and financially clumsy grant arrangement would cease and the local authorities would be left to administer the remaining few minor services of a purely local nature (the provision of wash-houses, for example), levying their local rates to meet the cost.

A question arises from this idea; is local government useful? Local administration has rarely been custom-built to fit the function; more usually it has grown up with the function, often bit by bit, and has been tailored periodically to fit the changing pattern of design. A century ago, when State services began to develop, their administration was put into the hands of the local authorities and local boards set up for the purpose; it was the simplest solution. The local councils were on the spot, they had some form of organised administrative machinery at the time, however poor, and they had the power to raise money locally by levying rates. It seemed most appropriate that the State should develop services, which in any case were of a partly local nature, through this existing machinery.

Since then, there have been adjustments and redistributions of the burden of services between central and local government, and since the 1950's a number of services have been taken over by the State in the manner proposed. Such functions include the hospital service, the gas and electricity industries and the main part of the poor law service, all of which were at one time local authority functions. Further adjustments will no doubt be made in the future, perhaps by the transfer of responsibility for highways to the State.

The question of which national services are suitable for local administration has always been difficult for Parliament. The doctrine of general and particular interest, too, which no doubt seemed quite clear a century ago, has been modified over the years. At that time there was the greatest reluctance to permit any local rate to be levied for education; there was thought to be a risk that its distribution would give rise to religious argument. It is likely that even such a basic service as the relief of the poor would have been frowned upon by the earlier economists like Ricardo or Malthus.

The point at which a service should cease to be local and become national, however, is a matter involving wider issues than we are here concerned with. However, the services entrusted to the local authorities over the years remain in their hands and the artificial financial relationship with central government still continues.

The reasons for this are not only convenience and the chance of history. Even if it were considered practicable now to dispense with the experience and established administration of the local authorities on the grounds of efficiency, it is doubtful whether such a step would ever be taken, for there are strong political arguments against it. A powerful national government where all authority is concentrated at the centre goes against our conception of what is right. Totalitarian or dictatorial government is abhorred and the independence of individuals, and therefore of local groups of individuals, greatly prized. Civics (the science of citizenship) is taught in schools, and the man-in-the-street is encouraged to take an active interest in the work of the Government. This is democracy. This is the British way of life, and it is unlikely to change.

It can therefore be assumed that the State will continue to value the local authorities and be extremely wary about adopting any measure which would limit local initiative and independence. The semi-State services will continue to be the responsibility of the authorities on the spot, and the financial relationship between these authorities and central government will remain as a sensitive, delicately adjusted and ever-changing factor.

All these views have recently been clarified by the Government[7] in the following terms:

Central government's role is:

1   to ensure that the local services reflect national priorities and are provided at broadly comparable standards.

2   to ensure that local government's spending plans do not conflict with the Government's economic objectives.

3   to ensure that the activities of one authority do not have adverse effects on another.

4   to encourage co-operation between local authority and other complementary services.

5   to ensure that the financial arrangements lead to efficiency.

6   to safeguard the interests of vulnerable minority groups whose interests may only get a proper hearing at national level.

7   to encourage and maintain local democracy.

British local government, then, once described as one of the most original ideas of the nineteenth century, is an administrative device of great simplicity which enables Parliament to retain active central control of the local handling of affairs. It is profoundly democratic in design and in its application it has continued to adapt to the needs of the day. In the process it has become flexible and very responsive to the requirements of areas as different as Aberdeen with its oil concerns and Belfast with its backdrop of urban warfare.

7   Green Paper: *Local Government Finance*, HMSO, 1977.

On-the-spot public and social services which any advanced society nowadays requires could, of course, be provided by other means; other countries such as France and Germany do provide them differently, but despite its faults, the British local government system works well and allows for local needs to be taken care of by local people, within a framework of national uniformity.

Effective local government depends on a number of things:

a)   imaginative and resourceful leadership from elected members and paid officials working together as a team

b)   Command over resources through time which every local council has at its disposal

c)   the use of up to date management techniques

d)   an understanding of how to use an administrative device like the local government system and the power which goes with it to improve the situation.

Suggestions for further reading

R Buxton, *Local Government,* Penguin, 1973
Local Government in England and Wales: A Guide to the New System, HMSO, 1974
Local Government Finance, Cmnd 6813, HMSO, 1977
Lord Redcliffe-Maud and B Wood, *English Local Government Reformed,* OUP, 1974

Questions

1   On what basis are local rates assessed?
2   What is a "rate support grant"?
3   What are the principal services provided by a non-metropolitan district?
4   How do local councils obtain money for capital purposes?
5   What are the principles on which the local government system is based?
6   In what respects is a local authority a "political-management system"?
7   Name the metropolitan counties.
8   Is local government a good idea?
9   From whom does a local authority obtain its "authority"?

9
The local government service

Challenge and opportunity

Between the years 1964 and 1967 when the Mallaby Committee was enquiring into the staffing of local government in England and Wales, the National and Local Government Officers' Association wrote in evidence to the Committee that, in their view, local government,

"concerned as it is with human life from the cradle to the grave, engaged as it must be in a ceaseless war against our common enemies of poverty, sickness, ignorance, isolation and maladjustment, and capable as it should be of transforming the whole pattern of environment and welfare, presents challenges and opportunities unequalled in any other employment".

It is unlikely that they exaggerated.

Local government is about the public administration of services and functions as varied as slum clearance and social work, education and public libraries: all the services which Parliament has delegated to it over the years and which are now considered essential to modern communities. It is concerned with the complex and shifting relationship between the environment, the available administrative structures, the technologies in use and the needs the services are designed to meet. The task of guiding and operating these services provides opportunities for improving the quality of life which are not found in many other vocations.

There are at present some three million people employed by the local councils throughout the country. Most of these are essential manual workers and policemen, teachers and technicians of many different kinds, but others, in the same way as civil servants, form an administrative, professional and clerical group. It is with the work of these that this chapter is mainly concerned. Local government staff have been described as a "second-line Civil Service", and there are undoubted similarities between the administrative work performed by civil servants at national level and that which is done locally by local administrators. However, the local government service has its own traditions and its own special characteristics and requirements and while local government officers seek a close relationship with their Civil Service counterparts, the two occupations are not identical or interchangeable.

Unlike civil servants, who are appointed on a national basis and are therefore subject to transfer between Departments and even to different parts of the country, local government officers are employed and paid by their respective local authorities and unless they choose to change their jobs, will continue to carry out their duties in a home situation. They do have rights under the Local Government Superannuation Act, but their terms of employment mainly depend on their individual letters of appointment. These are normally in line with conditions of service laid down by the National Joint Council for Local Authority Staffs, whose agreements are honoured by both employers and officers. Since the latter are usually members of a trade union such as NALGO as well, their interests are adequately protected at local and national levels.

A local authority may, of course, employ those staff which it considers necessary to carry out its responsibilities. By law, it is required to appoint properly qualified chief officers such as Education Officers, Chief Constables, Directors of Social Services and Fire Officers, and the approval of the appropriate Minister in central government may be required to engage and dismiss these people.

These officers are the employees of the council which appoints and pays them and offers them security of employment and while, as senior officers, they may work closely with elected representatives, they do not take orders from any individual councillor. Chief officers are responsible through their committees to the council, from which their instructions come.

Most local government officers in the course of their daily work come into contact with the public for whom they are providing a service. Service to the public is the guiding philosophy of their work, and this service outlook is probably the value they most share with civil servants. Like civil servants, too, they are closely involved in ongoing democratic processes by which local people look to their elected representatives to safeguard their rights and freedoms. Questions affecting these rights and freedoms can arouse heated controversy so that, as with civil servants, a feel for the political nature of the work is called for. Yet the politics remain local and the issues involved tend to be parochial; it is this very parochialism which gives the local government service its special flavour.

While the structure of the British Civil Service has slowly grown to maturity and has developed through successive reforms during the past 150 years so that it now occupies a position of considerable prestige, local government has only recently begun to pay similar attention to its own staffing requirements. For many years the standards of competence and efficiency varied between the hundreds of different councils and although the bigger authorities have always been able to recruit very able administrators, smaller councils have not always been so fortunate. The reforms of the early 1970's have begun to change this.

Recruitment

The powerful new authorities set up under the Local Government Acts of 1972 and 1973 lost no time in recruiting staff at all levels to fill the additional posts which were becoming available. New departments and sections of departments grew, and with them, officials with titles that often sounded strange to an older generation of ratepayers. At the same time, many of those who had spent a lifetime in council offices found themselves being offered early retirement on acceptable terms and so chose to leave the service. This wholesale turnover and renewal of local council staff did not escape comment from some sections of the public, many of whom were highly critical of what was seen at the time as an extravagant spending of ratepayers' money and an unnecessary tampering with styles and struc-tures which had stood the test of time and to which everyone had grown accustomed.

The modernisation of local government, which was the object of these upheavals, could only have been made possible by a staff able to carry this out. Attracting adequate staff was considered to be a matter of incentives; local authorities would have to offer rewards and attractions comparable with those being offered by competing employers in order to attract and retain staff of the quality they needed. This was exactly what they did.

Any large organisation which deliberately sets out to recruit to its service high-calibre staff in large numbers and at relatively short notice has to recognise that by doing so, it is denying these workers to other sectors of the economy. The more people who are brought into local government, the less there will be to serve the needs of commerce and industry. The organisation must also be able to justify its course of action in terms of the skills it is looking for. Once the decision had been taken and the approval of Parliament obtained, the question of incentives remained: what could a local authority offer that would seem attractive to the better qualified school leavers and university graduates, and what would encourage them to continue and to make their careers in the local government service? How could the job be made to seem important?

Good salaries are only one feature of any job. Traditionally, local gov-ernment is a white-collar occupation with security attached to it; it offers satisfactory pension schemes and conditions of work are good with no particular obligation to work away from home. Furthermore, in the new structures that were being developed and with the training programmes these offered there promised to be ample opportunities for advancement. Beyond the nine-to-five principle lay the chance for personal involvement, and as the recruiting booklet of one major authority put it: "You will be doing work which is of both local interest and national importance". For many young people today, there is an undoubted appeal in this, which is lacking in factory or shop work, and which promises to satisfy idealism and the desire to be of use.

A package based on these features proved effective: between 1972 and

1976 staff numbers in local government increased by more than 11%.

Labour force (in percentage)	1971	1975	1976
Central government:			
Civilians	6.4	7.7	8.1
HM Forces	1.5	1.3	1.4
Local government	10.9	12.0	12.2
Public corporations	8.2	8.1	7.9
Private sector	72.9	70.8	70.4
Total employed labour force	100	100	100

Fig. 13 Personnel in local government (*Social Trends*, 1977)

The new staff of authorities reformed after 1973 found themselves involved in a new-look local government. Not only were structures changed and functions reallocated, but new departments were formed and new appointments made, so that staff already in post as well as transferred staff and those being newly appointed found themselves having to adapt to new practices and procedures.

Career entrants into local government are nowadays recruited in a number of ways. School leavers may join as cadets or clerical assistants, or as technical, professional or administrative trainees. In most authorities induction courses are available with comprehensive training programmes designed to help new entrants become familiar with their work and introduce them to the different departments of the authority they have joined. Opportunities are usually available, too, to enable new entrants to develop their knowledge and experience through training schemes of different kinds.

Thus, professional trainees can enter the fields of administration, accountancy, surveying, housing management, consumer protection or environmental health. Training is a continuous process during the period of service with the authority but it is normally related to a particular area of work, for example, administration.

Administrative staff are involved in the general administration of the authority's work and the improvement of its organisation. They give advice on the formation of policy and are involved in staff management, committee and secretariat work. Training schemes, involving part-time day release for courses leading to the Higher Certificate in Public Administration, or in some cases to relevant university degrees, therefore provide the background to learning on the job. During the period of their training the normal process of socialisation also plays its part in turning raw apprentices into local government officers with a perception of and a feeling for the work. Graduate entrants are encouraged by most authorities and there are, of course, higher grades for those who are already professionally qualified at the time of recruitment.

More than 40 years ago, the Hadow Committee's opinion on the recruitment and training of local government officers was that

"every local authority should entrust to one committee all questions affecting the recruitment, qualifications, training and promotion of officers".

Today the logic of that view would no doubt be widely accepted. Matters affecting something as important as staffing should not be left to the whim of individual committees and departments but should be the special concern of those who are best qualified to deal with them. Most authorities now have Establishment Committees and Personnel Departments which serve that specialist purpose.

Manpower services

The kind of matters which are the concern of Establishment Committees (or Manpower Services Committees) include:

Providing a recruiting service
Interviewing and appointing officers
Making periodical staff reviews
Promotions
Arrangements for training schemes
Arrangements for inter-departmental transfers
Grading, salary scales and superannuation
Periods of probation
Questions affecting discipline
Staff welfare and development

In local government, as in the Civil Service and industry, the personnel function has grown very rapidly in the past few years. This reflects the increased complexity of legislation on pay, working conditions and the health and safety of employees. The increasing need, too, for skills in wage negotiation and for good industrial relations is illustrated by the variety of key workers in local government engaged in essential services like refuse collection. The disruption of community life which can result from industrial action by dustmen or firemen or public transport employees and others makes it important to develop conciliation procedures which may help to minimise the disruption.

This is of course delicate work; the technical aspects of personnel work, at one time a blend of routine record-keeping and elementary welfare, have developed into a highly professional activity with skills and procedures of its own which owe a great deal to the behavioural sciences. Job evaluation, job enrichment, career planning, joint consultation machinery; these are more than just a collection of fashionable new ideas. They are concerned with morale, and in the last resort, morale is what the personnel function is all about.

In the larger authorities, the work of Personnel or Manpower Services Departments covers more than just appointment procedures, promotions and grading scales. Nowadays it is occupied with manpower planning, which aims to ensure an adequate flow of well-trained staff. In present circumstances, market forces alone can no longer be relied upon to guarantee that flow, so steps must be taken deliberately to create the staffing mix needed now and for periods in the future. This means that detailed information must be compiled from records which are prepared at the most basic level. These records can be used to prepare estimates of staff joining and leaving the service for whatever reason and to prepare forecasts of the changing needs of the service so far as these needs can be identified.

A few of the larger authorities have so far taken the lead in this, acting as pace-makers for other authorities, but manpower planning is still at an early stage of development. Establishing a system which will work satisfactorily is likely to be expensive, and the main barriers to progress have been resources and the financial stability necessary for detailed forward planning. Uncertainties and sudden changes of course are not helpful.

Manpower planning has so far tended to be incremental and concerned with short-term considerations as the following example illustrates. Following the publication in 1972 of a White Paper announcing central government's intention to expand nursery education, some local authorities proceeded to recruit nursery nurses. Shortly after this, the Government was obliged by a sudden downturn in the economy, to notify a cutback in its allocation of grant which affected policy on a number of services. These authorities were then left with nursery nurses who could not be used for the purpose intended and who had to be absorbed as far as was possible in other tasks.

This kind of experience is so obviously counter-productive that it poses the question whether any comprehensive manpower planning by individual local authorities is a practical proposition. It also forces supporters of the technique to be specific about the results they expect the technique to achieve.

The term manpower planning needs to be defined with some care, for it has sometimes been used in an imprecise way in press and other reports. Over-optimistic claims have been made for it as a technique and these have not been borne out in practice. There is, for example, a tendency to confuse attempts at forecasting manpower requirements with the more straightforward planning which is needed to enable an organisation like a local authority to keep itself supplied with staff.

Forecasting of any kind is never easy and it is always surrounded by an aura of mystery; most administrators treat it with caution and respect, while recognising that it is an indispensable part of their equipment. Manpower planning has been variously described as "ensuring an adequate flow of well-trained staff" or as "providing within the confines of a budget the right number of staff of the appropriate skills at the right time to meet the demands of the work to be done".

There are important areas for investigation where personnel requirements are concerned. They take a number of forms and are best described as manpower studies. In any large organisation it is desirable to have a manpower group which can devote special attention to manpower studies and to the development of an adequate and updated information system about its employees which can serve as a basis for these studies. It may be possible, for example, to identify patterns of joining and leaving the service over a period of time and to relate these to the likely need for labour during the same period. To do this with any degree of success an organisation needs to be very clear about its objectives and to have a special awareness of the effects of change.

These two factors—objectives and change—are fundamental in any analysis of engagement forms and other documentation about staff which are part of general manpower studies. Employment "profiles" could be prepared from basic employment records and these could follow the progress, say, of a new intake of apprentices through their training period up to the point of their absorption into departments. The profiles could be used in conjunction with what is predictable about change, to help set up training schemes to re-train staff to tackle new tasks, for over lengthy periods of time it is unrealistic to suppose that job descriptions will not change or that the need for specific jobs will continue.

A possible model for a manpower programme with the needs of a local authority department in mind would be as follows:

a)   identify the department's aims

b)   specify the environmental and other changes needed to achieve these aims

c)   detail the tasks employees must carry out to bring about these changes

d)   analyse the tasks and develop job descriptions, training programmes and recruitment procedures

e)   structure the tasks in terms of levels of responsibility and training

f)   engage the required personnel or redeploy existing staff

g)   repeat the process continuously

Again, manpower studies may concern themselves with productivity and efficiency and with the best possible use of available staff by means of manning standards and task specifications. In a police force, for example, the time spent by police officers in routine patrolling and supervisory activities could be contrasted with the increasing statistics of crime. Priority tasks could similarly be discussed and agreed with social workers and with other employment groups. In any local authority there is scope for improvement, and cost savings to be made by such means.

At national level, manpower planning exercises have been carried out by central Departments for the past 20 years or so, and in particular by the former Department of Labour's Manpower Research Unit, the Advisory Council on the Personal Social Services and the Department of Employment's Manpower Services Commission, which is representative of employers, trade unions and other interests. In the Health Services, too, medical and nursing studies are relatively well developed and the Civil Service Department has established staff records which assist in central establishment work.

The purpose of these exercises has been to try to determine the pattern of employment as it has been developing and as it is likely to develop in the future. The methods used, like all forecasting, consist of analysing past employment trends and modifying them according to known future plans and developments. As such they represent a careful assessment of probabilities, based on the best evidence available at the time.

At central government level, it is, of course, important to establish total manpower levels and the future distribution of staff allowing for changes in technologies and skills. Factors such as likely population growth, birth rates, retirement choices, and new and declining occupations will influence these levels. Manpower levels are basic and fundamental and everything depends upon them. Moreover, the fair distribution of employment throughout the regions is a major element of national economic policy at present, and the ability to control such movements depends on information which is as reliable as possible.

At local level, especially in the big authorities, the need to control the skilled labour needed by the services has become increasingly obvious. Manpower planning, defined[1] as

"the identification and measurement of potential future imbalances in labour supply and demand and the development of plans or policies designed to avoid or minimise the incidence of such imbalance",

may help to ensure that over a period of time the required numbers of policemen, community workers, draughtsmen, surveyors and others will be available. As in any large-scale organisation, the question of continuity and succession is critical.

The problems associated with manpower planning are considerable. Within the education service alone, it would be necessary to forecast the supply and demand not just of teachers, but of teachers of the numerous subjects taught in schools and colleges at different grades, and then to plan to attract these skills into the service and develop them to suit the changing needs of the service. In some services, for example the armed forces, this is very effective. Manpower planning clearly cannot be left to chance or to market forces; the imbalance that suddenly became apparent in the output of primary teachers in 1977 and the resulting disorganisation of careers and closure of colleges could all have been avoided by using even the most basic manpower planning techniques.

Planning—planning of any kind—is exceedingly difficult, but it is worth doing well. The overall needs of local government, including manpower

1   L C Hunter and D J Robertson, *The Economics of Wages and Labour*, Macmillan, 1969.

needs, should be properly planned and integrated with other parts of the economy. To do this effectively, integration and co-operation and co-ordination between all the various parts of the economy are needed. So far this has not been achieved, although there have been a number of interesting experiments in corporate planning carried on by individual local councils.

Suggestions for further reading

Staffing of Local Government, HMSO, 1967
G Stainez, *Manpower Planning*, London, 1971
The Social Services Year Book

Questions

1 What is "personnel management"?
2 What factors would influence manpower planning in local government?
3 How do local government officers differ from civil servants?
4 To whom is a local government official responsible?
5 What are the functions of a local authority's Manpower Services Committee?

10

Local bureaucracies

Departments and committees

The day to day work of every local authority revolves around the routine needs of its various committees and the changes which they bring about within the system. These committees must be serviced by committee clerks and they have to be provided with a continual flow of prepared information in the form of agendas and minutes and back-up papers supporting the projects and proposals under discussion. Resource committees, in particular, have to deal with a large volume of statistical and accounting material, with estimates and accounts and with analytical statements of all kinds. These are usually of a technical nature and they require to be explained and their underlying arguments made clear.

The use of a committee structure for discussions is very well established in local government, and is in many ways ideally suited for its purpose. Committees provide a rational basis for participating in the work of the authority and for elected members and appointed officials to come together in an exchange of views and opinions. In the democratic tradition, decisions are far more likely to be sound if taken by a group than by any one official, however skilled he may be. At the same time, there are some obvious defects, including the tendency of committees to blur responsibility and to waste time in discussion which often seems more concerned with point-scoring than with rationality.

Each individual department has its special needs and emphases and values: the schemes of administration for schools and colleges, or an education department, the law and order aspects of a police department, the care and commitment of a social services department. In each case, front-line workers such as teachers, policemen, social workers and firemen are matched by administrative staff who help to organise the service and provide for its needs.

Local government officers must be aware of these needs and be responsive to the ebb and flow of council business and the pressures they cause. They must also learn to regard the departments not so much as a series of separate empires but as different aspects of the same thing, namely: the provision of a total service to the ratepayers of the council. A study of the activities of departments reveals the overlaps between them and the inter-connectedness which emphasises the corporate nature of the work. In this sense, departments within an authority constitute a kind of corporate bureaucracy.

Any local authority carries on its business through a network of operating units like its own committees and sub-committees, the management committees of external agencies such as community schools and homes and institutions, the many voluntary committees and the committees of other subsidiary organisations. A key problem is to help all of these groups to blend and fit into the common policy of the council. For some purposes, joint committees may provide the co-ordination which is required, at other times some form of bridging or consultation may be needed. The following example shows how closely functions of the Social Services Department are impinged upon by the other major departments:

Education is concerned with:

   a)   the availability of a child guidance service
   b)   truancy and children whose school performance is adversely affected by home and other social conditions
   c)   provision of education for the under-fives, including pre-school playgroups
   d)   the education of children in care of the local authority
   e)   the education and training of houseparents

Police duties include:

   a)   juvenile warning schemes
   b)   Court work connected with children
   c)   liaison on probation and other social work enquiries
   d)   dealing with individual cases of people in difficulty
   e)   community involvement

Housing deals with:

   a)   rent collection
   b)   eviction policy
   c)   house letting policy for people in need
   d)   community development schemes
   e)   the provision of sheltered housing and houses designed for the elderly
   f)   the provision of recreational and social facilities in housing schemes

Other departments and agencies outside the local authorities also have an interest in these matters; they concern people's needs and these do not conveniently slot into the administrative arrangements of any particular committee. In the illustration given, the Health Services, the Department of Social Security, the Department of Employment and possibly the Prison

Service, too, will all have a contribution to make, which underlines the need for a corporate planning approach with policies and programmes that interlock.

Part of the routine of council work is the whole array of filing systems and office machinery, communications and arrangements for information handling, the detail of resource management and the law. In addition, the secretariat and public relations work serve the political need to inform the public. Local government departments thus operate in a highly mechanistic fashion, but at the same time, they must be able to call upon a mixture of personalities devoted to creative change, for at the heart of local government lies this paradox of continuity and change; both are its goals.

Every local council traces its origins and its power base through patterns of local democracy which combine to demand the provision of a range of services. These are administered through a hierarchy of committees and sub-committees, each served by elected members and advised by paid officials, the whole being co-ordinated by a Chief Executive working with a management team. The corporate nature of all these separate services is emphasised by the authority's Policy Committee and finally in the council chamber itself. In these ways all local authorities bear at least some resemblance to the ideal type of organisation once described by writers such as Weber in the early years of the twentieth century.

In this ideal organisation—a bureaucracy governed by rules and regulations—each worker fills an allotted niche, working according to a job specification which is handed down to him. His work is supervised and controlled by a superior, a departmental manager, and the whole enterprise is headed by a Director. The personalities of the people involved are not considered particularly important but the post they fill is.

In a hierarchy like this it was thought that the "organisation man", wedded to his job, owing allegiance to his superiors and acting in a disciplined and respectful manner towards them, would flourish, and the ideal of a rationally functioning and controlled organisation in which everyone played his part under the leadership of his omniscient superiors could be achieved. In a well-structured organisation in which everyone knew what was to be done and did it without question, it was thought that there could be only one result: maximum efficiency, the reward of effective management.

This image of smoothly functioning organisations operating in robot-like fashion belongs very much to the early twentieth century. The notion of an organisation being like a machine, a mechanism, an apparatus, is met with again and again in literature; Kafka, Wells and Orwell were all fascinated by the thought.

Rigid authoritarian organisations have long gone out of fashion if, indeed, they were ever more than drawing board models. From the late 1920's the idea of an organisation as some kind of impersonal machine-like creation began to be displaced by the realisation that the components that really mattered were the people. A reaction slowly set in against the cog-in-a-wheel view of the individual, routinely working from nine-to-five, and the emphasis shifted away from the machine to human beings and to enquiries into how people behaved in real life and how they related to one another at work.

Psychological studies which have been made during the past 40 years have provided an insight into the human condition in the work place. The administrative process in local government, just as in industry or in the armed forces and elsewhere, has now come to be regarded more as a set of relationships than of hierarchies; relationships, for example, between structure and goals, between environment and technology, between needs and resources. Traditional authoritarian administrations may have tended to think of people as just so many units making up an efficient organisation, but this view has had to be increasingly modified during the past 50 years.

The so-called human relations school which led these changes began in America with investigations into patterns of work performance in industry, and grew through the contributions of a number of academic sociologists, psychologists and other researchers. Their findings, when applied in practice, were shown to be effective and productive and prompted new approaches to administration which have been continuing right up until the present time. Administration today sees the organisational problem as something rather more intricate than any machine.

As organisations, modern local authorities are run by many different people working together against a continual background of consultation and discussion, with policies being formulated and decided upon by committees and groups of specialists responding to pressures from many different sources. These sources include central government, trade unions, local business interests, ratepayers, voters and community agencies, and decisions about what has to be done—important decisions like whether to finance the building of a new civic theatre or close a community home or use powers of compulsory purchase—must try to reconcile all these various interests as far as possible, while keeping the council's objectives in mind.

A local authority is, of course, bureaucratic, It would be impossible to conduct its affairs without structure and regulation and control. What has become apparent in the past few years is the complexity of the human resources which go to make up local authorities or central government Departments or Area Health Boards. However, certain questions still need to be considered, for example, to what extent should ordinary people in localities and in neighbourhoods be actively encouraged to participate along with councillors and officials in the process of administration? To what extent, indeed, would they want to be involved in these processes since, for the most part, the services and functions of local government are of a technical nature, not likely to be understood by most people?

An important element in the new local government legislation of the early 1970's was the emphasis it placed on participative democracy and the need to bring ordinary people into the process of government. The county council and even the district council can seem very remote from the point at which the real issues are daily taking place. Apathy among local electorates feeds on this remoteness and as a practical measure to strenghthen local democratic processes, parish councils in England were given increased power and their position in the local government scene improved considerably. In Scotland and Wales provision for new community councils was included in the reorganisation Acts; boundaries were established for the councils and, sometimes reluctantly, they have come into being one by one.

These organisations are extensions of local bureaucracy and are easily controlled. Like similar arrangements for local health councils, local school councils and other forms of community groupings, they are basically reporting agencies, except that they can encourage and voice genuine neighbourhood opinions and feeling. When this happens organisations take on a new meaning. Public service can be carried out within communities and it is perfectly possible and acceptable for public spirited members of the community working in a voluntary way to count themselves as public servants; perhaps the ideal type of local authority is to be sought at this grass-roots level.

Professionals in organisations

Local government is skill-intensive and within the service as a whole there is a growing need for all manner of highly specialised tasks such as systems analysis, personnel management, educational psychology, computer technology and various aspects of work in the Courts. Most of these services are provided by qualified staff who are members of professions. Thus, lawyers and accountants, architects and civil engineers all interact in a municipal setting with social workers and teachers, and while all of these are local government officers in the first instance, owing their allegiance to the councils which employ them, they are, at the same time, members of associations as varied and distinguished as the Law Society or the Royal Institute of British Architects.

Bodies like these set their own standards of entry and registration based on the completion of a prescribed period of training and the passing of examinations. They also have their own ethical codes which are monitored by their own disciplinary committees. These arrangements ensure the presence throughout the service of a relatively large body of men and women who see their ultimate source of authority as lying outside their employing council. When conflicts arise between the expectations and norms of that council and those of the professional community, the claims of the profession tend to prevail. There are, undoubtedly, large areas of practice where it would be quite impossible for a council as a bureaucratic organisation to lay down hard and fast rules of work and expect them to be obeyed.

There have been many examples in recent years of social workers who have refused to agree to evictions from housing tenancies or teachers who have refused to perform "non-professional" tasks like the supervision of meals; in all these cases, the challenge to the established authority of the council has been hard to accept. Questions about who is running the organisation are difficult to avoid.

What, then, are professionals, for it is important to try to establish working arrangements to integrate them with elected members and other of their fellow workers? It is easy to see that doctors and clergymen, lawyers and airline pilots are professionals, but it is harder to justify why: what differentiates them from bus drivers and office workers?

Various attempts have been made to define the nature of a profession. In each profession there exists a systematic body of knowledge and expertise which is not easily or readily accessible to the general public. Those who have acquired this knowledge take care to preserve and develop it within a closely guarded circle, and the public recognise their exclusive right to practise in what amounts to a closed shop. This kind of general description can be applied to council legal staff, for example: only they are able to carry out the intricate conveyancing associated with housing and property; they alone have the skills necessary to represent the council in the Courts. So no one seriously disputes the right of a lawyer to be considered as a member of a learned profession.

Since belonging to a profession carries with it a unique status, as well as possible financial rewards and the power that goes with it, membership of a profession is a desirable goal to aim for and, as a result, a number of "semi-professions" have emerged in recent years. The doctors and the clerics have been joined by the nurses and the planners, the librarians and the social workers, all claiming exclusiveness and recognition and all backing their claims with varying degrees of validity.

The professional's problem of divided loyalties in a bureaucratic organisation is highly significant. It must be tackled because of the need to co-ordinate and to adjust to change with the minimum of disruption. Whether this is achieved by adapting professional groups to the organisation in some way, or by adapting the organisation to suit the needs of the professionals, will depend upon the circumstances of the case: a compromise must ultimately be struck.

Democratic administration in Britain both at central and local level, depends on two very different groups of people, both servants of the public, namely, elected members and appointed officials. Members are responsible to their electorates while officials are responsible to their employing authority and to no-one else. Members are birds of passage who may only be in office for a year or two until they are voted out; officials may spend a whole working life in a department and learn its ways in intimate detail. Members are amateurs, and officials, professionals, where the work of administration is concerned.

The member's contribution is only amateur to a degree however; much of his contribution comes from his close experience of the people and their concerns in his part of the local area. Local government is concerned

"beyond the wider issues of state, with more immediate responsibilities. Such responsibilities cannot be effectively discharged unless people with first-hand knowledge of all sections of the local community are represented on the council."[1]

Before the First World War, local government was mainly performed by independent councillors who sought public office in the interests of the local community spurred, no doubt, by the usual mixture of personal motives. This situation has changed during the past 50 years, and the local government scene has become increasingly dominated by party politics with politically controlled councils backed by party machinery.

There are arguments for and against this development. Some feel that it is wrong for purely local issues to be affected by party politics and individual councillors bound by a party line. On the other hand, parties do introduce support and discipline and a sense of unity which would otherwise be lacking. Despite the pros and cons, party politics is now a fact of local government life to which one must adjust.

In local government, councillors in committee agree among themselves on council policies while officials advise and assist them in the decision-making process. When policies are decided, these same officials see that they are implemented. The official is the unbiased expert, the councillor, the representative of the people; it is the councillor who will have to justify courses of action to his ward electorate and it is on their behalf that he agrees to certain actions. As Herman Finer says,

"the councillors have the opportunity of permeating the expert with the will of the community; they let the official know both what the public will not stand and what it insists upon having . . . . it is the committee's business to introduce and impose the sense of proportion".

Outside the formality of committees, however, barriers between councillors and staff have dropped a little so that communication has become less superficial and more professionally creative. As C F Darlow remarks,

"councillors decide the policy. But what goes on beforehand: the process of investigation, argument and consultation which leads up to the actual decision—is quite a different story".

The notion of a partnership, with the official taking the lead, would not be very far from the mark.

In the most progressive authorities, mixed officer-member groups have become a regular feature of local administrative practice and study groups like these, taking topics such as "the elderly" or "handicapped children", examine them in depth against the background of the service as a whole. As a means of control such groups represent good management practice. Moreover, they help to develop team attitudes among councillors and staff.

1 *Management of Local Government* Vol 2, 1967.

The relationship between councillors and permanent staff is complex and interesting and the success of Government both centrally and locally depends a great deal upon the relationship working well. There is scope for a much closer analysis of the way it works and the way it ought to work than has so far been attempted—the way it copes with apathy, ignorance, self-interest and external pressures, for example.

In local government, effective management depends a great deal on the agreement of councillors and officials, of trade union members and professional workers with the source of authority to which each is responsible; officials often have to become diplomats and mediators.

Control

One of the great advantages offered by most professional groups is that they usually have established codes of conduct and values which are relevant to their particular field and which generally operate in favour of their clients. In this way, the confidentiality of records and of personal disclosures will be absolutely protected by lawyers, teachers and social workers alike; the accuracy of statistical presentations will be guaranteed by accountants, together with impartiality and a striving after the truth; and no architect or engineer (with one or two unfortunate exceptions) would accept a bribe for favours shown to contractors. A general duty to take care will ensure that the quality of professional work (which can be measured against standards regularly being achieved elsewhere) is kept uniformly high, in addition to the control exerted by environmental restraints referred to in Chapters 2 and 3.

Not only will these standards be supervised by the local authorities themselves through their individual departments and Establishment Committees, but more importantly, they will be enforced by the external disciplinary committees of the professional bodies concerned. "Unprofessional conduct" is a judgement which can ruin a promising career in the private and the public sectors alike, and no professional worker would normally consider acting outside the limits set by his professional association.

The Institute of Chartered Accountants in England and Wales sets out fundamental principles in its *Ethical Guide* in the following terms:

1 In accepting or continuing a professional assignment or occupation a member should always have regard to any factors which might reflect adversely upon his integrity and objectivity in relation to that assignment or occupation.

2 A member should carry out his professional work with a proper regard for the technical and professional standards expected of him as a member and should not undertake or continue professional work which he is not himself competent to perform unless he obtains such advice and assistance as will enable him competently to carry out his task.

3   A member should conduct himself with courtesy and consideration towards all with whom he comes into contact in the course of his professional work.

4   A member should follow the ethical guidance of the Institute and in circumstances not provided for by that guidance should conduct himself in a manner consistent with the good reputation of the profession and the Institute.

With appropriate variations, similar codes are prescribed by other professional bodies and an examination of these will reveal how closely they restrict their members and bind them to a common outlook and a uniform standard of performance.

Where elected members of local councils are concerned, the same high standards of integrity are expected although it is more difficult to judge and enforce these standards. Councillors represent a wide cross-section of a local population, and their backgrounds vary considerably; herein lies the strength of the local government system. Businessmen who have made their way in the world in the face of competition and the pressures of profit-making, sit in committee alongside housewives with family commitments and doctors bound by medical ethics. All have different outlooks but a common purpose.

Amidst the cut and thrust of local politics it is difficult for the most honourable of men to discern, at times, what is the right thing to do. Events move fast and conduct which may have seemed reasonable at the time can only too easily be adjudged immoral after the event. The press, which is the main guardian of public morality, must itself be judged by these same high standards of integrity.

All councillors are subject under the Prevention of Corruption Acts to prosecutions brought by the Attorney General, who is advised in such matters by the Director of Public Prosecutions. Both councillors and local government employees are required to declare any financial interest they may have in matters arising from their council work, and they would normally prefer not even to be present at committees in which they may have a business interest.

There are many other ways in which a conflict of interest may arise; these might include the taking of gifts or hospitality in return for favours, attendance allowances wrongly claimed either by genuine mistake or by intention, the use for private gain of information received in the course of membership or employment in a local authority. The opportunity for fraud and corruption or misunderstanding of the law abounds in local government as in any other large-scale organisation, but because the confidence of the public is so closely involved, it is especially important that controls should exist.

There is nothing specially new about the problems of local government; they are all experienced by all large administrative structures. These problems surface in a variety of forms every so often, so it is advisable that they are periodically restated and redefined.

The Mallaby Committee wrote:

"During the period of our work we have seen local authorities criticised for the increase in their staffs, the growth of their expenditure and for the burden of the rates. We have also seen local authorities attacked for the inadequacy of their services and exhorted to do what they may not already be doing. There is no limit to the demand for social services and the physical environment is seldom equal to the demands which the public makes on it. But society can only have the services and amenities which its resources will allow . . .".

Local councils have a considerable command over manpower resources and capital assets. They also have access to very large annual sums of money. However, the quality of their councillors and of the staff they can command is even more important, and for this they must compete in the open market with other sectors of the community whose manpower needs are equally pressing. Local government is only one aspect of the life of the nation but it must see that its own staff needs are met.

Suggestions for further reading

Conduct in Local Government Vol 1, HMSO, 1974
A Etzioni (ed), *The Semi-Professions,* Free Press, 1969
The Municipal Year Book

Questions

1 Explain the term "corporation"?
2 Mention two important differences between the "members" and the "officers" of a local council.
3 Describe the different kinds of committee which are found in local government.
4 What is a profession?

11
Financing the public sector

The need for money

The public sector and its surrounding environment, discussed in Chapters 2 and 3, includes central and local government as well as all the other public bodies which are considered necessary for the purposes of government. In any country, these elements combine to provide public administration, and together they play a major part in the economy of the nation.

The economy of the United Kingdom can be simply described. Its people inhabit a small and overcrowded island with few natural resources of consequence apart from coal seams and some offshore oil. Unable to produce more than a part of its food requirements it is obliged to buy in the rest from abroad. To pay for this and for imports of raw materials it survives by selling its services and manufactured goods to other countries and over the years it has become relatively proficient at this. It is a trading nation, and like any other trader, if it is occasionally unable to balance its accounts it borrows money.

At the same time, the United Kingdom is a developed country, whose people have become accustomed to efficient government and a high level of public and social services. All of this costs a great deal of money and absorbs a sizeable portion of their income. In 1976, the total value of all the goods and services produced in Britain, together with net income from abroad—that is to say, the gross national product—amounted to some £110 000 million. Of these resources, expenditure on public services took just over half, or £58 000 million. Sums of money of this order are very large indeed, and within the so-called public sector, they are spent by central and local government and the public corporations on the various social and environmental services, on defence and law and order, on financial assistance to industry and on interest on borrowed money; on all the things, in short, that government is concerned with.

It is with this fraction, with public expenditure, that this chapter is concerned, for it is a political responsibility to decide how large the fraction should be at any time. Between 1970–71 and 1976–77 total public expenditure programmes were allowed to grow in real terms by about 27% until measures were taken in 1976 to reduce that very rapid rate of growth.

Year	Public expenditure	Gross national product	Percentage of public expenditure to gross national product
	£ million	£ million	%
1966	14.448	33.470	43
1967	16.672	35.255	47
1968	18.290	37.723	48
1969	18.954	39.836	47
1970	20.706	43.924	47
1971	23.199	49.656	47
1972	26.254	55.492	47
1973	30.500	64.815	47
1974	39.188	74.958	52
1975	51.410	93.978	55
1976	58.506	110.259	53

Fig. 14 Public expenditure and the gross national product (derived from the National Income and Expenditure tables 1966–76, Central Statistical Office, 1977)

In taking decisions about this and about precisely how the fraction devoted to public expenditure should be spent, any Government must be able to count on the continuing support not only of its creditors but also of the millions of people who elected it in the first place. These people, while always anxious to improve their living standards by having better health services and schools and houses and holidays, may differ in their ideas as to who should pay for such commodities: whether it should be left to themselves to do so as private individuals, or to central government to spend their money on their behalf. Government must expect to make expenditure decisions under political pressure from many different quarters and in the face of political beliefs which differ from its own.

Programmes of public expenditure which were almost non-existent 100 years ago, nowadays range over a great variety of necessary activities: schools and universities, hospitals and shipyards, old people's homes and motorways, and the large sums spent on these programmes need to be carefully managed. How public authorities decide this expenditure and how they find the revenue to pay for it is the concern of public finance and there can be little doubt that finance is the central pivot round which any public administration scheme must turn.

Any Government must strike a balance between a variety of desirable objectives which seem to be contradictory. As managers of the economy they must, for example, try to see that industry produces enough goods at a competitive price for export abroad, while leaving sufficient to satisfy home demand and to invest for the future. They must ensure, so far as they are able, that the gross national product increases by a little each year without causing inflation to grow, and that people have jobs and security and reasonable public services without feeling that they are being over-taxed to pay for them. Fundamental to all these objectives is the question of the size and shape of public expenditure, and basic to this is Parliament's granting of public money.

Each year to this end the House of Commons traditionally allocates time to consider the **supply estimates**. These are the sums which the various spending Departments of Government have estimated they will need to meet the commitments of the coming financial year which runs from April to April. By the time they finally receive Parliamentary approval in early spring, they will have gone through a long-established procedure involving Departmental collation, Treasury scrutiny, discussion and pruning. The estimates will be presented to the House of Commons, arranged under set headings and classifications and, once approved, these "votes" are incorporated in the year's Appropriation Act. Without this Parliamentary authorisation, no expenditure may take place.

There is an interval of several months from the end of the year to the time the Appropriation Act reaches the Statute Book, so the House of Commons authorises expenditure during this period by a "vote on account". Special arrangements are available to deal with any additional estimates which may become necessary later in the year. During the fiscal year the Departments undertake spending with Treasury approval where required, and at the end of each year the Departmental accounting officers submit an account of the exact amount of cash the Department has spent out of its allocation, to the Comptroller and Auditor General. This officer's report on the accounts is submitted in due course to the Public Accounts Committee.

The Public Accounts Committee, originally established in 1861, is a select committee of the House of Commons whose terms of reference are to examine the accounts, and although it does so after the expenditures have taken place, it has nevertheless a very important and powerful role in the investigation of waste, inefficiency and maladministration. Its reports are debated in the House of Commons and receive considerable press coverage and public attention. This Committee ensures that the cycle of application, authorisation, spending and report back to the people is brought full circle.

The supply estimates procedure is time-honoured and is intended to leave control over central government expenditure firmly in the hands of Parliament. The underlying principle is that of representative democracy, for the granting of public money and the imposing of taxation is the function of Parliament, not of the Queen nor of the Government nor of any other body.

Raising the money

The budget

Side by side with these arrangements, annual procedures, also of long-standing, are put in hand in order to raise the money to meet Government expenditures. These procedures culminate, usually in late March or early April, with the Chancellor of the Exchequer introducing his **budget** proposals. In a statement and report to the House of Commons, he outlines the state of the economy and proposes such changes in taxation as are considered necessary to yield sufficient revenue to meet anticipated expenditure.

Any such changes will have been intensively considered by a Budget Committee of the Treasury in the light of preliminary forecasts of revenue and expenditure, of projections of public investment, of short-term economic forecasts, of advice given by a great many organisations and interest groups ranging from the Institute of Chartered Accountants to the Child Poverty Action Group, and of the political and economic needs of the changing situation.

The Chancellor's budget proposals are debated in the House of Commons and are duly incorporated, together with any amendments, in a Finance Act which becomes law during the summer. Tide-over arrangements for the few months between the budget and the appearance of the Act are provided for by the Provisional Collection of Taxes Act 1913. Under this Act any changes proposed by the Government in Income Tax and Customs and Excise duties immediately become law if they have been adopted by a Resolution of the House.

Government expenditure takes two forms. Most of it is met out of what could perhaps be described as the Government's current account: the Consolidated Fund. One type of expenditure is authorised by the Appropriation Act on Supply Services as described, and this includes the cost of defence, the social services and the general administration of the country. The second type of expenditure is that which has been authorised by statutes other than the Appropriation Act; for example, permanent

		£ million
Government expenditure:		
on supply services	X	
on Consolidated Fund services	X	X
less		
Government revenue from taxation, etc		X
Government borrowing requirement		X
add		
Local authority borrowing		X
Public corporation borrowing		X
Public sector borrowing		X

Fig. 15   Borrowing in the public sector

expenses such as the management costs of the national debt, the financial provision for the royal family and the salaries and pensions of judges.

Government expenditure also includes loans to the nationalised industries, and to local authorities and other public corporations, and these are normally charged along with any Consolidated Fund deficit to the National Loans Fund. In his budget speech the Chancellor gives details of transactions through this Fund, and these are published in a White Paper which is issued to the public just before budget day.

Once the Finance Act comes into force, tax revenue flows into the Consolidated Fund held at the Bank of England from which central government expenditure is met. The main purpose of the budgetary procedures described is, indeed, to raise the very large sums of money needed to pay for Government services. Nowadays, it is common for Chancellors to introduce "mini-budgets" at other times of the year in addition to the annual budget if the developing economic situation calls for it, since events move much more swiftly and dynamically these days than when the mechanics of the budget were first being drawn up in the eighteenth and nineteenth centuries.

Apart from its money-raising qualities, the budget also has far-reaching effects on the country's general level of expenditure and of national economic activity, so that for many years it has been used by Chancellors to try to achieve a balance between the demand for and supply of goods and services. Since the budget affects the way people spend their money, it can be used to stimulate economic activity or to influence levels of employment or (by increasing taxes without at the same time increasing Government expenditure, for example) to control inflation. Thus there is a clear relationship between the control of the flow of funds by Parliament by means of the Finance Act and the Appropriation Act, and the economic policy which is based on this flow.

This system, which allows annual expenditure to be paid for out of a fund which is annually topped up by assessed taxes may appear simple but it is, in fact, very subtle. Many learned books and papers have analysed the system, and though suggestions have been made to improve it, no alternative has so far been found which has promised more effective results. Not for 70 years—not since the days of the so-called "assigned revenue" system of allocating the proceeds of particular taxes to pay for particular Government purposes—has the earmarking of revenue through separate funds been used. Financial control has been strengthened if anything by arrangements which are simple and free from unnecessary complication.

In the process of evaluating policies which involve the raising and spending of money, many different factors are taken into account; political factors, economic and social factors, factors involving likely collective advantages to be gained and factors influencing costs. In the public sector questions of cost are of fundamental importance not just for the usual financial reasons, but because the public spending involved uses up huge resources in ways which affect the lives of everyone. Resources are not unlimited and it is necessary to make sure that they are properly used and that policies involving them are not wasteful. The effects on the general public of public expenditure are important, so that when central funds come to be distributed—in paying rate support grant to the local authorities or as part of the Urban Programme or in allocating agreed sums to the National Health Service each year—the relative needs of different parts of the country are taken into account.

These needs may vary from time to time and adjustments made accordingly; the principle at stake is equity and fairness between one part of the country and another. The National Health Service allocation, for example, is distributed by the Department of Health and Social Security to health regions on the basis of population assessed in terms of regional death rates and patient numbers. The resulting regional and area budgets represent a clinical and political judgement about health needs, which are carefully examined and possibly contested by medical and other interest groups.

Taxation

Central government expenditure, then, is normally funded by taxation which is either direct or indirect and is collected by the Boards of Inland Revenue and of Customs and Excise.

Direct taxes include income tax, corporation tax, capital gains tax, capital transfer tax and petroleum revenue tax, while **indirect taxes** bring in all the customs and excise duties on tobacco, oil, alcohol and on motor vehicle licences as well as value added tax. Each of these taxes is capable of raising large sums of money in a highly flexible way, while at the same time having important secondary effects which can be used to achieve social and economic objectives. Thus, a Chancellor may manipulate the range of taxes at his disposal so as to stimulate the motor car industry or to respond to the anti-smoking lobby or, by varying income tax allowances, to help the elderly or the disabled or young families within the community.

A Chancellor can reduce marginal tax rates to create the same effect as an increase in wage rates; and by increasing Government expenditure without increasing taxes he may stimulate demand for goods and services. The tax system is a highly sensitive collection of parts which can be taken apart and put together again in many different ways to produce the sort of economic effects which seem desirable at any given time: a veritable chinese box.

While some individual taxes within the tax structure may be thought of as regressive in the sense that they press more heavily on those less able to pay, or progressive in that they demand more from the better-off sections of the community, the combined effect of the tax structure as a whole is progressive, so that "ability to pay" is the value underlying the system. That being so, some redistribution of resources is continually taking place between upper and lower income bands.

About three quarters of public spending is paid for by taxes and customs and excise duties, and by local authority rates which are, in fact, a local tax and as such, part of the general tax structure. The remainder is paid for by social security contributions, the trading income of the nationalised industries and income from property. In years when spending exceeds revenue, the shortfall is financed by public sector borrowing.

Taxes are annually assessed on individuals and other tax-paying bodies by the local tax offices within the tax regions into which the country is divided. In some parts of the country, assessment record-keeping has been computerised and the Inland Revenue is at present making arrangements for a system of self-assessment to replace existing controls, as it does in some other countries.

The collection of revenue is administered through local collection agencies which are unconnected with the assessment offices; the principle of separation in the functions of cash-handling and recording is an old and well-tried one. Adam Smith's "canons of taxation", set out in *The Wealth of Nations*, originated in the eighteenth century, but they are equally applicable to modern conditions. They run as follows:

1   The subjects of every State ought to contribute towards the support of the Government as nearly as possible in proportion to their respective abilities . . .

2   The tax which each individual is bound to pay ought to be certain and not arbitrary. The form of payment, the manner of payment, the quantity to be paid ought all to be clear and plain to the contributor and to every other person.

3   Every tax ought to be levied at the time and in the manner in which it is most likely to be convenient for the contributor to pay it.

4   Every tax ought to be so contrived as both to take out and keep out of the pockets of the people as little as possible, over and above what it brings into the public treasury of the State.

Principles like these emphasise the fact that public administration is balanced between the needs of Government and the needs of the individual. In matters of administration, particularly financial administration, such relationships are important. A fairly obvious link exists, for example, between the tax system and the system of administering social security benefits, for the one is to all intents and purposes the reverse of the other. Those whose income is sufficient pay taxes; those whose income is insufficient, by whatever test society applies, pay no tax but instead receive cash benefit. It has often been suggested that the logical next step would be to bring together the functions of the Inland Revenue and the Supplementary Benefits Commission and provide them with a common technology and a unified structure.

The human right to shelter has been recognised by the United Nations Organisation for many years. One of the present aims of Government is to reduce homelessness, and taxation and other policies have been extensively developed for this purpose since the end of the First World War. Tax incentives are given to those who are saving to buy their own homes whilst tax-subsidised houses are available to local authority tenants. Since most people pay taxes and rates, all are to some extent subsidising each other. It is hard to identify which section of the community bears the greatest burden in this exercise in resource distribution: whether it is rent and rate paying council tenants or the tenants of private landlords or owner-occupiers paying mortgage interest. Reforming such a system would be complicated by the sheer variety of interests pressing for matters to be left exactly as they are so as not to upset the balance.

The political and administrative problem begins to come into focus. The delicate balance between the choices of action and the instruments of finance—taxes, rates, interest rates, wage and salary levels, benefits and allowances—all make a clear-cut and wholly rational system of housing support unlikely.

Other sources

This chapter has so far been concerned with the financing of central government, but it is important to remember that the public sector also includes local government and the public corporations. Local government is of course financed by Government subsidies and local rates, as described in Chapter 8. The financing of the public corporations will be dealt with in Chapter 13.

Spending in the public sector may have consequences for communities which go far beyond the mere construction of motorways, housing estates, schools, hospitals and ships, and the employment opportunities these projects create. Thus, a decision to adopt one policy rather than another could have far-reaching social effects on individual members of the public so it is important to be aware of the "real" resources involved in the decision.

Similar considerations apply to transfers of cash to and from the Common Market. Since 1972 Britain has been one of the nine member countries of the European Economic Community and, as such, contributes to the annual European budget in accordance with a formula agreed in Brussels. Among other benefits which may derive from membership of the Community, Britain receives allocations from European funds.

Grants and loans for different purposes are available to local authorities and to industry under a variety of Community policies. These include:

a) grants from the European Social Fund
b) grants and loans from the European Coal and Steel Community
c) grants from the Community's Agricultural Fund
d) loans from the European Investment Bank
e) grants from the European Regional Development Fund

In most cases, funds are only available with the agreement of and, usually, with contributions from the appropriate public authorities at national level and the industry involved.

The European Social Fund
Organisations running Government approved training schemes can apply to the Department of Employment for 50% grant aid towards the cost of projects for the training or retraining of people leaving agriculture or the textile industry, handicapped people, immigrant workers, the unemployed in less developed regions, people in industries affected by decline or technological progress.

The Regional Development Fund
Companies, nationalised industries and public utilities as well as local and regional authorities may apply to the Departments of Industry or of the Environment for investment grants or interest rebate grants for eligible projects. These include:

    a)   industrial and service investments which create at least ten new jobs or maintain existing ones
    b)   investment in basic services
    c)   agricultural investment in disfavoured and hill-farming areas within priority areas.

The European Coal and Steel Community Retraining Fund
Organisations running Government approved retraining schemes for coal and steel workers may apply to the Department of Energy or the Department of Industry for 50% grant to finance retraining or resettlement schemes for coal and steel workers threatened with redundancy.

The European Investment Bank
Any investor may apply direct to the European Investment Bank in Luxembourg for a loan to finance either development in the less developed areas of the Community, or development which would be of interest to several member States.

Agricultural Investment Funds
Any investor may apply to the Ministry of Agriculture for a 25% grant towards the cost of improving agricultural processing and marketing for the modernisation of farms.

Research Funds
Funds are available at the European Commission in Brussels to finance research into fields such as energy, environmental protection, scientific communication and coal and steel research.

Fig. 16   The main sources of finance from the European Community

At European level, transfer payments like these are intended to assist particular areas and industries and to provide for particular needs as defined in the regulations of the funds. Britain is affected by European legislation and financial arrangements in many ways and it is increasingly difficult to study public administration in a purely British context.

Suggestions for further reading

L Hey, *The Economics of Public Finance*, Pitman, 1972
A R Prest, *Public Finance in Theory and Practice*, Weidenfeld and Nicholson, Latest edition
E Taylor, *The House of Commons at Work*, Pelican, Latest edition

Questions

1 What is the Committee of Supply?
2 How does Parliament provide money for Government purposes?
3 What taxes are levied in Britain?

12
Allocating resources

Planning

Chapter 11 examined the need for and the raising of *money* but it is not so much with money as with *resources* that Government is really concerned i.e. the way in which these resources are allocated and the way in which their allocation is controlled.

The traditional procedures which enable Parliament to exercise year by year control over the revenue and expenditure of central government—namely the budget and the estimates—are powerful but they go only a short way in meeting the needs of a modern administration. They fail to allow full democratic control of policy-making or of the planning of public expenditure over the longer periods which are more appropriate for large, ongoing programmes such as defence or support for the arts or education.

The Plowden Committee, which reported to Parliament in 1961, made a number of recommendations to deal with this shortcoming. It spoke of the need for regular surveys of public expenditure as a whole, for a period of years ahead and in relation to expected future resources. It also called for more effective arrangements for central decision-making. As a result, procedures for the preparation of annual public expenditure surveys have been developed since 1961.

In May of each year, the Public Expenditure Survey Committee (one of the sub-committees of the House of Commons Select Committee on Expenditure) is supplied by the Treasury with a report compiled by the spending Departments. This deals with a period of five years ahead and costs policies on current programmes and possible additional programmes. In turn, the Public Expenditure Survey Committee reports to Ministers showing where present policies are likely to lead in terms of public expenditure over the next five years and what would be achieved by a range of alternative policies.

This report and a medium-term assessment of the economy prepared by the Treasury are discussed at Cabinet level and decisions are taken about a total figure for public expenditure and the proportion of this figure to be allocated to each public expenditure programme. In December the Chancellor of the Exchequer presents a survey to Parliament in the form of a White Paper which outlines public expenditure for each sector for the current year and for the next four years. Each year the survey rolls the figures forward a year, the "current" programme being followed by more or less committed Departmental expenditure plans in the second and third years, while the fourth and fifth years remain provisional for the time being. Plans which have been proceeding during this five year period may be modified or changed but usually not later than the third year which is often seen as the "focal" year.

The annual White Paper on Public Expenditure thus outlines a five-year rolling plan expressed, for easy comparison, at constant prices. Programmes based on policies which have been adopted in Government legislation are set against a short-, medium- and longer-term background.

In discussing matters of public finance it will be apparent that the subject is technical and sometimes abstract and not easy to describe simply. The decision-making processes outlined involve an immense amount of background work, the collection and assimilation of technical, statistical data relating to the economy and the reconciling of differing points of view. As Lord Diamond has said:

"The task . . . is that of winning agreement on a precise figure within or at least very close to a band of figures from colleagues who are going to find it difficult to come to an agreement; and to win it in such a way that there will remain a sufficient fund of mutual goodwill to enable the same colleagues to resolve similar difficulties in other areas of government which are bound to arise in the very near future".

The skills which go into the production of a White Paper on Public Expenditure range from economic expertise to the ability to gather and present large amounts of complex information in usable ways.

The White Paper presents this information in such a way that public expenditure is dealt with by programme and in total, as well as by economic category. It also classifies public spending by programme groups, economic categories and spending authorities. The totals of planned expenditure are arranged so as to contain a contingency or emergency reserve for each year designed to cover approved increases which were not foreseen at the time of publication. In the normal way additional expenditure is offset within existing Departmental totals but where this is not possible, the Treasury may allow the additional expenditure to be paid for out of the contingency reserve. It therefore acts as a buffer area.

Control over resource allocation

There is undoubtedly a need for control over public spending—not just after the money is spent but before—and in 1912 a Parliamentary commit-

£ *million at 1977 survey prices*

	1977–78	1978–79	1979–80	1980–81	1981–82
1 Defence	6 255	6 289	6 494	6 660	6 660
2 Overseas aid and other overseas services	1 351	1 722	1 860	1 958	1 962
3 Agriculture, fisheries, food and forestry	899	706	654	649	642
4 Trade, industry and employment: refinance of home shipbuilding and fixed rate export credit	−174	145	−44	−114	−30
other	1 970	2 798	2 632	2 589	2 547
5 Government lending to nationalised industries	420	1 350	1 550	1 350	1 100
6 Roads and transport	2 590	2 563	2 583	2 572	2 554
7 Housing	4 475	4 702	4 814	4 948	4 995
8 Other environmental services	2 532	2 594	2 626	2 643	2 657
9 Law, order and protective services	1 906	1 948	1 947	1 970	1 992
10 Education and libraries, science and arts	8 010	8 102	8 143	8 205	8 255
11 Health and personal social services	7 390	7 537	7 652	7 776	7 927
12 Social security	13 226	14 063	14 172	14 458	14 602
13 Other public services	844	854	865	865	886
14 Common services	883	910	952	986	1 022
15 Northern Ireland	1 742	1 815	1 811	1 796	1 808
Total programmes	54 320	58 100	58 711	59 310	59 577
Contingency reserve	—	750	1 500	1 750	2 000
Total	54 320	58 850	60 211	61 060	61 577
Debt interest	1 900	2 000	1 900	1 800	1 600
Total	56 220	60 850	62 111	62 860	63 177
Total programmes, contingency reserve and foreign and market borrowing of nationalised industries	54 850	58 550	59 611	60 860	61 237

Fig. 17 Public expenditure by programme

tee, the Estimates Committee, was set up to achieve this. It was never outstandingly successful, chiefly because the estimates were based on Government policies so that it was difficult for any committee to interfere with them without also appearing to interfere with policy. This has always been a sensitive area and alternatives to the Estimates Committee were regularly proposed from the early 1930's onwards until its terms of reference were eventually widened and taken over by a new committee of Parliament, the Expenditure Committee.

Since 1971 the Select Committee on Expenditure has had functions which include:

a) consideration of papers on public expenditure presented to the House of Commons
b) consideration of such estimates as seem to it appropriate
c) consideration of how the policies suggested by the figures of expenditure and in the estimates may be carried out more economically
d) examination of the form of papers and of estimates presented to the House of Commons

As a select committee of great importance, the Expenditure Committee has power to send for persons, papers and records; it may use expert advice and may sit regardless of whether the House of Commons is in session. It may also appoint sub-committees to which it may refer matters relating to expenditure. The sub-committees appointed in this way include those on:

a) Trade and Industry
b) Employment and Social Services
c) Defence and External Affairs
d) Education and Arts
e) Environment and Home Office
f) Public Expenditure

Each sub-committee concentrates its enquiries on a particular range of Government business. The Public Expenditure Sub-Committee, for example, is particularly concerned with financial control over the very large expenditure incurred within the public sector.

From about the time of the Plowden reforms, too, the practice has grown up of conducting full-scale examinations into the programmes of Government Departments under the title of Programme Analysis and Review (PAR). PAR studies, which are selected and carried out in depth by groups representative of the Department under review and the Treasury, are intended to arrive at an informed view of the value of particular programmes and to report to the Minister concerned. Specialist study groups of this kind are a logical part of the control process.

Programmes for providing school meals, health centres, housing, family income supplements, special prison units and so on are all established as a result of Parliamentary discussion and debate under constant external pressures, with the aid of Departmentally prepared costs and statistics in support of arguments or in answer to Parliamentary questions.

What were once seen as important reforms, were concerned with rising standards of living at the time they were introduced and with the balance between poverty and growth. Since the economic situation is constantly changing, policy has to react to these short-term changes, while at the same time taking a longer-term view of the needs of the country. Programmes which were once considered highly desirable are not necessarily still suited to present requirements. Periodic reviews—which are good management practice in any case—help to prevent programmes stultifying and becoming out of date.

Pressures for change are also bound by priorities of one kind or another and in some services there may not be much room for manoeuvre, for example, more than 65% of central government expenditure on services is at present subject to cash limits. The main exceptions are services which are affected by demand, such as social security where external factors such as unemployment levels make it impossible to achieve absolute administrative control. Cash limits which are fixed by the Treasury each year impose a planned "ceiling" on spending by central and local government and the nationalised industries as part of the effort to restrain the growth of public expenditure.

A major factor in the expansion of Government expenditure in recent years has been the growth in welfare payments including Supplementary Benefits, Family Income Supplements and other social security benefits. Since the welfare legislation of the late 1940's which followed on the Beveridge Report of 1942, there has been a general commitment to welfare in Britain which has now reached the point where it is an expected public provision. The principle of State-provided welfare is a very old one—the "alimenta" in the Roman Empire of the second century is an early example—and other European countries have welfare provisions in greater or lesser degree. The principle once established, however, is hard to change; welfare tends to grow rather than diminish, and in the end political control becomes a matter of necessity.

Public expenditure, though it directly affects all Departments of Government, is traditionally the concern of the Treasury, the central finance Ministry in Britain. The Treasury, responsible as it is for the development of overall economic policy, maintains very close links with the finance divisions of Departments, advising them in their preparation of annual estimates and helping them to ensure that funds allocated to them are properly spent. Its public services sector controls total public expenditure and individual programmes.

The co-ordinating and controlling influence of the Treasury in exercising the "power of the purse" and in modifying social policies, is sometimes resented by those who feel that policy should be determined without an overriding regard for expenditure alone. Yet idealism in social policies has to be tempered by a knowledge of what people are prepared to pay; Government strategy is concentrated above everything else on how to win the next election, and gaining sufficient support from its electorate is not something which can be left to chance. The Government plans its public spending and raises revenue to match it; if the resulting tax burden is felt to be too heavy, then social policies are likely to be regarded sceptically by the people of the country and their representatives. In short, new programmes are evaluated differently depending on the economic circumstances of their introduction.

Apart from PAR exercises, the control exercised over public expenditure by traditional formal bodies such as select committees also plays an important part in influencing policy. When the Public Accounts Committee reported in 1973 on apparently inappropriate financing arrangements for North Sea mineral rights, the reaction of Parliament, and indeed the public, was quick and effective in bringing about an alteration in existing fiscal and administrative policies.

Looking forward

In 1971, the incoming Government set up for the first time a Central Policy Review Staff, a body of 15 or so selected people, which was intended at the time to act on the Cabinet's behalf by producing analyses which would help in arriving at policy decisions. The Central Policy Review Staff have undertaken a number of studies on which reports have been submitted; independent of the Cabinet Office they have been able to look at developing policy ideas in a more detached and perhaps logical way than the more committed Departments and, as their name suggests, to relate individual policies to central strategy and aims.

The role of the Central Policy Review Staff is to provide the Cabinet and the Prime Minister with an informed and co-ordinated view of the situation so that the trends of the complete range of Government policies at home and in the European Community can be assessed as a coherent whole. In addition special futures studies have been made of issues like population, transport, overseas representation and the growth and decline of particular industries. The "think-tank" aspect of the work of the Central Policy Review Staff is perhaps its most useful contribution. There is a case for a central policy-influencing organisation of this kind, and it seems likely to remain a feature of future administration.

There is a sense in which Cabinet Ministers and their Civil Service advisers, particularly those concerned with public sector finance, live in a two dimensional world: a world in which the national scene is being simultaneously scanned from two points of view—the immediate present and a point perhaps 15 months in the future. Nationally, adjustments have to be made for the day to day changes in the political, economic and social life of the country, while at the same time an impression has to be formed of what conditions will be in 6 months, 1 year, 15 months time. The clearer and more refined this impression can be, the better, and to this end information has to be assembled and looked at from different viewpoints.

Analyses of national income and expenditure have been made for a number of years and are published annually by the Stationery Office as the Blue Book. The national income represents the total income of the population of the United Kingdom, but it can also be taken as equivalent to the national product or, in other words, to expenditure on consumption goods and services plus investment.

The Blue Book deals with essentially the same information as the Exchequer accounts, published as the Chancellor's Financial Statement and Report at the time of the budget; both offer a view of central government finance. However, the Exchequer accounts are kept on a simple cash basis whereas the National Income and Expenditure Blue Book presentation deals in large estimated figures which are classified in different ways and cover the calendar year rather than the financial year.

National accounts which illustrate the interaction of the different sectors of the community and their contribution to the national income are very useful in planning and policy-making. However, in addition to planning, expenditure must be controlled as it occurs and information on actual spending must therefore be collected. Since 1976, an improved financial information system has been developed by the Treasury to provide a flow of figures which can be used by Departments for control purposes. The figures enable the Departments to check their allowed expenditure in the Public Expenditure Survey and the supply estimates, and to monitor their own cash limits. Such flows of figures represent an impressive array of figure information.

Volumes of statistics, too, are developed by the Central Statistical Office and the Statistics divisions of Government Departments. Many of these series are published by Her Majesty's Stationery Office appearing in such forms as the Monthly Digest of Statistics, Economic and Social Trends, Financial Statistics and the Indices of Retail and Wholesale Prices and of Industrial Production as well as the Family Expenditure Survey. These and the collections upon which they are based enable projections of trends to be made.

For many years the Treasury has used projections like these to help with forward planning; the extent to which they are used in the budget process and in the Public Expenditure Survey has already been noted and no Government today could survive for long without them. Forecasting depends on using records of past events and experience to extrapolate a little way into the future. During the past 15 years or so, ways of forecasting the national income have been developed to the point where the Treasury forecasts the economy by computer. Based on some 800 equations, the value of a macro-economic model like this is that it can suggest how the economy would be affected by changing the situational "givens".

It goes without saying that something as shifting and complex as the national economy is extremely difficult to condense and simplfy: using past data to predict how people are going to react in a set of future circumstances which can only be guessed at is not something which can be done with any degree of accuracy. It is all too easy, too, to develop economic and social indicators which are intended to chart the economy or to provide pointers to developing social trends and then to imagine that they represent the truth. The truth is not to be wheedled so lightly into a figure.

However, those who work with forecasts are no doubt aware of the risk of error and make allowance for it. In the last resort the justification of economic and other forms of forecasting is that they provide the opportunity for educated guessing. In the "real" world as in the world of public finance it may be better to forecast than not to do so.

Public finance, then, once described as "the supply and application of State resources", is one instrument of Government policy which—like regional policy or monetary policy—is used to pursue national economic goals. These goals include the defence of the country, the achievement of full employment combined with growth, the provision of public goods and services, and the control of poverty through the redistribution of wealth. In developing social and economic strategies to meet these goals, the Government needs to consider not just where and how it proposes to raise the funds it requires, but also the manner in which these funds are to be distributed for, as we have observed, this will have far-reaching effects on individuals and on the effectiveness of particular policies.

Suggestions for further reading

Lord Diamond, *Public Expenditure in Practice*, Allen and Unwin, 1975
P Else, *Public Expenditure, Parliament and PPB*, PEP, 1970
Heclo and Wildavsky, *The Private Government of Public Money*, Macmillan, 1964

Questions

1 What does the Central Policy Review Staff do?
2 Explain PESC, PAR, and PAC
3 How does the Blue Book on National Income and Expenditure contribute to policy-making?
4 Describe the composition and functions of the Select Committee on Expenditure.
5 In what ways does Parliament control public spending?

13
Independent public bodies

Central control

In the summer of 1974 a chemical factory run by Nypro (UK) Ltd at Flixborough in Humberside blew up with sudden and devastating force killing or injuring some 130 people, wrecking hundreds of homes and causing widespread repercussions throughout the whole of the textile industry. The explosion had, it seemed, been caused by an escape of cyclohexane vapour which had spontaneously ignited; the destruction of the plant and the surrounding countryside was total.

It is unlikely that many people realised until the report of the enquiry, which was set up by the Secretary of State for Employment to investigate the affair under section 84 of the Factories Act 1961, that the company was in fact an industrial unit jointly owned by two Governments through shares held by their respective nationalised industries, namely, Dutch State Mines and the National Coal Board. Thus the company, like so many quasi-public firms nowadays, illustrates the fact that no clear distinction can be made between the private sector and the public sector; there is a large middle zone in which industrial, trading and other organisations operate independently.

In this grey area are public corporations operating commercial activities such as airways and atomic energy and television. Here, too, the many hundreds of non-profit-making bodies operate, some of them with annual budgets running into millions of pounds, much of it devoted to research. On the far fringes are the planemakers and the firms handling defence contracts, the shipbuilders and computer firms. At times these may be producing private goods and at other times public goods. If the latter is the case the Government is their customer and their pricing policy may have little to do with any conventional commercial considerations.

In this zone, companies are often engaged in work which is new, unique, very costly and of national importance. Their Directors may be bound by the Official Secrets Act and they may work in close harmony with civil servants; they may literally exist only by virtue of Government loans. Although these companies may be concerned with profitability, their responsibility generally rises above commercial interests and extends to the community as a whole; "the public interest" is a value which becomes equally as important as business commonsense. Organisations like these need forms of control over policy and operational efficiency which—like themselves—are exceptional and out-of-the-ordinary.

These independent public bodies take so many different forms and exist for so many different reasons that they are far from easy to classify. They range from big and basic nationalised undertakings like British Rail to public corporations like British Steel or to simple funding agencies like the Arts Council. However, some guiding principles by which these organisations operate can be established.

From time to time during the history of the United Kingdom, Governments have found it necessary to set up special administrative authorities in order to deal with a particular task. These authorities have been allowed relative freedom from Government control to help them operate more effectively. Chartered companies in the seventeenth century like the East India or the Darien had more than just commercial motives in mind and so, too, did the seventeenth century monopolies operating under licence such as the glassmakers and the soapboilers.The borderlands of Wales, the swamplands of the Fens, the Debateable Area on the Scottish Border are all early examples of administrative problems which were solved by creating separate ad hoc authorities vested with special statutory powers. This is an old and universal principle; Roman government was studded with one-off bodies.

During the nineteenth century, many such authorities were brought into being by various Acts of Parliament and were entrusted with strictly defined duties limited to one function or to one part of the country. In this way corporate bodies such as poor law boards, turnpike trusts, boards of health and school boards proliferated and contributed to a characteristically Victorian brand of administration which was patchy, experimental and cautious. Modern local government learned its trade, however, from these ad hoc boards, for by the end of the century most of them, along with their accumulated expertise, had been absorbed by the new local authorities and had been finally brought under tight and tidy democratic control.

Yet, as time passed a variety of functions remained which seemed to be more suitably administered by agencies other than central or local government. In the 1920's, for example, it was easy to justify a separate board for early broadcasting which would be free from political interference, and similar arguments could be applied to the various marketing and regulatory bodies such as the Herring Industry Board which were later developed. Other specialised functions of a technical or commercial nature, such as forestry or the generation and supply of electricity, which were basic and national in scope, required management structures which would enable them to function effectively but with some degree of autonomy and the minimum of political interference.

By the end of the Second World War the Government saw that public ownership was the most appropriate way to run industries like these, and it became necessary to introduce administrative machinery to deal with them. Much experience was already available for the purpose. The close wartime control over basic industries and services such as coal, steel, transport and the hospitals had given Civil Service Departments experience of working with external agencies. The experience was extended into the peacetime control of the economy which formed the basis of the economic and social reforms the Government was proposing.

In the late 1940's, many nationalisation Acts were passed bringing public corporations into being. Each had a corporate status and powers and functions extending over the whole country. They were also relatively exempt from the normal processes of Parliamentary accountability. Today these corporations are, as the Government has made clear[1], major users of national resources, employing 7% of the country's labour force.

"In 1976 they contributed about 10% of the total output of the UK economy. They dominate four strategic sectors of economic activity: energy, public transport, communications and iron and steel. They supply basic goods and services to industry and essentials of life to individual consumers. They are themselves major customers of some of the capital goods industries and the scale of their purchases means that some of these supplying industries are heavily dependent on their strategic decisions and investment. In short, the nationalised industries have a pervasive influence throughout the economy on investment, employment, industrial costs and on the cost of living".

Herein lies the essential problem of public ownership: how to construct an organisation which will work with the freedom, drive and commercial secrecy of any private enterprise firm, yet remain subject to democratic control? It is a problem which has never satisfactorily been solved. The independent public bodies are for the most part big, powerful and essential. They employ huge workforces and use vast resources of capital and revenue in conditions bordering on monopoly; any disruption in the services which any of them provide would quickly lead to breakdown and dislocation in the life of the country. The implications for public order are clear and the problem of control is pressing and fundamental.

Public corporations

What, then, are these independent bodies? Like other European countries, notably France and Italy, Britain has used public corporations as an important method of administering public services. In recent years the method has been developed to the point that while many such bodies now exist the

1 White Paper: *The Nationalised Industries,* 1978.

public at large is not generally well informed about them. Can they be rationally classified in any way? A short selection of the more important bodies would include the following:

Power, energy and resources

The British Gas Corporation
The Central Electricity Generating Board and Area Distributing Boards
The Electricity Council
The North of Scotland Hydro Electricity Board
The South of Scotland Electricity Board
The Northern Ireland Electricity Service
The United Kingdom Atomic Energy Authority and its statutory companies
The National Coal Board (and its wholly owned subsidiary companies: NCB (Ancillaries) Limited, and NCB (Coal Products) Limited)
The British National Oil Corporation
The British Steel Corporation
The National Water Council and regional water authorities

Transport and communications

British Rail
British Transport Docks Board
British Airways and its Divisions
Civil Aviation Authority
British Airports Authority
British Waterways Board
National Ports Council
British Shipbuilders
British Aerospace Corporation
Post Office

Environment

National Parks Commission
Nature Conservancy
Commission for the New Towns

Advisory

The Commission for Racial Equality
The Arts Council
The National Consumer Council
The National Economic Development Council

Research

Agricultural Research Council
Science Research Council
Social Science Research Council
Natural Environment Research Council
Medical Research Council

Industrial support

The National Enterprise Board
The Scottish Development Agency
The Welsh Development Agency
The Marketing Boards
The National Film Finance Corporation
The Herring Industry Board
The White Fish Authority

Even such an abbreviated list shows the very wide range of activities now carried on by these independent public bodies, some of which are commercial-type public corporations, others, research organisations set up under Royal Charter, others of an advisory nature or designed to channel financial resources where they are most needed. The variety of forms and structures lends a remarkable flexibility to a system which was largely created over the last 30 or 40 years. It is a new, third force in public administration alongside central government Departments and local authority services.

New, independent bodies continue to be appointed to deal with new needs. When oil was first discovered in commercial quantities in the North Sea in the 1960's the task of drilling and exploration was quickly taken on by the big international oil companies, operating for profit. These companies—the so-called "Sisters"—between them not only possessed a great deal of technological skill and expertise, but also had access to risk capital which was simply not available elsewhere; as development agencies they were absolutely essential.

Government action thus became necessary to construct an administration through which the benefit of these new-found national resources could be felt by the nation, while at the same time maintaining the operators' commercial interest in continuing to work the oil fields. Fields were identified, a petroleum revenue tax was introduced, and in 1976 a new public body—the British National Oil Corporation—was formed to take over the offshore interests previously supervised by the National Coal Board and to hold the Government's participation interest in production licences.

The Corporation has a Board with a Chairman and members appointed by the Energy Secretary. It has wide powers to explore, produce, transport, refine and to buy and sell oil. Through this independent statutory agency, Government control over the industry has now been sufficiently extended to safeguard the national interest. By means of the Corporation amenity and security can be protected. State participation in private holdings can be secured and a check can be established on when and at what rate particular UK fields are to be exploited.

The BNOC, like the other independent bodies, is uniquely designed to deal with a special need. Like other such bodies, too, it has its own terms of reference and its own objectives, but there are many more points of difference than similarities.

There is no standard organisational model for the public corporations and no one constitution is identical to another. However, each has a governing body with a Chairman and Board members, often drawn from industry, who are normally appointed by the Minister of the sponsoring Department. Each is a corporate body, independently financed by its own activities or from the public or the Treasury, and responsible for running itself.

Neither managers nor staff in these organisations are usually civil servants and, though the Minister may give general directions as to how the organisation should be run so as to be in line with current Government policy, it is the duty of a board to conduct its affairs according to best commercial practice. It is largely independent in its day to day work and is ultimately accountable through its Minister to Parliament. It is this very accountability which has so often in the past 20 years proved difficult to achieve. As the McIntosh Report stated, in 1976:

"there is confusion about the respective roles of the boards of nationalised industries, Ministers and Parliament with the result that accountability is seriously blurred."

The accountability of public corporations is periodically put to the test using statutory methods of control but Boards also have a responsibility to inform their Ministers who, in turn, must inform Parliament and the people of the country of the current state of affairs; they, in the long run, have to pay for the service.

Since 1955, for example, a House of Commons Select Committee on the Nationalised Industries has had power to examine the reports and accounts of those nationalised industries with controlling Boards appointed by Ministers and not completely supported financially by the Exchequer. Since its introduction, the Select Committee has had its powers of supervision widened to include the Independent Broadcasting Authority, Cable and Wireless Ltd, and certain aspects of the Bank of England. It has produced a series of reports for Parliament on the different industries which have usually been informed, constructive and very critical.

In 1978, the Select Committee published a penetrating report on the British Steel Corporation in which the attention of Parliament was drawn to the very large financial losses then being incurred. The Committee sought access to confidential Steel Corporation documents. In the process the

Committee successfully forced the Chairman of the British Steel Corporation to give the information they required by using the constitutional device of having notice served upon him by the House of Commons Serjeant-at-Arms. The whole issue was raised of the amount of confidential information which Members of Parliament are entitled to have about any nationalised industry.

In the case of the Steel Industry, problems caused by world price movements and foreign competition had been made worse by overcapacity and antiquated plant at home, and numerous suggestions were made by the Select Committee with a view to improving matters. Among many other things the Committee questioned the value of the Department of Industry's close control and monitoring of the Corporation. It also unfavourably criticised the methods of financial forecasting which were being used by the Corporation and the Treasury.

Apart from these investigative activities of the Select Committee, each of the nationalised industries has for many years sponsored consumers' or consultative councils through which recommendations by the user public can be processed.

Periodically, too, matters affecting the nationalised industries and other independent public bodies get an airing in Parliament in the course of debates on their annual reports or in answers to Parliamentary questions about matters of policy. However, the management are granted a considerable degree of independence in their day to day administration.

All the independent public bodies have certain characteristics in common, namely:

a) they have corporate status
b) their constitutions, powers and duties are laid down by statute or by Charter
c) they can exercise discretion and are independent in their operations
d) they are subject to some degree of control by Government
e) the public has a controlling financial interest in them

Financial control

Many of the independent public bodies are directly financed by Parliament. In some cases these grants are intended simply to cover their running costs. In other cases, the bodies concerned act as distribution agencies, placing funds where they can best achieve the results intended by Government policies. The largest independent public bodies are concerned with providing public services of a commercial nature, but without the competition which is usually associated with business. They have their manufacturing costs and fix their prices and, like any commercial concern, they may earn profit or they may incur loss. In any case, they are accountable to the public which has not been slow in recent years to call for refunds and tariff reductions where excessive profits have been reported in the annual financial statements of certain boards.

The various Acts governing the public corporations require the Boards of these independent bodies to keep accounts and to publish them each year, and to conduct their business in such a way that receipts will balance with payments "over a period". This is, of course, more likely to be achieved by some corporations than by others; financial targets have been agreed between the Government and the various Boards setting out specified rates of return on capital which may be expected in each particular corporation.

All the nationalised industries operate with large amounts of capital and in some cases—the Gas Corporation, the Post Office and the Airports Authority are examples—current capital requirements are met out of revenue. Whether each of the different industries can finance itself, however, depends upon many different circumstances such as market demand, pricing policy, changes in productivity and even the weather. All have, too, "wider obligations than commercial concerns in the private sector". Accordingly, where new investment cannot be met from within the corporation itself, the Government may arrange funding by grants or interest-bearing loans from the Exchequer. In some cases, too, borrowing from the market either at home or abroad may be required and the degree to which each corporation requires funds forms the basis for the annual cash limits imposed upon each nationalised industry by the Treasury.

In practice these arrangements are applied differently between one independent Board and another mainly because of the special circumstances which apply in different cases. Two very contrasting bodies, both of which were brought into existence in 1946, serve as good illustrations.

The National Coal Board was one of the first of the great public corporations. It was taken into public ownership under the Coal Industry Nationalisation Act 1946 with the express purpose of taking over responsibility for all the mines in Britain. To-day it is one of the largest organisations in Europe and owns many other activities such as brickworks and chemical plants.

Coal, which is one of the few natural resources that Britain owns in any abundance, is produced at coal fields grouped into 12 areas throughout the country, each controlled by a Director who is responsible to the National Coal Board. The value to the nation of this primary source of energy and its future prospects is too great to calculate; adequate control of policy and efficiency is clearly a necessity. The question that has to be decided by Parliament is the extent to which control is best left in the hands of technicians and specialists and how far that control should be supervised by civil servants and by Parliament itself.

The Arts Council of Great Britain, established in 1946 by Royal Charter, is a very different kind of organisation, but is also important in its own way. Its members are appointed by the Secretary of State for Education and Science and its aim is to encourage a greater knowledge and understanding

	1978–79 Forecast: £m
Capital requirements	
Investment	4 009
Working capital	358
	4 367
less Internal funding	2 099
	2 268
External funding	2 268
less Government grants	732
Net borrowing	1 536
British Aerospace British Shipbuilders	35
Short-term borrowing Leasing	−130
Estimated shortfall	−400
Adjusted net long-term borrowing	1 050
Overseas loans	−290
UK loans	−10
Net Government borrowing	1 350
By loans	918
and public dividend capital	432

Fig. 18 Financing the nationalised industries

of the fine arts. As an independent public body, it co-operates with Government Departments and local authorities, using the annual grant it receives from Parliament to exert its influence in the fields of music, drama and the visual arts. Support for the arts comes, of course, from many different sources, both public and private; the Arts Council plays a central role in helping to organise this support and thus supervise Government patronage.

Independent public bodies like the public corporations and other Boards which are run by virtue of their statutes and Charters are all examples of the State's response to special administrative needs. In recent years the State has also obtained holdings in individual companies.

The Industry Act 1975 established the National Enterprise Board to develop and assist the national economy, to improve industrial efficiency and international competitiveness and to safeguard employment. The Board is a public corporation with a full-time Chairman whose Board members are appointed by the Secretary of State for Industry. It draws its funds partly from the National Loans Fund and partly in the form of public dividend capital voted by Parliament—similar to industrial share capital—on which a dividend is payable to the Exchequer where appropriate.

The Board's main function is to provide finance for industrial investment, particularly for the expansion and modernisation of the means of production in industry. Its financial and advisory services may also be used to promote industrial restructuring. In addition the Board acts as a holding company for shareholdings in industrial companies which it has acquired either through its own financing activities or through their having been transferred to the Board by the Government.

An arrangement like this, however desirable it may seem, brings the Government directly into the business arena and obliges its servants to adopt a business outlook. The inconsistency which Adam Smith noted between "the functions of trader and Sovereign" is no different to-day to what it was nearly 200 years ago. When, occasionally, private firms which have been helped by Government loans and shareholdings fail and have to go into liquidation, the public inevitably questions the stewardship of public money.

The Industry Act allows the Government to determine the Board's financial duties, to set limits to borrowing and may impose certain restrictions on the Board's freedom to acquire shares in companies without the Government's prior consent. As a source of capital finance, the National Enterprise Board chooses to assist those firms which, in its own commercial judgement, appear to offer prospects for growth if given adequate backing, but in doing so, it must bear in mind the guidelines laid down by the Minister.

The National Enterprise Board has acquired holdings in a number of sectors of industry, notably in the computer field, in electronics and in high technology; its investment proposals are outlined in its Corporate Plan. Some of the Board's holdings have been well-publicised: British Leyland and Rolls Royce are two big firms which have been much in the headlines in recent years, partly because of their financing problems and partly because they are so closely identified in the public mind with British industry.

Other firms in which an interest has been taken include Ferranti Ltd, Dunford and Elliott Ltd, Sinclair Radionics Ltd, ICL Ltd, and many others. The National Enterprise Board has also been prepared to participate in joint ventures with other private sector firms in bidding for overseas contracts which nowadays tend to be very large and possibly too great a burden for any one firm to handle on its own.

The National Enterprise Board differs from other nationalised industries in that its activities are not confined to any one sector of industry but extend over a much wider area in such a way as to influence industrial performance. Remote-controlled underwater craft, machine tools, corrugated fibreboard and plastic mouldings are only a few of the different fields in which it has an interest through its holdings. Since it has access to very large amounts of public money, it can take decisions which may contribute to the long-term strengthening of companies engaged in these fields and so help the economy of the country as a whole. It has been seen as a bridge between the public and the private sectors.

As with other independent bodies, the need for accountability persists. The sums of public money which are deployed by the National Enterprise Board are so large that the decision-making processes and the outcomes of decisions need to be supervised with the greatest of care and tested against sound financial standards. Nor is finance the only test. The activities of the NEB, like those of other independent public bodies, are fundamentally concerned with power, and the public has a right to know how that power is exercised.

Suggestions for further reading

A H Hanson (ed) *Nationalisation: A book of Readings,* Allen and Unwin, 1963
The Nationalised Industries, Cmnd 7131, HMSO, 1978
A Study of UK Nationalised Industries, NEDO, 1976
R E Thomas, *The Government of Business,* Allan, 1976
W Thornhill, *The Nationalised Industries,* Nelson, 1968

Questions

1 What are cash limits?
2 What is the function of the National Enterprise Board?
3 How do the nationalised industries pay for their capital assets?
4 What are the reasons for having organisations which are independent of central or local government, to deal with: a) television broadcasting? b) coal production? c) race relations?

14
Health and voluntary agencies

Health services

The National Health Service is somewhat different from the other public bodies. Described in recent Government papers as a State agency, it exists in its present form as the result of the amalgamation in 1947 of many services which were then being separately and haphazardly provided; hospitals and doctors, dentists and midwives, chemists and opticians. During the ensuing 30 years, all these functions have been welded together into a health service which, despite its shortcomings, still represents perhaps the most important social reform of the twentieth century.

The Health Service was established by the National Health Service Act 1946, and was introduced by the post-war Labour Government as a major part of the new welfare services then being developed. The integration of its varied but related services put the ideals of the Welfare State, outlined in 1942 by the Beveridge Committee, into practice. Under the Act, hospitals were taken over by the State from local authorities and voluntary boards which had previously been responsible for them. Executive councils were set up to organise general practitioners and other health workers, while local authorities were given increased powers to provide local health and public health services.

The three part system which emerged was based on four assumptions. Nowadays these are taken for granted, but at the time they were new:

1   There should be national ownership and direction of the Service
2   Responsibility for finance should be at national level
3   Administration should be decentralised, regionally and locally
4   Every citizen should have an absolute moral right to such a measure of good health as society is able to give him

The health services were nationalised amid controversy and opposition; large numbers of the medical profession were unwilling to co-operate in making the new scheme workable almost until the Bill became law. Their reservations were perhaps understandable: doctors and consultants were being asked to abandon well tried methods of conducting their business in favour of new and untried procedures. Doubts about becoming employees of the State were added to misgivings about what was often thought of as "socialised medicine".

In the event, Aneurin Bevan, the Minister of Health, made certain concessions to the pressures which had built up over the Bill and introduced an element of choice for patients. A "private" sector in medicine was preserved and the results of this compromise have persisted to the present time. Private consultation and treatment, hospital pay beds, nursing homes and provident societies operate side by side with the State-provided services, although not on a very significant scale, for the great majority of the population nowadays uses the National Health Service facilities. Britain, however, has an international reputation for certain medical specialisations and many people come to this country from overseas for treatment they may not be able to obtain elsewhere; this treatment is given privately.

The social changes which the National Health Service epitomised at the time of its introduction were radical and profound. After the deprivations of the 1930's and '40's, Welfare State ideals seemed right and appropriate, and the goal of universally available care of equal standard for everybody was then, and is now, the value upon which the system is based.

The tripartite system of local health authorities, regional hospital boards and executive councils with which the new Service started, continued for the next 25 years with relatively few alterations being made to that basic structure. During that period, however, the flaws in the system became increasingly apparent. The most important of these was the difficulty of co-ordinating the three parts of the Service. Patients with long-term and chronic illnesses in particular, required hospital care and community care on an integrated basis and this was hard to achieve with structures which were separate and isolated even from the other associated social services.

At about the same time as the re-organisation of local government, the health services in England, Scotland and Wales were completely reorganised in 1974 following a series of White Papers, Green Papers and consultative documents. Northern Ireland's re-organisation had taken place in the autumn of 1973.

Although separate legislation applies in Scotland and in Northern Ireland, all four parts of the United Kingdom have broadly similar health service structures and Ministerial responsibility is divided between the Secretary of State for the Social Services and the Secretaries of State for Scotland and Wales. Though lacking the independence and freedom to operate and make decisions which other corporate bodies enjoy, the National Health Service in Scotland and Northern Ireland has a separate kind of responsibility.

In England there is a three-tier structure consisting of 14 regional health authorities, each with at least one medical school and responsible for regional planning and allocating resources to the 90 area health authorities. As far as possible, the boundaries of these regional and area authorities have been made to correspond to those of the local government areas they serve.

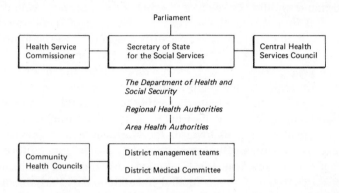

Fig. 19 The framework for the National Health Service in England

Just as area health authorities are accountable to regional health authorities as corporate bodies, so regional authorities are accountable to the Department of Health and Social Security and through that Department to Parliament itself. Control is thus direct but it is also bureaucratic.

The main burden of the service is carried by the area health authorities which are responsible for assessing health needs within their areas and for providing services to meet these needs. The management of an area is in the hands of a Chairman appointed by the Secretary of State and a representative Board which includes doctors and nurses. The running of the services provided by an area authority is based on health districts covering populations from 100 000 to 500 000 including within them district general hospitals. District management teams carry out health policies at local level, co-ordinating services and supervising the planning of health care for particular groups of patients such as children, the elderly and the mentally and physically handicapped.

One of the new ideas introduced by the re-organisation Acts was that of Community Health Councils. These represent the patients and consumers of the Service and there is one for each health district. Its members are appointed partly by the local authority and partly by voluntary bodies and the regional health authority. The intention of these new organisations is to enable local people to play a part in the running of the Service by collecting and conveying opinions, suggestions and complaints to those who are responsible for it; in this way they resemble the consultative councils of the nationalised industries.

An added democratic safeguard is provided by the Health Service Commissioners for England, Wales and Scotland, whose job is to investigate complaints from members of the public who consider they have suffered injustice or hardship as a result of maladministration or failure of the

Service. The Commissioner's business is to investigate claims by individuals, not by public bodies such as local authorities or other independent public bodies.

When the National Health Service was originally set up its founders intended that it should be free to everyone. Free treatment would, it was hoped, result in a substantial increase in the level of health among the population, which could only have beneficial effects on the economy of the country. To a large extent it has remained a free service.

Over the years, however, charges have been introduced for part of the cost of certain kinds of treatment such as prescriptions, dental work and glasses, though exemptions from these charges are given in cases of need. In addition to these charges, part of the national insurance contribution paid by people at work goes towards the National Health Service. Apart from these two sources of income, however, public expenditure on the Health Service is met from the Exchequer. Finance for the health programme, as discussed earlier, is funded and allocated by Parliament as part of its overall planning of public expenditure and is distributed to regions, areas and districts on a formula basis related to priorities and objectives for the Service as a whole.

A "free" service as large and varied in its application as the National Health Service makes great demands on resources; these resources need to be rationed in some way and planning is required in order to establish priorities. These plans are outlined in the Public Expenditure Survey, but periodical planning documents are more specific about the Government's intentions for the next few years and in demonstrating how health and other social services are interconnected.

Since 1974 the Department of Health and Social Security has used a financial planning system for the health and social services, based on programme budgets. Within the National Health Service itself, a planning system has operated since 1976 which distinguishes between strategic planning and short-term operational planning. Consultation at different levels of the Service plays an essential part in this.

Beyond the next few years, plans and programmes are much more difficult to forecast. In 1975 a Royal Commission was appointed to

"consider in the interests both of the patients and of those who work in the National Health Service the best use and management of the financial and manpower resources of the National Health Service".

The health services are currently being reviewed with this in mind.

The Royal Commission saw the need to examine the relationship between Parliament and the Service in the following terms:

"we shall need to consider . . . . the accountability of Ministers to Parliament for the health services for which they are responsible, including whether Parliament is able to exercise effective control over the Service and whether Ministers with health service responsibilities should be answerable for all that goes on in these health services: and the responsibility of the Accounting Officers at the Health

Departments for all National Health Service expenditure;
— whether it would be possible, or advantageous for the Service to be 'taken out of politics' by putting it under the control of an apolitical central agency;
—the effectiveness of community health councils and lay members of health authorities in ensuring that services are responsive to local needs and the method of appointing these bodies;
— the proper scope of worker participation in running the service;
— whether the public is given enough information of the right sort and the role of community health councils in supplying it.''

Service	Population base	Level of provision (per 1000 appropriate population)			Throughput	
		Departmental guidelines	1975/76 Out-turn	1979/80 Illustrative projection	1975/76 Out-turn	1979/80 Illustrative projection
		Available beds			**Cases per bed**	
Acute inpatients	Total	2.8	3.4	3.1	24.3	28.2
Obstetric inpatients	All births	—	37.6	32.8	32.8	37.5
Geriatric inpatients	65 yrs and over	10.0	8.5	8.4	3.6	3.8
					Occupancy rate	
Younger disabled inpatients	15–64 yrs	—	0.04	0.06	79%	85%
Mental handicap inpatients	Total	0.68	1.2	1.1	92%	92%
Mental illness inpatients	Total	0.5 ⎫	2.1	1.9	87%	86%
Elderly severely mentally infirm inpatients	65 yrs and over	2.5–3.0 ⎭				
		Places				
Non-psychiatric day patients	65 yrs and over	2.7	1.1	1.0	—	—
Mental illness day patients	Total	0.65 ⎫	0.29	0.36	—	—
Elderly severely mentally infirm day patients	65 yrs and over	2.0–3.0 ⎭				
		Staff				
Health visiting	Total	0.33	0.15	0.18	—	—
District visiting	Total	0.40	0.25	0.32	—	—

Fig. 20   Levels of provision in the hospital and community health service

At present, the National Health Service is an independent public body only to the extent that it exists to serve a particular function. In spite of the corporate status of its area and regional boards, it is in all other ways the agent of its Department and, as such, subject to detailed Parliamentary control. When the Royal Commission reports to Parliament in due course and the shape of the National Health Service for the next quarter century becomes clearer, it is unlikely that control will be relaxed.

Voluntary agencies

A discussion of independent public bodies would be incomplete without referring to the network of voluntary organisations which abound in Britain at the present time. There are well over 100 000 registered charities of all kinds, including the highly efficient operations of Oxfam and Shelter, all of which are supervised and annually reported upon by the Charity Commissioners in England and Wales. Organisations like these have interests which range from prison welfare to concern with old age. Some, such as the Haemophilia Society, have specialised aims applicable to minority groups; others, like the Women's Royal Voluntary Services or the British Red Cross Society have a more general purpose. Some, like the National Marriage Guidance Council, are large and Government supported; others are smaller and more local. While a third of such societies date from the last century, the majority are of much more recent origin.

All of them have an inbuilt survival regulator. Being self-supporting, they will automatically collapse unless there is continuing public demand for their services. Conversely, their services will be as good as the public are prepared to pay to make them good. Finance is therefore of major importance to every voluntary society.

The public image of the voluntary society—a small organisation haphazardly and inefficiently competing with the services provided by law and run by amateurs—dies hard; only a few societies still look like this. The vast majority of agencies to-day are modern and national in their outlook and have their own brand of professionalism together with a strength which comes from voluntary enthusiasm and community support. Many of them co-operate with the local authorities to provide a service, and apart from the freely-given services which they are able to call on from a wide range of professions, many agencies nowadays employ full-time professional workers and run training schemes for their non-professional workers.

Since they are voluntary, these agencies are frequently able to undertake research, experimental and development work which could not so readily be handled by a local authority operating as it does within a statutory framework. In this way these agencies are a testing ground and a workshop for new ideas, and the feedback from this work to the statutory services may be of considerable importance. This, indeed, has been the pattern of development for many years; in Britain self-help has usually preceded State aid.

Where the services being offered in this way are adequate, they have been encouraged to continue, with financial assistance, either in partnership or in close association with the local authorities. The public social services to-day are thus provided by central and local government authorities with the active assistance of a national network of local non-Governmental agencies.

Politically, such a system has a great deal of strength as it relieves Government of the burden of having to provide services directly. The weakness of the system is one of control, for while central government could persuade the voluntary services to fit into the national pattern of administration, the services can always opt out; Departmental circulars and directives are not likely to carry much weight in the face of opposition from voluntary memberships. An attempt has been made to co-ordinate voluntary service through the Home Office Voluntary Services Unit and the Volunteer Centre (a central information bureau) but control remains a continuing problem.

This relative failure to control voluntary organisations centrally is unfortunate, for it may result in inefficient organisation within agencies which in themselves are worth preserving and developing. Finance is an important instrument when questions of control arise either at local or national level.

How, then, do the voluntary organisations finance themselves and how does central government ensure that enough financial encouragement is provided to keep them in existence? All voluntary societies are perpetually short of funds and the search for cash sources is continuous and often pursued with great determination. Apart from possible tax and rating reliefs and relatively minor fund-raising activities such as fetes, bazaars and flag-days, the main permanent sources of finance are:

a) grants from central government
b) grants from local authorities
c) grants from trusts and foundations
d) subscriptions
e) donations and legacies
f) interest on invested funds

The traditional dependence of voluntary bodies on private charitable subscriptions has decreased; public sources have, in the past 20 years, become much more important. Where it is Government policy to support and develop a given voluntary activity, a specific grant may be made for a period of years to the national co-ordinating society. Locally, too, voluntary bodies are frequently able to persuade their local authority to make an annual contribution to their funds, though the amount obtained will vary from one area to another and will depend on local committees and even on local politics.

The variety of such arrangements and the opportunities for democratic participation provided by the voluntary organisations make them a very useful feature of the public service. In recent years this usefulness has been fully recognised and new ways of helping them to integrate with central and local services have been sought.

The theme of control is fundamental to any discussion of the independent public bodies and the problem remains of how to arrange for organisations to be free to develop and exploit opportunities which benefit the public, with the minimum of supervision.

When a public body like the National Enterprise Board or its regional equivalents in Scotland or Wales take shares in or advance cash to a firm in the private sector, it usually has wider aims in mind than simply securing a fair return on capital invested. Support to particular industrial concerns may have a social goal to prevent or reduce local unemployment or to obtain some technological spin-off, to begin some new development or even to maintain national prestige. All these goals may be very much in the public interest, but they may distort the conventional business environment so that markets may be entered which would never otherwise have been reached. Whatever goal is aimed at it is important that it should be explained and that Parliament should have a clear understanding of what it is, for the one enduring principle in a democratic society is that of public accountability.

The independence of public bodies whether they are local authorities, public corporations, health boards or other statutory and non-statutory undertakings is only relative. The constitutional authority of Parliament is supreme and the power of individual executive Departments of central government theoretically unassailable. If independence is granted, then it is a calculated degree of independence; control still remains.

Suggestions for further reading

Health Services in Britain, HMSO, Current edition
The Reorganised National Health Service, Office of Health Economics, 1977
J S Ross, *The National Health Service in Great Britain*, OUP, 1952

Questions

1 What is the purpose of a Community Health Council?
2 To what extent is the National Health Service a free one?
3 How do voluntary organisations find the money they need to provide their services?

15

Integration

Central administration

Chapter 1 argued that "administration" is the co-ordination of men and materials within organisations for the accomplishment of identifiable purposes. It was also suggested that administration is organisationally based. Later chapters indicated the importance of the various organisations which, together, comprise the system of British public administration: central government Departments, nationalised industries, local authorities, "quasi-independent" bodies and the like.

The many different types of organisations and the ways in which they are interrelated, make the system highly complex. Variety is found not only between these organisations; within each organisation considerable differences arise. In the case of Government Departments, for example, the "style" of administration may vary considerably between one Department and another. A Department operating over the whole geographical area of the United Kingdom may need to adopt administrative practices not required in a Department operating mainly in London. Similarly, considerable differences exist between local authority units. Working practices in a large local authority may be different from those in a small one. Administrative styles in local authorities whose councils are dominated by party politics may differ from those in which such political influence is small or non-existent.

Such variety in organisations within the public sector has, itself, resulted from a variety of causes. Administration developed in a very piecemeal way in Britain; administrative practices and organisational forms are not usually the result of grand organisational and administrative designs but of pressure of circumstances and events. Chapter 5 drew attention to the various pressures which led to the establishment of particular Government Departments and the process of "fission, fusion and transfer" which has marked the development of central administration.

Attempts to establish the "one best way" of allocating functions between different Departments have generally proved unsuccessful, as discussion of the Haldane Report demonstrated, and such allocation has usually proceeded on an ad hoc basis: some Departments have been established according to one principle, others have followed entirely different ones. As Government has grown, new needs have been met by setting up new types of organisation and by adopting new administrative ideas. The setting up of the National Health Service and the establishment of the quasi-independent agencies illustrate this process. Chapter 7 examined the Fulton Committee's suggestions for adopting new organisational practices in certain Departments and establishing "hived-off" agencies to put new administrative ideas—such as accountable management—into practice.

Examination of the administrative system over a period also shows the importance of fashion in ideas about organisation. During the post-war years there was a tendency to decentralise important headquarters functions of Government Departments to large regional organisations—a policy which was subsequently reversed, but later showed signs of returning. During the 1960's and early 1970's, there was a strong tendency towards establishing large Departments to incorporate the work of many previously separate organisations. Now, it seems, this process has gone out of fashion. These last two examples show that theories about how best to organise and administer are debatable matters. There is no one correct way to carry out the work of Government—experiment and compromise may be in order.

The foregoing shows the variety of administrative machinery in Britain. While many critics complain that the administrative system is inadequately integrated to meet the demands made upon it, it is important to note that it has not been constructed completely at random or without any attempt having been made to ensure that all the parts fit together into a unified whole. An interesting feature of the British administrative system is that, as Government activity has increased and brought with it greater administrative variety, increased efforts have been made to set up procedures and machinery to unify the system.

Achieving unity

Administration is a purposeful activity. An administrative/political system is concerned to achieve certain set objectives or goals. Administrative activities and the organisations within which they are conducted aim to produce specified end results—better housing, adequate welfare benefits, a well-equipped army and air force, the building and maintenance of hospitals, schools and so on. A **rational** system of administration is one in which the goals of the system are clearly established and in which the *means* are available for achieving those objectives. Two basic activities are therefore involved in any well structured administrative system.

Firstly, objectives must be laid down so that all the participants in the system know what it is that they are trying to achieve. The goals or ends of the system must be clearly specified. Closely connected with the activity of establishing what goals the system can and should achieve is that of establishing priorities. Governments and their supporting administrative systems must face the fact that many things may be in short supply, for example, money and knowledge, whereas the demand for these resources may be limitless. In conditions of scarcity, Governments must lay down priorities and settle on the best possible means of achieving their objectives.

The second major function of any administrative system is that of providing the means to achieve the ends or goals. This involves establishing effective organisational machinery, training personnel in appropriate skills, establishing an adequate budget procedure and so on. Organisation provides an authority structure through which orders are given and supervision made of the activities of individuals and groups. It also provides the major means of achieving administrative goals and a system of communications. Orders flow down the hierarchy of the organisation while important "feedback" information from the bottom of the organisation may be communicated to those at the top. This is essential if key administrators are to understand the effects that many of their decisions have on the people directly affected by them—clients, customers, and so on.

Organisation, as one writer has remarked, is important for effective goal achievement wherever two or more individuals work together to undertake a task which one man, acting alone could not carry out. The tasks of Government clearly fall into this category: they are large-scale and their successful completion requires the co-operation of large numbers of people and the use of large amounts of money and other resources.

Another key task in any administrative system is that of achieving harmony between the various parts so that people and the organisations within which they operate can work together without conflict. The pieces of the administrative jig-saw must be fitted together to prevent overlapping between jobs and organisations. This process of harmonisation is often called integration or co-ordination or control, and it is of central significance in understanding administration.

Integration is the activity of unifying the work of individuals, groups and organisations so that they all work together effectively for the achievement of common objectives. The importance of integration, co-ordination and control is so great that many textbook writers on organisations and administration argue that it is the primary purpose of the administrator. Chapter 1 indicated that administration is an organisationally based activity: the very word organisation implies integration, co-ordination and control.

To suggest that integration or co-ordination is being achieved within the system implies two things; firstly, that attempts are being made to prevent damaging conflict between the various parts of the system, and secondly, that the parts are working together to achieve stated purposes. Integration also implies "control". It was suggested earlier that administration is a rational activity; ends are stipulated and then means are developed to achieve those ends. In such a system, ways must be found for ensuring that there is a proper relationship between means and ends.

Control describes the processes whereby the system is watched and supervised in the interests of efficiency, accountability and the other environmental values already referred to. It is essential in a democratic system of government that public servants are regularly supervised to make certain that they do not exceed their powers and that they carry out their duties efficiently.

Integration is necessary in a system of government administration for very obvious reasons. The public sector is so large that if the various parts are not harmonised a great deal of money and manpower could be wasted. Secondly, "public" administration is highly visible. We are all affected by it and rightly demand that civil servants, local government officials and other members of the system work together to produce the best results. Public administration operates within a political context. In a democracy, public officials are ultimately responsible through politicians to the electorate. The need to control and co-ordinate the system is equally as important as in a privately-owned organisation. Parliament, the Ombudsman, consumer groups and so on rightly demand that the system should be responsive to outside requirements and demands and all insist upon high standards.

Size, too, is an important factor affecting the need for co-ordination and control. Some of the organisations which have been examined are extremely large and complex and the bigger and more complex an organisation becomes, the more attention must be paid to the problem of integration and control. This becomes yet more difficult when the organisation is decentralised with a large number of regional and local centres.

No system of administration and no organisation can sensibly function for long without establishing means for co-ordinating and controlling the activities of its members to ensure that they are all working together to achieve its purposes. Such co-ordination and control is essential when that system is subject to ever increasing demands and when resources are limited. The British system of administration has grown in importance and complexity in recent years and as Government activity has increased, so questions of co-ordination and control have become more crucial.

Integration takes place at two levels in any administrative system. Firstly, agreement must be reached on what should be done (this is the policy-making function) and secondly, on how to achieve the ends or goals desired (this is the policy-implementation function). Clearly, in a complex system of Government administration it would make little sense if everybody pursued their own goals irrespective of what other members of the system were doing, neither would it be sensible for everybody to follow completely different administrative methods to achieve those goals.

The co-ordination of policy-making and policy-implementation

In 1918 in its examination of the structure and functioning of central administration in Britain, the Haldane Committee insisted that central government should consider what goals should be pursued and what priorities established. In other words, policy-planning should be considered.

As Haldane made clear, the Cabinet is the key policy-making body in Britain. In fact, the Cabinet performs a dual role; firstly, it decides policy (lays down goals) and, secondly, it oversees the co-ordination of administrative machinery to achieve those goals. The Cabinet is thus the pinnacle of the political (decision-making) process and of the administrative (decision-implementing) process. The Haldane Committee described the three main areas of the Cabinet's power:

a)   it decides on the policy to be submitted to Parliament

b)   it has supreme control of the national executive in accordance with the policy prescribed by Parliament

c)   it co-ordinates and defines the activities of the several Departments of State.

In theory, the Cabinet is the fount of all policy-making. This pre-eminent position is a traditional one, and constitutionally the Cabinet is supreme. In fact, much of the work involved in policy-planning is conducted outside the Cabinet in the Departments and in important inter-Departmental committees of civil servants. The point was made earlier that these administrative officials are often the source of political decisions. Many proposals for new policy come from the Departments and often come up to the Cabinet for approval. This shows the importance of the Cabinet as a "final court of administrative appeal". Disagreements within the Departments and between Departments on the question of what policies should be adopted and followed are often settled at Cabinet level. Occasionally, the Prime Minister as the most senior Cabinet member rules on what policy alternative is to be followed if such disagreements arise. Disagreements are quite frequent when the Government discusses expenditure. Although integration of policy and administration is very important, disagreements can arise over the proportion of expenditure granted to particular Ministers and Departments.

Many Departments can be classified as spending Departments. If they are successfully to accomplish their designated tasks they need massive sums of money from the Treasury each year. As the central finance Ministry, the Treasury must keep a close control on the level of Departments' spending and ensure that sums of money allocated to them are spent on the purposes for which the money is intended. In a situation of limited finance, it is natural for Departmental Ministers to "fight their corner" in Cabinet and ensure that they obtain as much for their individual Departments as they can. Thus they will come into conflict with other Ministers fighting for the same thing. Ministers who are "successful" in the eyes of their civil servants are those who can ensure that their Departments get as good a deal as possible.

The size of the Cabinet has already been discussed. As with most committees, size is a very important factor in deciding how effective it will be as a body. With 20 or more members, the typical Cabinet is too large to be effective in policy-planning. In practice, therefore, much of the detailed work of policy-planning at Cabinet level is delegated to Cabinet committees. These are composed of members of the Cabinet and sometimes non-Cabinet Ministers and junior Ministers and they greatly ease the work of the Cabinet. They enable much detailed work on policy matters to be considered closely, leaving the full meetings of the Cabinet to deal with questions of principle. Ex-Prime Minister Sir Harold Wilson has noted that since the Second World War, every Government has relied heavily on such committees and their number and importance is steadily increasing. Undoubtedly, the increase in the volume of Cabinet business will encourage this tendency.

Cabinet committees also play an important role in co-ordinating policy. Differing points of view can be aired in such committees and the presence of non-Departmental Ministers introduces valuable outside experience to the discussions. Nevertheless, the system has been criticised especially for the secrecy which surrounds the committees. Relatively little is known about the composition, size and numbers of Cabinet committees: such information is kept closely guarded. They do, however, take important decisions in the name of the Cabinet and can sometimes act independently of the Cabinet and the Prime Minister. The convention that Cabinet committee membership and deliberations are well kept secrets has arisen from the fear that if it was widely known that particular Ministers were serving on a Cabinet committee dealing with controversial policy matters, interested individuals and groups might try to put pressure on them and influence their decisions.

One point is worthy of note regarding the importance of Cabinet committees. It is said by some commentators that the British system of Cabinet government, involving collective Ministerial decision-making, is being displaced by a system in which the Prime Minister takes all the important decisions to which the Cabinet automatically gives its approval. The most important spokesman for this new theory of how British government works, is the late Richard Crossman. According to his view, the Prime Minister is becoming more and more like an American President with a weak Cabinet. Against this view, Sir Harold Wilson—arguably one of the most "presidential" Prime Ministers of recent years—has suggested that Cabinet committees are an important means of preventing just such a tendency, for their existence and operation makes the Cabinet more effective and better able to prevent the emergence of Prime Ministerial government. They thus ensure that Departmental Ministers play a full part in Cabinet discussions.

Cabinet committees have also helped to keep down the size of the Cabinet. It is not necessary to enlarge the size of the Cabinet to include all Government Ministers if both non-Cabinet Ministers of senior rank and their junior counterparts can be involved through Cabinet committees. The Cabinet must be kept small if policy-planning is to be efficient. From time to time other methods of achieving this have been tried.

Between the years 1951 and 1955, an experiment with co-ordinating Ministers (known as the overlord experiment) was tried. It involved appointing non-Departmental members of the Cabinet to co-ordinate the work of Departments whose Ministers were not in the Cabinet. Thus, instead of having separate Ministers in the Cabinet to represent Departments concerned with food, agricultural policy, transport, fuel and power, Ministers responsible for the co-ordination of food and agricultural policy, and transport, fuel and power were appointed. The experiment was not very successful and was subsequently abandoned.

In the first place, the overlord experiment raised problems of Ministerial responsibility. It was difficult to decide who was responsible to Parliament for the work of the Departments concerned—the overlord or the non-Cabinet Minister. This inevitably caused non-Cabinet Ministers to feel that they were playing second fiddle to the overlord. The experiment also separated responsibility for policy-planning—the job of the overlord—from the day to day Departmental administration. This was a completely artificial distinction and one which completely contradicted Haldane's principles of Cabinet government; namely, that the Cabinet is not only concerned with policy-formulation but with ensuring that policy is put into practice.

No further experimentation with overlords has been attempted since 1955. Instead, other ways of using Ministers in a co-ordinating role have been used. Sometimes non-Departmental Ministers (or "Ministers without portfolio" as they are properly known) are used to handle affairs which cross conventional Departmental boundaries.

Since the end of the 1960's, the size of the Cabinet has been kept down by amalgamating Departments into so-called giant Departments under the control of Secretaries of State assisted by several junior Ministers. This practice differs from the overlord experiment in that the Secretary of State quite clearly remains responsible for both policy-planning and co-ordinating administration within the Department: responsibility for the two functions is not divided as it was in the 1950's. The attempt to set up such giant Departments as the Department of the Environment, and similar attempts to achieve administrative co-ordination will be examined later in this chapter.

The Cabinet and its organisational support

In carrying out its functions of policy-making and administrative co-ordination, the Cabinet does not work in isolation. In practice it is supported by an impressive administrative machinery. Before the First World War no minutes of Cabinet meetings or records of Cabinet decisions were kept. Under the pressures of wartime administration, the Prime Minister David Lloyd George established a Cabinet Secretariat. Staffed by civil servants (and assisted by temporary advisers), the Cabinet Secretariat helps Ministers carry out Cabinet business. It records the proceedings of the Cabinet and prepares an agenda for meetings of the Cabinet and its committees.

The Cabinet Office

Under the direction of the Prime Minister, the Cabinet Office comprises the Cabinet Secretariat, the CPRS and the Central Statistical Office. All three together co-ordinate the central government machinery. While the Cabinet Secretariat serves Ministers collectively in the conduct of Cabinet business, and the CPRS provides a major source of policy advice, the Central Statistical Office provides statistical information necessary for constructing important economic and social policies and for forecasting the likely impact of Government policies.

The importance of the Cabinet Secretariat derives from its central role as a co-ordinating agency. It circulates papers to all members of the Cabinet thereby ensuring that they are kept well informed about policy decisions made in Cabinet and it keeps in touch with the progress of decision-making, thereby ensuring that policy decisions are linked to administrative action. The Secretariat also performs an essential role in preventing Cabinet Ministers being swamped by work; inspite of the massive increase in the tasks of central government throughout recent years, the number and frequency of Cabinet meetings has remained suprisingly stable.

The Cabinet Secretariat, however, is not merely a note-taking and agenda-producing machine; it has an important dual role in central government. Apart from keeping minutes and documentary records of Cabinet proceedings (a document-producing role), it acts in a policy advice role to the Prime Minister. The Permanent Secretary to the Cabinet—a civil servant of the highest rank—is also the Permanent Secretary and Chief Adviser to the Prime Minister in the same way that every Minister is served by a Permanent Secretary and Chief Adviser. The Permanent Secretary offers the Prime Minister advice on the general management of the Government. Although the Cabinet Secretariat acts in a policy advice role in relation to the Prime Minister, it is not the only source of advice the Prime Minister can rely on. A distinction must be drawn between the Cabinet Secretariat and the Prime Minister's Private Office in Downing Street.

The Private Office looks after the daily personal needs of the Prime Minister—keeping his diary, looking after his constituency affairs and so on. In addition to the civil servants who assist the Prime Minister in this way, it has become standard practice in recent years for Prime Ministers to set up a personal advisory team including senior policy advisers from outside the Civil Service. Undoubtedly, one of the objects of such appointments is to increase the variety of advice offered to the head of Government. These advisers assist the Prime Minister in the same way that temporary advisers in the Departments assist their Ministerial heads. (See Chapter 6.)

Assisting the Cabinet in its policy co-ordinating function since 1970 is the new Central Policy Review Staff (CPRS)—also known as a "central capability unit" or "think tank". A relatively small group of 15 to 20 people, both permanent and temporary civil servants, the unit was formed to act as a monitoring agency for the whole Cabinet by producing analyses of important problems to enable Ministers to make better, well-informed decisions, and to keep a close watch on the overall strategy of the Government. Lord Rothschild, the first head of the CPRS has insisted that it has a very useful role to play in providing Ministers with an alternative point of view on important matters to that put forward by their Permanent Secretaries and other important civil servants in their Departments.

Since its birth, the CPRS has examined the possible effects of Government policy in such areas as Concorde, regional economic policy, energy policy and the future performance of the United Kingdom economy compared with that of other members of the European Economic Community. Occasionally, it has ruffled a few Civil Service feathers in its investigations. Its report in 1977 on the working of the Foreign Service—that part of the Civil Service dealing with Britain's relationships with foreign countries—was not universally popular and a misreported speech by Lord Rothschild in 1973 led to disagreement between him and the then Prime Minister, Edward Heath. In an organisation deliberately intended to take an independent line, occasional embarrassments are likely to occur when its recommendations do not agree with announced Government policy, but one recent commentator on the work of the unit, Mr Christopher Pollitt, has concluded that

"it is unlikely that future Prime Ministers will be content to return to a situation in which the Cabinet Office and their own Private Office are their only sources of sustained and systematic non-Departmental advice".

Recent criticism of the working of the CPRS arises from its tendency to act as the eyes and ears of the Prime Minister rather than the Cabinet. Many people suspect that it has become an extension of the Prime Minister's Private Office rather than an organ of Government serving the collective body of the Cabinet and there are fears that such a development will work to the advantage of the Prime Minister and undermine Cabinet government.

Inter-Departmental committees

The network of Ministerial committees is an important aid to the Cabinet in the conduct of its business, but no less important is a network of inter-Departmental committees at "official" level within the Civil Service. These committees are composed of civil servants concerned with the co-ordination of Departmental policy. Like their Ministerial counterparts, inter-Departmental committees are shrouded in secrecy—for much the same reasons. Many of them report to the Cabinet committees and, like individual Ministers, civil servants are not usually identified with particular policies.

Ex-Ministers have, on occasion, indicated that such committees play an extremely important role in the system of government. They prepare the ground for subsequent discussion by Cabinet committees and iron out important policy differences between Departments. So successful are they in these activities that Ministers sometimes complain that the Cabinet is often presented with a "fait accompli". Much Cabinet discussion is based on submissions to the Cabinet from committees of civil servants. Ministers are, by tradition, excluded from the meetings of such committees, a fact which has led to (Ministerial) complaint that the decision-making power of the Civil Service is on the increase.

The Treasury and the Civil Service Department

One of the most important central government organisations attempting to co-ordinate and control the system of administration is the Treasury. It is one of the oldest of the central Departments and has enormous prestige within the system. It is considered the most important of all the Departments and is really the "Department of Departments".

The position of the Treasury as the central Department of Finance enables it to oversee all other Departments. Before the Civil Service Department was created, the Treasury had three broad functions:

The establishments function

The central position of the Treasury in the administrative system early led to it being given responsibility for:

a) the financial affairs of the nation
b) management of the Civil Service
c) central control of the machinery of government.

With the development of a unified Civil Service in the mid-nineteenth century, the Treasury was the obvious Department to supervise the pay, promotion, discipline and conditions of service of civil servants.

In this establishments role, the Treasury has contributed to the unification of the Civil Service and the standardisation of methods and working practices. In 1919 the Treasury set up a division concerned with establishments questions. Soon after its creation this division itself set up a Special Investigation Section staffed with investigation officers concerned with giving advice to Departments on questions of office procedure and the correct methods of keeping records. In 1941 the Investigation Section became known as the Treasury Organisation and Methods Division (O & M) and was also concerned with Departmental efficiency.

Recent criticisms

As we have seen, the Civil Service has been subjected to a barrage of criticisms during the past few years. In the past, those criticisms were directed at the system of central co-ordination of administration.

In 1958 the Select Committee on Estimates commented critically on the system of Treasury planning and control of expenditure. It suggested that Treasury control of Departmental expenditure was unsystematic and was based more on an examination of past expenditure than forecasted expenditure. At best, policy proposals involving expenditure were only considered one year ahead: little or no attempt was made to forecast the likely effects for more than one year ahead. In short, the Committee were suggesting that no-one was performing a strategic planning role in British Government, at a time when important technological and social projects involving a long time span were being developed. As a result of the Estimates Committee criticisms, the Plowden Committee on the Control of Public Expenditure was set up. It reported in 1961.

Plowden was very much a document of the 1960's. Many hostile critics of British public administration had bemoaned the fact that decision-making within and between Departments was disjointed and unco-ordinated. The Plowden Report argued that projects involving large sums of money should be assessed in the context of what Government was trying to achieve and that regular "forward looks" over a five year period should be made to ensure that a corporate planning approach to decision-making was adopted. In the past, controls on expenditure had been short-term and had concentrated on the legal aspects of expenditure—ensuring that public expenditure was incurred only on projects and programmes expressly approved by Parliament. What was also needed was an analysis of the aims of government to ensure that they were consistent and co-ordinated. The Report argued that regular surveys should be made of the whole of public expenditure in relation to resources available and that improved methods for measuring and handling questions of public expenditure should be adopted.

The Committee advocated that the Treasury should henceforth devote itself to broad questions of policy. The individual Departments, it said, should pay greater attention to questions of internal management and especially to methods and techniques employed to good effect outside the system in the private sector of industry. The Treasury could give them valuable assistance and advice in this. In order to enable the Treasury to carry out its work of expenditure appraisal more effectively and, at the same time, provide the Departments with up-to-date advice on the best methods of management and organisation to adopt, the Committee insisted that the Treasury's own organisation should be reviewed.

This internal Treasury reorganisation, in fact, occurred very soon after the Plowden Report appeared—in 1962. The changes were designed, in the words of the Prime Minister, Harold MacMillan, to enable the Treasury

"to develop more effectively the methods of financial control and the wider responsibility for management which were outlined in the Plowden Report".

Basically, the Treasury was split into two sides: a pay and management side, dealing with questions related to the internal management and effectiveness of Government Departments, and a finance and economic side, dealing with questions of public expenditure and the management of the economy.

One of the most important consequences of the Plowden Report was the establishment of an important inter-Departmental committee of officials known as the Public Expenditure Survey Committee (PESC). This Committee, composed of the finance officers of the major spending Departments, prepares an annual report showing what public expenditure is likely to be incurred by particular policies over the next five years and what would be the financial effects of pursuing alternative policies. Each year the Treasury produces a Medium Term Assessment of the state of the economy for the same period as that outlined in the PESC report forecasting the rate of economic growth (on which many Departmental policies depend for their success), the likely state of the country's balance of payments situation and other key economic indicators.

The object of both exercises is to encourage better attempts at five year planning by the Departments, a more accurate review of priorities by Ministers and a better informed Parliamentary discussion of expenditure proposals. Since 1969 the Public Expenditure Survey has been published as a White Paper.

The Treasury reorganisation of 1962 was designed to give it a better internal structure to enable it to cope with its dual functions of dealing with the financial aspects of Government administration and with questions relating to the "machinery" or organisation of public administration in central government. However, it was not the last time that the Treasury was subjected to criticism during the decade which followed.

In 1964, with the coming to power of a Labour Government committed to stronger economic planning, it was decided to establish a strong Department of Economic Affairs. This had a responsibility for the "management of the economy as a whole". The Cabinet clearly felt that the transfer of many of the Treasury's functions to a new Department was necessary if the economy was to be expanded. It would also allow the Treasury to improve its work as administrative co-ordinator.

However, the Department of Economic Affairs was to prove short lived. In fact, its attempts to stimulate expansion and its much vaunted National Plan in 1965 which forecast a 4% annual growth rate in the economy were both failures. In a series of short-term economic crises which persistently dogged the Labour Government from 1965 onwards, the DEA's reputation diminished and the Treasury was able to re-assert its old dominance. The functions which had been transferred from the Treasury to the DEA were transferred back to the Treasury when the DEA was wound up by the incoming Conservative Government in June 1970.

Of more lasting significance to the Treasury than the establishment of the DEA was the setting up of the Civil Service Department in 1968. This Department took over the Treasury's responsibility for establishments

work and machinery of government work. The Fulton Report insisted that
the "new look" Civil Service should

"constantly review its tasks and the possible ways in which it might perform them;
then consider what new skills and kinds of men are needed and how these can be
found, trained and deployed".

Fulton argued that the new management style of the Service should be
supervised by a new Department if it was to operate successfully. The pay
and management group of the Treasury—the product of the Plowden
reforms—had, according to Fulton, never been "a fully-developed directing body at the centre with complete overall authority to manage the Civil
Service"; the central management role of the Treasury had been performed
in a patchy way.

According to the Committee reforms in the Civil Service would inevitably increase the role of central management of the Service and this would
enlarge the responsibilities of the Treasury—already coping with financial
and economic policy and the control of public expenditure—so that "there
would be reason to fear too great a concentration of power in one Department". According to Fulton, the function of central financial control
should not be combined with that of trying to increase the professionalism
of the Service. The management of the Service required a "separate and
different" expertise from that required by the management of Government
finance and the control of expenditure. Accordingly, the pay and management divisions of the Treasury were transferred to the newly constituted
Department.

The major point which emerges from this survey of integration and
co-ordination is that greater administrative variety has been paralleled by
attempts to achieve greater co-ordination. Alterations in the system of
public expenditure forecasting, in internal Treasury organisation, and in
the attempt to set up a Civil Service Department were aimed at improving
the strategic effectiveness of Government administration. The attempt to
improve the forward planning of the system was linked during the 1960's
with an attempt to produce better co-ordination. This decade—a decade of
change—was one in which a new "synoptic" style of government was
introduced. The word "synopsis" refers to a general survey. Central
government reforms were aimed at taking a general survey of the various
functions of Departments, independent agencies and so on, so that
comprehensive reviews could be made of the overall aims of Government
and an across-the-board survey made of the resources available to achieve
them.

A dominant management philosophy of the decade was that of
"management-by-objectives and corporate planning". This philosophy is
founded on two basic ideas. Firstly, it involves the idea of objectives and
priorities being clearly established so that everyone in the system knows
what they are supposed to be doing and is then given the appropriate
resources (in terms of manpower, material and money) to be able to

achieve it. Secondly, it involves the notion of making a comprehensive review of the objectives and resources of the entire system so that all the parts function together smoothly and without unnecessary friction and disagreement. The Fulton Committee recommendations on the Civil Service (for example, in the recommendation for the adoption of "accountable management") evidently had the idea of clearly defined objectives very much in mind.

Improvements in the machinery of government reveal that "corporate management" was also very much an ideal of the time. This is emphasised by an important policy document produced by the incoming Conservative Government in 1970, the White Paper entitled *The Reorganisation of Central Government*.

Like Fulton and Plowden before it, the White Paper argued that "the objectives of Government should be clearly identified and policy options costed". The Civil Service should also be given clear goals to aim for and have "more sharply defined responsibilities". In addition, the work of Government Departments should be clearly linked to the overall objectives of Government. Following Plowden's lead, the White Paper put forward the view that improved policy-making would result from analysing existing and proposed Government policies and their expenditure requirements. The document reviewed the new system of Public Expenditure Surveys developed as a result of Plowden and argued that these had provided a rational and systematic basis for allocating resources to the public sector.

Inspite of improvements in forecasting techniques, the White Paper considered that important statements about the aims of expenditure were still absent. This made it difficult for Ministers' plans to be properly tested against overall Government strategy and made detailed analysis of existing programmes cumbersome. The recommendation of the White Paper was, therefore, that the existing public expenditure system should be further strengthened. A system for regular reviews of expenditure as described in Chapter 12 should be adopted which would enable Ministers to identify and discuss questions of policy.

The White Paper concerned itself not only with questions of setting out aims and objectives, but also with the broad machinery of government—the distribution of functions between Departments and improving the Cabinet's ability to assess the programmes of Departments.

Concerning the allocation of functions, the White Paper proposed that Departmental boundaries be re-drawn

"to improve the framework within which public policy is formulated by matching the field of responsibility of Government Departments to coherent fields of policy and administration".

In practice, this meant grouping functions together in giant Departments to create areas of unified policy. Such a reconstruction of Departments, it was felt, would enable clearly defined strategies to be developed within closely related policy areas. Conflicts would also be more easily resolved within large Departments rather than between many small Departments. The White Paper also suggested that the Cabinet Office should be strengthened; one important consequence of this was the creation of CPRS, already discussed.

Following the White Paper, the Government set up "giant" Departments to amalgamate the work of previously separate Departments: the Department of the Environment was created out of an amalgamation of the Ministries of Housing and Local Government and of Public Building and Works, and the Department of Trade and Industry was created out of the Board of Trade and the Ministry of Technology. The Department of the Environment was created, as its name suggests, to deal with the problems of the physical environment in a co-ordinated manner, and so avoid conflict between Departments which had previously dealt with this question from different perspectives. The Department of Trade was created to "avoid separating responsibility for nationalised industries and privately-owned industry".

The other major innovation brought about as a result of the White Paper was the introduction of PAR (Programme Analysis and Review). While Public Expenditure Surveys, introduced after Plowden, were designed to relate public expenditure programmes to the national economic resources likely to be available, PAR was a method for obtaining clearer Departmental aims and priorities. It was thus a necessary follow up to the earlier reform.

While PAR is still very much alive, the giant Department was dealt a blow when the incoming Labour Government partially dismantled the Department of Trade and Industry in 1974. This illustrates an important point: the advantages of trying to achieve the maximum co-ordination between organisations in the public sector may be partially outweighed by disadvantages which reveal themselves inside the organisations in question. Creation of such giant Departments as those proposed in the 1970 White Paper causes problems of internal organisation. One prominent civil servant, Sir Richard Clarke, has remarked that Ministers and civil servants within a giant Department must "work as a team together, and this requires good temperaments and good organisation".

Integration – local government

So far this chapter has concentrated on the problem of integration in central government organisations and, in particular, on relations between one set of organisations, namely central government Departments. This concentration is justified, for the Departments are undoubtedly of key importance in central government. However, problems of co-ordination also reveal themselves in other organisations in the public sector.

Central-local relations

During the years leading up to the introduction of the Local Government Act 1972 (in Scotland, the Local Government (Scotland) Act 1973) a great deal of attention was given to the kind of management structures which would best suit the requirements of modern local government. A great deal of local experimentation took place with ideas like city managers, reviews by firms of management consultants and the adoption of management techniques and services from industry.

Local authorities, as J D Stewart[1] observed, were in reality "political-management systems" which were being asked to take intricate and complex decisions about all sorts of matters of direct importance to everybody. They should therefore have available to them adequate management tools to meet these needs.

The Maud Committee[2] and the Mallaby Committee[3] both proposed important changes in the internal organisation and staffing of authorities, while the Redcliffe Maud Report[4] spoke of "ensuring that the best and most modern managerial methods were adopted".

Perhaps the most influential of these enquiries was the study group on Local Authority Management Structures set up by the Government in 1971, the so-called Bains Committee, which reported in 1972. From this Committee and its Scottish counterpart, the Paterson Committee, derive many of the administrative practices which have come into regular use in recent years: the closer working relationship between elected members and officials, the development of a corporate outlook, programme development, the appointment of Chief Executives, the use of management teams and the improvement of decision-making facilities.

These Committees were advocating a total style of management which would permeate the whole of an authority's activity. The aim was

"to achieve a situation where the needs of a community were viewed comprehensively and the activities of the local authority were planned, directed and controlled in a unified manner to satisfy those needs to the maximum extent consistent with available resources."

Corporate management would set out to identify existing needs and emerging problems, establish aims and analyse ways of achieving these aims. It would develop and put into operation programmes of action covering several years in the future and it would systematically review ongoing programmes, comparing achievement with intention. The key to providing such an integrated system of management was a framework that "would link together all the various aspects at both member and officer

1 J D Stewart, *Management in Local Government*, Charles Knight, 1971.
2 Committee on the Management of Local Government, 1967.
3 Committee on the Staffing of Local Government, 1967.
4 Report of the Royal Commission on Local Government in England, 1969.

level". Following central government's ventures into Programme Analysis and Review (see Chapter 12), many local authorities began to appoint multi-disciplinary policy analysis teams to investigate selected areas of their work.

The re-thinking of the early 1970's, which was intended to revitalise local government and shake off a dusty nineteenth century town hall image has been slowly showing results during the latter part of the 1970's. A variety of attempts at corporate management following the example of large-scale industrial practice have been introduced; computers have provided a basis for management information systems, while new methods of monitoring the performance and effectiveness of council activities have been devised. Local government is becoming streamlined and equipped to tackle the challenges of the 1980's.

The fragmentation of local services and committees which was apparent during the 1960's led to a drive towards a more synoptic style of local government. This sought to achieve the necessary integration by means of policy and resources committees, management teams and chief executives.

Corporate management is a means of integrating organisations with many different divisions and parts which, left to themselves, might independently pursue their own narrow goals. These parts need direction, for without co-ordination, their efforts would be piecemeal and fragmented. In industry corporate planning has been found to counteract this tendency.

Corporate planning as defined in its central government context is a systematic way of choosing an organisation's objectives, policies and strategies. It sees the organisation as a whole and each issue is assessed both for itself and for its effects on all other parts of the organisation. This approach to management has been found useful because it is integrated and complete and because it encourages separate groups to·work together towards common objectives. This "unity of action" is after all what the process of co-ordination seeks to achieve. If corporate planning can assist the process then it is a valuable tool.

Corporate management at the local level was intended to help councillors and chief officers to view the overall operations of their authority and to develop a co-ordinated approach to local administration. The procedures have been briefly discussed in Chapter 8 and the corporate approach in general has been a recurrent theme in this book. It was felt that integration might be achieved, for example, by rearranging committees and Departments on a "programme area" basis, bringing together activities which have a common end result. Where several Departments fell within one programme area it would be possible to establish programme area teams of officers drawn from different Departments and disciplines.

Associated with these ideas was the idea of the wider community. The concept of community interest, as the Bains Committee noted,

"must involve not only the new local authorities but also other voluntary and public agencies including particularly the new area health boards and regional water authorities".

Corporate management can, of course, mean many different things. In the larger authorities it can mean very thorough and detailed procedures administered by specialist personnel, whereas in smaller authorities it may be much less developed. What is appropriate for one authority may not be appropriate for another, and as the Paterson Committee pointed out:

"while the principles are applicable to all authorities the scale and extent of their application must clearly be tailored to suit the needs of and the means available to each particular authority".

Corporate management is more a *style* of management than a technique, and it has been adopted in local government in recent years with many good results. The preparation for the Housing (Homeless Persons) Act 1977 (which was intended to deal with the complex problem of homelessness in its different forms) provides a good example of corporate management in practice. Before the Act came into effect, the central Departments concerned issued a circular to local authorities drawing attention to their new obligations and outlining the way in which these might be fulfilled. The organisations affected by the Act included, in addition to the housing authorities, agencies such as the Greater London Council, New Town Corporations and the Commission for the New Towns, the special housing associations and social service Departments. The circular emphasised the duty of such organisations to co-operate with each other and with the various voluntary bodies concerned with the problem.

Co-ordinated action like this which recognises the contributions to be made from every quarter illustrates the style of corporate management which has established itself in administrative practice. It is right that action should be taken by the different parts acting as one and it is right that they should confer together and consider the different ways in which their agreed intentions may be achieved.

Criticisms of corporate management have been largely to do with structure. The allocation to different authorities of functions (like housing and planning and personal social services) which have considerable areas of overlap has sometimes caused delays and frustration. Corporate management has sometimes been criticised, too, for giving rise to unnecessary paperwork and reports, for causing more meetings and for increasing staffing costs. On the other hand most authorities are better organised than they were before, they no longer work in isolation and their management systems introduce greater efficiency and more rational decision-making.

Suggestions for further reading

A H Hanson and Walles, *Governing Britain,* Fontana, 1976
CPRS, A Joint Framework for Social Policies, HMSO, 1975
The Reorganisation of Central Government, Cmnd 4506, HMSO, 1970
J Stanyer and B C Smith, *Administering Britain,* Fontana, 1976
J D Stewart, *The Responsive Local Authority,* Charles Knight, 1974

Questions

1 How may corporate management contribute to securing co-ordination in a local authority?
2 What do you understand by "joint funding"?
3 What is "hiving-off"?
4 What do you understand by "rationality"?
5 Why was the CPRS established?
6 Why is the problem of integration of central importance in understanding organisation?
7 Outline the functions of the Treasury and the Civil Service Department.
8 How may corporate management contribute to securing co-ordination in a local authority?

16
Continuity and change

The drive to efficiency

The theme of change has been stressed constantly throughout this book. A comparison of the systems of public administration in the nineteenth and the mid-twentieth centuries reveals the tremendous demands now made upon Government. The shape and overall structure of Government Departments, for example, has been reformed and amended to meet new, and often unforseen, demands. At local government level, too, attempts have been made to achieve greater integration and control over the many different tasks faced by local authorities.

Over the last 10 to 15 years many experiments have been performed with the techniques used by central and local government personnel. "Environmental" demands for public administration to be conducted efficiently and for public officials to be held properly accountable have continued while, additionally, efforts have been made to ensure that public organisations are responsive to changes in the nature of the tasks which they undertake.

Previous chapters have examined the various ways in which reform has been attempted and the pressures which have encouraged reform. In the case of central government organisation, it was suggested that disappointments in the performance of British Government after the Second World War gradually and inevitably produced criticism that the working practices and personnel of central administration in Britain were out of step with changing reality. At local government level, criticisms were voiced about the management structure of local authorities. The traditional method of committee work, in particular, was blamed for helping to fragment the work of the local council which made co-ordination between related services hard to achieve.

British public administration covers not only the work of central government Departments and local authorities, but has become increasingly diversified due to the large growth of so-called "independent public bodies''. The new importance of such bodies indicates the movement of public administration into commercial, scientific and industrial areas: something which could hardly have been envisaged a century ago. All these developments question the traditional values and structures of public administration.

The 1960's was a decade of reform. It was a period during which many commentators on both central and the local government argued that the methods and management practices of any modern efficient business concern should be adopted in the management of the public affairs of the country. The Plowden Report insisted that not enough attention was paid in central government to detailed questions of "management"; the Fulton Report argued that too few civil servants were trained in the skills of management despite being engaged in management tasks.

The various investigations into the working of local government in the 1960's and early 1970's—the Mallaby Report 1967, the Maud Report 1967, and the Bains Report 1972—all recommended changes in the training and deployment of staff. They also recommended that corporate management programmes drawn from experience in the private sector should be introduced. This chapter examines how far the techniques and management practices used in private industry suit the aims and philosophy of public administration.

Chapter 1 suggested that although the private sector and public sector organisations have certain points in common, there are important differences between them. These similarities and differences help to show how relevant the best commercial practices are to the public sector organisation.

Bureaucracy and management

The various reform documents which have appeared in the last few years have a common theme; that the structures and working practices of bureaucratic organisations in the public sector are not best suited to the performance of many of the tasks now faced by the modern public administrator. It has recently become fashionable to insist that public sector organisations, in comparison with their private counterparts, are ineffective and unable to cope with changing circumstances.

Efforts to import a "management" philosophy into central and local government organisations have been based on two contrasting views of organisation and working practices in the public sector and the private sector. Firstly, the public sector—Government Departments, local authorities and so on—is often considered to be "bureaucratic". The assumption here is that such a system of organisation has important negative characteristics.

The second view is that the private sector has adopted working practices which enable it to avoid many of these negative features. It has sometimes been described as having a "management" system or philosophy which has allowed greater initiative and encouraged procedures capable of coping with a changing society. These two contrasting views will now be examined.

Chapter 4 argued that public sector organisations are usually organised bureaucratically. The environment of public sector organisations demands consistency, fairness, and impartiality for clients of the system and also sets high store by accountability and public responsibility. Such values inevitably lead to the development of a hierarchy of authority whereby all members of the organisation rely on a rule system and codified instructions and guides to action. This kind of system also has tremendous advantages.

Impartial rules mean that the customers or clients of the public sector organisation can rely on their cases, petitions and applications for help from central and local government being treated reasonably and with the same degree of help and care shown to everyone else. Desmond Keeling, in a recent book on central government, described such an organisational system as one in which the prime object of the administrator is to avoid making mistakes and to bend over backwards to treat those affected by the organisation in the same way that a judge deals with individuals appearing before him in court. He will try to treat them impartially and fairly and will follow precedent—that is, how similar individuals in similar circumstances were treated in the past. His behaviour is bound by rules and intended to avoid uncertainty. Most commentators on the working of large organisations believe that such a philosophy inevitably creates characteristic bureaucratic patterns—hierarchy and rules.

Keeling goes on to identify what he calls a "management" view of organisations. This philosophy contrasts with that of the bureaucratically run organisation because its emphasis is on a different set of values. Firstly, the concern of the decision-maker is not so much concerned with avoiding mistakes as with achieving success after taking reasonable risks. His prime concern is not so much to achieve consistency and fairness—although he may take both into consideration—but to achieve commercial success. Secondly, management systems, while having to rely to a degree on hierarchy and rules will, often, use a much more flexible system of organisation. Such a system may be "organic" in contrast to the "mechanistic" system of bureaucracy. These two concepts will be explained.

At the beginning of the 1960's writers on organisations identified two different ways of running organisations. The first, the **mechanistic** type, broadly conforms to the notion of the "bureaucratic" organisation (described in Chapter 4) with its pyramidal form of organisation, reliance on rules and standard procedures and avoidance of novelty and uncertainty.

In the **organic** form of organisation, there is impatience with such devices as lengthy hierarchies and written rules. Instead, the organisation is kept deliberately loose and flexible. Responsibilities are not given to individuals because of their positions within the hierarchy; instead, members of the organisation are encouraged to display initiative whether they are at the top or the bottom of the organisation. These features have been widely felt to contribute to the success of the organisation in coping with change. Organisations, so structured, are considered more flexible than their bureaucratic counterparts.

This illustrates the fact that the management system of the private organisation is widely seen as being more in tune with contemporary social conditions than the bureaucratic—or mechanistic—organisation, supposedly typical of the public sector. As Government has taken on more and more "commercial" tasks—such as the responsibility for managing a nationwide telephone system, or the management of ordnance factories and dockyards—many critics have suggested that more flexible patterns of organisation and working practices should be developed.

The reasoning and force behind such arguments can be seen in two important reviews of the work of central and local government in recent years: the Fulton Report and the Bains Report on local government organisation.

Fulton revisited

In order to understand the Fulton Report the basic philosophy or view of the organisational world upon which its findings were based must be assessed. The Report gives the impression that the structures and personnel of modern central government are not suited to the tasks which they are trying to accomplish; the notorious opening paragraph of the Report stated that the contemporary Civil Service is more suited to the demands of the nineteenth century than to those of the twentieth. The Report saw the Civil Service as a bureaucratic structure, demonstrating all the weaknesses of the bureaucratic organisation—namely, inflexibility and the inappropriate division of responsibility. The class structure of the Service hindered prompt decision-making, since too many matters had to be referred to the top of the hierarchy for a final decision. In addition, too few administrators understood the various techniques used by managers in the private sector to improve the quality of their decision-making.

While the bureaucratic structure of the Civil Service made it easy to define the area of a civil servant's responsibility, it was not easy to give individuals—especially those low down the hierarchy—the authority to make their own decisions. Greater decentralisation of decision-making was essential in order to encourage and reward initiative. To this end, the Committee recommended the establishment of "accountable management", that is, holding individuals and parts of organisations responsible for performance measured "as objectively as possible". Such a system of decision-making would require new methods of financial control and a modification of the traditional Civil Service system of accounting.

Two other extremely important recommendations of Fulton were that each Department should have a central "management services" unit to ensure that its operations were being conducted with maximum efficiency by means of a flexible, coherent system of management. In addition, policy-planning units should be established to consider priorities and programmes for the future. A standard criticism of bureaucratic organisations is that they are too concerned with past performance instead of seeing how new approaches to problems could bring increased future benefits.

Fulton's findings are full of references to what its members considered to be the best practices in outside industry. The Committee's views about personnel of the Civil Service were founded on a view of personnel practice as it was assumed to work in private industry. Reward for merit rather than seniority was seen as a typical industrial—"management"—philosophy which greatly contrasted with Civil Service practices where the relatively inefficient could be unduly rewarded simply on the grounds of the length of their service or seniority. Again, delegation of responsibility to relatively junior management was far more acceptable in private industry than in the Civil Service.

Fulton's proposals for the introduction of "accountability centres" were part of an attempt to introduce a more "organic" style of working into Government Departments. The aim here was "flexibility". This was reflected in Fulton's view that the traditional Departmental structures in central government were inappropriate for their changing tasks. There were too many layers in the hierarchy of many Government Departments leading to constant upward referral of decision-making to superior officers which resulted in delay in communication and lack of responsiveness.

The Bains Report on local government

In 1971, a working group was set up by the Secretary of State for the Environment to examine the management structures of local authorities and to consider how the most efficient use might be made in the future of the manpower and other resources which they used. The working group came to be known as the Bains Committee after its chairman M A Bains, Clerk of Kent County Council.

In examining the work of local government, the group produced a Report which, in certain particulars, bears a resemblance to the Fulton Committee Report. Just as Fulton criticised the Civil Service for retaining practices which were more suited to Victorian times, so Bains reflected that "the management structures of many local authorities remain those which emerged from the development of local government in the nineteenth century". What was therefore needed, they concluded, was critical self-examination and change within the system.

One of the characteristic weaknesses of local government identified by Bains was the tendency for fragmentation of the services and functions performed by the local authority. Each major service in local government is under the direction of a committee of elected members and permanent officials—the latter with a high degree of professional expertise in their own area of administration. Undoubtedly, this division of functions has brought advantages. Specialisation of function is one of the characteristic features and strengths of the bureaucratic organisation. It enables members and paid officials to concentrate on a specific part of the work of their authority and encourages the development of expertise. There are, however, two sides to the question.

Specialisation can lead to a situation in which the members of an organisation spend so much time on one aspect of the work that they tend to forget the relationship of that part with the rest of the organisation. Fulton had said that fragmentation and diffusion of responsibility were costly disadvantages of bureaucracy at the national level; Bains suggested that "departmentalism" in the local authority had similar negative results. Local authorities were not simply to be seen as collections of separate services. Those services collectively formed a bigger "corporate" unit. For better government at the local level it was essential that a management team of officers should be given the task of preparing plans and programmes for the future development of the work of the councils. In addition, a Policy and Resources Committee consisting of elected members and permanent officials should be established to advise the council on its future plans.

Bains' other important recommendations for local government were drawn from experience in industry. Personnel management—dealing with the "human resources" of the organisation—should, they argued, be improved, and many lessons could be learned from successful training programmes used in the private sector of industry. Again, "management services"—those services which help management to plan, control and improve the activities of the organisation (such as the use of computers, organisation and methods and work study)—should be improved. Many important lessons could be learned from examining private industry's use of such skills.

As with Fulton, the message of the Bains Report appears to be that public sector organisations were, and are, having to cope with rapidly changing conditions in their external "environments". Greater demands are being made on them and they are providing a greater range of services than ever before. Both Reports clearly advocate the use of skills and resources widely in use in private industry. Both appear to be saying that central and local government's bureaucratic standards and procedures were out of phase with changing reality. The accent of both Reports was on *modernisation* and *management*, in Keeling's sense of the word.

Assuming that the overall impressions conveyed by these and other reports—that bureaucratic procedures in public organisations lead to hesitancy, inefficiency and fragmentation—are accurate, the question remains as to whether the methods and organisational practices followed in the private sector can be imported for use in Government organisations and what, if any, are the obstacles and difficulties to be overcome in any such effort? The Conservative Government elected in 1970 made efforts to reorganise central government organisations along these lines; closer examination of this reorganisation is helpful.

A new style of government?

In June 1970, following its somewhat unexpected triumph in the General Election, a Conservative Government took office under the Prime Ministership of Edward Heath. In October of that year the new Government produced a White Paper setting out its recommendations for injecting new life into the machinery of central government. The White Paper summed up a decade of administrative reform which began with the publication of the Plowden Report in 1961. The philosophy upon which many of the White Paper's central recommendations were based is important.

The previous Labour Governments which had held office during the years 1964−70, were committed to an "interventionist" view of the role of Government: namely, that Government had a legitimate and necessary role to play in the economy and in society in order to achieve desired social objectives. As such, the Labour Government was committed to the idea of economic planning and the establishment of such organisations as the Department of Economic Affairs and the quasi-independent Industrial Reorganisation Corporation.

Such an "activist" view of the role of the State had been shared with previous Conservative administrations: the establishment of the NEDC in 1962, for example, was the creation of a Conservative Government. However, during their years in opposition (1964−70), the Conservative party developed a philosophy of "disengagement" which was based on the assumption that "that Government is best which governs least". Both the Conservative party and the Labour party were committed to Fulton's ideas: after all, who could disagree with statements that Government organisations should be made as efficient as possible and that the machinery of government should be modernised to cope with a changing society?

While Labour politicians tried to achieve this within the context of "large government", Edward Heath and other Conservatives were advocating a reduction in the size of the public sector and the consequent reduction in the role of the State.

Differences in party philosophies at this time are revealed by the varying reactions of Labour and Conservative spokesmen to Fulton's proposals for "hiving-off". The Fulton Report stressed the value of adopting a policy of accountable management within the Civil Service and insisted that such a policy could be best pursued where areas of Civil Service work were "hived-off" from the central government machine and relocated in semi-autonomous public boards or corporations. They would not be subject, to the same degree as the traditional Government Department, to detailed public and Parliamentary oversight: their managements could be given greater freedom from day to day external control. Such a proposal was clearly acceptable to the Labour Government in office when Fulton reported: after all, it was a previous Labour Government (1945–51) which had established important new semi-autonomous agencies (nationalised industries) immediately after the Second World War.

"Hiving-off" ideas were consistent with Conservative philosophy but, whereas Labour thought such agencies should be kept within the public sector, the Conservative approach to hiving-off was more radical. Convinced that there was too much central government, the Conservatives saw that "hiving-off" could mean that certain functions should be taken from Government altogether and relocated in private industry.

These different interpretations of hiving-off and accountable management reveal a very interesting fact: while "management" ideas were welcomed by both parties and were seen as providing the necessary framework for developing more flexible "organic" government organisations, the Conservatives went a stage further than Labour in insisting that true "managerialism" could only flourish outside the confines of bureaucratic government. With this end in view, the Conservative administration redefined the dividing-line between the public and the private sectors and established a team of businessmen within the Civil Service to encourage the adoption of sound business and commercial practices. The movement for "managerialising" the public sector had reached its peak.

Hesitancy

Chapter 1 indicated that the public and the private sectors have come closer together—for example in the emergence of "hybrid" organisations financed by public and private money, and in the problems which large organisations face in both the public and private sectors. Recent reform philosophies suggest that methods of working and management practices in the private sector can be transferred to the public sector organisation with beneficial consequences for the latter. However, since differences still remain between public and private organisations, this may not necessarily follow; the structure and methods of working appropriate to one type of organisation will not necessarily be suitable for another.

Where the work of a Government Department is routine and unvarying, and where consistency of treatment is essential, bureaucratic hierarchies with a high degree of centralised decision-making may achieve the best results. On the other hand, there can be little doubt that where speed and flexibility are needed, a more "organic" pattern of working may be better. The work of both private industry and Government organisations is extremely varied and no simple set of management practices and organisational arrangements can be guaranteed to work equally well in all organisations in either sector. The key problem for management and decision-makers in both sectors is to decide which arrangements will produce the best results. The difficulty lies in choosing from a wide variety of alternative methods and designs.

To be fair, neither Fulton nor Bains argued for the uncritical adoption of private management practices. Both recognised the importance of distinct differences in environmental values facing public and private organisations. Administration in Government organisations is carried on within a political framework. This point was recognised in the Fulton Report; it pointed out that while every effort should be made to modernise the Civil Service it should not be forgotten that it is politically accountable for its actions. It does not serve a narrow sectional interest (such as a group of private shareholders) but must serve the whole community. In the process, narrow concerns with efficiency and profit must be balanced against the need to achieve fairness and equality in dealing with members of the public.

Bains argued, along the same lines, that it is not possible to apply "straight business concepts" to management in local government. Bains suggested that "local government may well have lessons to learn from industry, but one must be wary of attempting wholesale transplants from one to the other". In other words, both Fulton and Bains commented on the different nature of the constraints within which management must operate in the public and private sectors.

Inspite of the reservations contained in both Reports, difficulties of bringing about fundamental change in the machinery of central and local government organisations are often not properly considered. At central government level, the existence of a political environment and the constraints which that imposes on public servants is highly significant. Fulton's suggestion that accountable management should be introduced into the public sector is an invitation to decentralise decision-making and give greater responsibility and freedom of operation to lower-level personnel. The "line" manager should, by this argument, be provided with sufficient resources to enable him to achieve his objectives and be allowed greater initiative and control over his subordinates. The model here is the lower level manager in private industry being given significant autonomy and hire and fire powers over his staff.

In the Civil Service, however, such a policy is fraught with difficulty. Members of the public dealing with Government Departments must be treated with fairness and equality, and, in addition, Government Departments' staff would quickly complain if they were treated differently (according to the whims of their immediate superior) from other civil servants in different parts of the Service. For these reasons, tradition has demanded a high degree of uniformity in conditions of service and standards of expected performance.

Accountable management also requires successful measurement of managerial performance. However, performance tests in government are not so easy to apply as they are in many private sector organisations. For example, no simple test of profitability can be applied to many of the functions of a Government Department. The danger is that efforts to quantify and measure performance according to a simple test may produce a false picture of the work conducted by many public servants.

The great variety of work performed by the Civil Service must be taken into account in any serious attempt to introduce novel forms of accounting and work measurement. While some organisations in the public sector may resemble profit-seeking organisations in the private sector others, such as those administering social service benefits, health services and the prison system, are of an entirely different nature. Different criteria may be needed to assess their performance.

Suggestions for further reading

The Civil Service, Vol 1, Report of the Fulton Committee, HMSO, 1968

Questions

1   How relevant are the management techniques used in the private sector of industry to the running of a Government Department?
2   How would you recognise an "organic" type of organisation?

17
Conclusion

Evolution and revolution

Many writers and commentators on British public administration have clearly been impressed with the changes which have taken place in the system of central and local government since the beginning of the 1960's. At least one of them has argued that the various changes which have been spawned since the publication of the Plowden Report represent a revolution in the way in which central and local government conducts its business.

Judged in terms of the number of reports and recommendations which have appeared on the subject of reform in public administration during these years, an unprecedented period of change followed Plowden. It may be that, under the pressure of greatly increased responsibilities, Government organisations have been forced to discard their time-honoured practices and adopt a new attitude to their functions and the means needed to achieve their aims successfully.

However, the metaphor "revolution" does not fully capture the essence of what has happened in public administration in the last 10 or 15 years. The phrase "dynamic evolution" is a more accurate description. "Revolution" conjures up an image of an over-turning—of Governments and social systems—and is too violent a description of change in the machinery of government. Certainly, important changes have occurred in the way central and local government is organised, but the phrase "dynamic evolution" conveys the nature of the changes which have occurred.

In large complex organisations, such as a Government Department or local authority, it is extremely unlikely that change can be introduced and achieved overnight; it can take a number of years for a change to work its way throughout an organisation. That real change has occurred is undeniable; the *Wider Issues Review*, a report produced by the Civil Service Department in 1975 tapped the opinions of serving civil servants and concluded that various attempts to reform the machinery of government in the past few years (including such innovations as the introduction of the so-called "giant" Departments following the 1970 White Paper) had had a profoundly unsettling personal effect on many of the staff involved.

Change in organisations does not happen in a vacuum. Chapter 7 indicated that public servants, as highly intelligent people, do not simply allow themselves to act the role of victim: they do not sit idly by and agree without question to changes introduced by politicians and the relative "outsiders" who regularly sit on committees of inquiry into their work and organisation. On the contrary, changes in the machinery of government are introduced into a social system within organisations, composed of individuals who may take an independent line when they fear that their routines will be disrupted and their interests threatened.

There are many examples of such resistance. When Edward Heath introduced his team of businessmen into central government with a view to modernising the system and recommending how parts of the machine could be hived-off to the private sector, there was widely reported indifference and in some cases hostility on the part of important civil servants to what many of them feared would be the break up of an effective and well-tried pattern of organisation. In 1969, the Post Office was reorganised—it changed its status from Government Department to public corporation, an example of hiving-off in action. The intention, consistent with the Fulton philosophy, was to encourage the adoption of a "business" outlook in the new organisation. Accountable management was planned and it was also expected that relatively subordinate line managers would be given greater individual control over the conditions of service of their staff. This latter proposal met with tremendous hostility from members of the minor and manual grades who felt that they might be victimised in certain cases by area managers with whom they had disagreed and might also lead to varying standards in work practices and in the standards of service they could offer the public in one area as compared to another. Nearly 10 years after the move to semi-independent status for the Post Office, this issue has still not been fully resolved.

The history of Edward Heath's attempts to introduce a "new style of government" also provides lessons for those seeking to introduce large-scale change in Government practices. This experiment was founded on the belief that Government should be made smaller and that modern methods of management could be more effectively introduced in organisations removed from the public sector altogether.

The first step in implementing this policy was an attempt to "disengage" the Government from a previous policy of giving support to ailing industries. It was announced that Government would no longer assist so-called "lame ducks" in the private sector. This policy marked the first step in a more radical attempt to reduce the role of Government. If it had proved successful there is little doubt that efforts would have been made to return certain Government functions to the private sector.

The case of the Post Office again provides a good example. During the passage of the Bill to change the constitution of the Post Office in 1968–69, Conservative spokesmen in Parliament argued strongly for hiving-off parts of the telephone function to private enterprise—including the potentially profitable activity of telephone installation. This doctrine was kept to during the 1970's and, in recent years, there have been indications that a Conservative Government would put this philosophy into practice. The policy of "disengagement", however, ran up against severe practical and political difficulties. During the early 1970's the state of the economy and consequent rise in unemployment forced the Government to reverse its previous policy. Only at the severe cost of increasing the already high level of unemployment could the Government continue to pursue this goal. In the event, the Government returned to a "consensus" view of the role of the State, and its achievements in reducing the size of the public sector proved minimal. It did not waver in its intention to improve the machinery of government, but in this it shared a commitment very similar to that of the Labour opposition.

Experiences such as these suggest that massive and rapid change in the role of Government and in the methods used to achieve the goals of public administration is unlikely. Nevertheless, very real changes have taken place in the last 10 or 15 years, and these illustrate the fact that a more "synoptic" style of management has come into being in the public sector.

Chapter 15 argued that an important problem needing attention in a complex and evolving system of administration is that of achieving a high degree of integration between its parts. The work of modern institutions of public administration has become ever more varied and complex. Real efforts have been made at both central and local government levels to adopt the much favoured "corporate" approach of private management. This has led personnel at all levels of public administration to review their roles and how they can best perform them, and to see themselves as part of a much larger and comprehensive system.

Change and the organisational future

A few years ago it was fashionable amongst writers on organisations to suggest that the day of the large bureaucratic organisation was over. Books and articles appeared in academic and management circles claiming that the virtues of the large bureaucratic organisation had become outweighed by its disadvantages. In fact, its very virtues had themselves become vices. Standardisation of procedures and long hierarchies of command—useful in unchanging conditions in which relatively straightforward tasks were performed—had become a positive handicap to a system carrying out more and more complex and varied tasks in a situation of environmental change.

More recently this black picture of bureaucracy has itself been criticised. It is too easy to criticise public officials and claim that they are worse than their counterparts in outside industry. On the one hand, public servants have shown themselves highly adaptable to a constant set of fresh demands made upon them by politicians and public alike. The many changes with which they are supposedly incapable of dealing have, in many instances, been brought about by public officials and the organisations within which they work. On the other hand, the picture of a thrusting, dynamic private sector often presented in contrast to the Civil Service and local government is too simple. There are examples of bureaucratic practices in large privately managed organisations. In some instances, private sector organisation does not look quite as effective and dynamic as critics of public administration sometimes claim. Attempts at modernising and changing the public services of the country may be in order, but such efforts must be based on a profound and realistic assessment of the achievements as well as the failures of the system.

Statements have been made from time to time that the demands of the future will enforce dramatic changes in the way in which administration is conducted as an activity in society. Undoubtedly, changes in the working lives of public servants and their counterparts in industry are under way. Some of the boredom and routine has been removed from jobs—a result which would have been inconceivable a few years ago. Changes have also taken place in the way organisations are structured and in the techniques available to improve the quality of decision-making and goal-achievement. Successful policies of coping with change must be founded on well tried and proven organisational structures and techniques. Bureaucracy will continue to exist to a large degree because it has proved itself adaptable and capable of coping with the pressures of a changing society.

Contemporary change and environmental values

A central theme of Chapters 2 and 3 and a large part of this chapter is the argument that public administration takes place as a set of activities within a set of "environmental" values. This sets it apart from private management; indeed, it is this fact of environmental difference which gives public administration its distinctive character. Public administration takes place within a "political" framework and the behaviour of central and local government officials is directly affected by this.

Such a system of values has, itself, been subject to a process of change in many important respects. In particular, the convention of Ministerial accountability at central government level has been gradually amended. This is a constitutional change of deep potential significance and recent events seem likely to continue this process.

In 1972 the United Kingdom added its signature to the Treaty of Rome, thereby becoming a part of the European Economic Community which at that time was 15 years old. The 9 countries of the enlarged Community together formed a powerful trading bloc with a combined population of some 253 million people, a Community with common economic and social aims and committed to finding mutual solutions to its common problems. A year later, when the European Communities Act 1972 came into force, the Parliament of the United Kingdom bound itself to observe policies evolved by the Community and accepted that Community "rights, powers, liabilities, and restrictions . . . should without further enactment be given legal effect or used in the United Kingdom".

From that point on the exclusiveness of the United Kingdom's public administrative system changed considerably; in many different areas ranging from fishing rights to farm subsidies, from health and safety regulations to environmental pollution, policies are determined in Brussels rather than in London. Moreover, under the European Treaties, Britain is required to work towards a "harmonisation" of her own practices and procedures and bring them into line with those of other member countries—metrication is but one example.

The European institutions created by the Treaty of Rome in 1956 include the Commission, the Council, a Parliament and a Court of Justice. Between them, they provide the basis for a European-style administration. The **Commission**, which is divided into 20 different Directorates-General with their specialised services—such as legal and statistical offices—is made up of Commissioners drawn from the 9 countries and served by civil servants from these countries. Its primary purpose is to plan policies and initiate Community action, to act as a mediator between Governments and to serve as a watchdog over standards.

The proposals of the European Commission are discussed and approved (or otherwise) by the European **Council** which is composed of senior Ministers representing each of the 9 countries. It is the Council which takes the important decisions, and veto powers are available whereby member countries can block proposals if they are felt to be against national interests.

The European **Parliament**, which is elected by direct universal suffrage throughout the Community, reviews the work of the Commission and the Council and, through its standing committees, consults with Commission representatives, national Ministers and officials, trade union and industrial bodies as well as other private groups. The final judicial body in the Community is the **European Court of Justice** which deals with disputes between member countries and between individuals or firms and Community institutions. It is not only an international Court but also a constitutional Court, an administrative Court and a Court of appeal. As well as these organisations there are many consultative bodies which play their part in the work of the Community—bodies such as the very influential Economic and Social Committee which is representative of employers, trade unionists and other interests.

The Commission, responding to pressures from various quarters and with the aims of its original legislation in mind, may decide to initiate some new course of action. A policy document will be drawn up by the appropriate Directorate General for discussion and once it has been agreed by the Commission the draft goes to the European Council. If approval is given there the draft is published as "secondary" legislation in the Community's Official Journal. Agreement is reached on policy by a process of compromise and consensus and along the way opportunity is given for consultation with the European Parliament, with permanent national representatives and with all the various groups which may have an interest in the particular policy.

Community laws in the form of regulations, directives and decisions are binding on member countries, though they vary in the way in which they are applied. All Community law having direct internal effect must operate as law in the United Kingdom without any further legislation, while Community law which does not have direct internal effect must be made effective by national legislation or simply by administrative action on the part of the appropriate Government Department.

Public administration in Britain has felt the effects of joining the EEC. Community membership has had an impact on both central and local government although local government is affected to a lesser degree. Some central government Departments are more affected by membership than others: this is especially true of the Ministry of Agriculture and Fisheries, Customs and Excise, and the Department of Trade and Industry. The work of these Departments is directly affected by community legislation. Other Departments, such as the Home Office and the Department of Education and Science, have been affected only slightly.

At the centre of Government there is a need to integrate and co-ordinate all the different policies which have been developed as a result of membership. The Cabinet Office has grown considerably in size as additional staff have been included to improve its capability for assessing the long-term implications of membership for British policy-making and administration. In Parliament, both Houses established select committees to consider EEC secondary legislation in 1972.

In the long-run, it seems likely that the administrative impact of the Community will be very great. Already, the work of certain key civil servants has been affected to a considerable degree and staff in the affected Departments make hundreds of visits to Brussels each year. In addition, civil servants must make themselves familiar with the work of the Community. To assist them in this, the Civil Service College mounted an intensive training programme just before Britain's entry into the Common Market and this programme continues.

Most commentators agree that the work of civil servants in the Community institutions is likely to bring about important changes in the pattern of constitutional government in Britain at some future date. This will inevitably affect the environmental constraints on administration. In particular the "visibility" of individual civil servants in Community institutions seems likely to erode still further the doctrine of anonymity. Traditionally, constitutional convention demands that Ministers take full responsibility for the activities of their officials and those officials are not identified with particular policies. The more individual civil servants are identified with formulating and implementing particular policies in Brussels, the more likely it seems that the convention of anonymity and Ministerial responsibility will be subject to further alteration.

During recent years, too, political pressures for a further allocation of powers to Scotland and Wales have been increasing—both countries have already enjoyed special arrangements for government for many years. The constitutional implications of such projected changes are of obvious importance as would be the changes in working practice which devolved forms of administration would bring with them.

Membership of the EEC and the move to devolution are just two of the many changes which are likely to have a profound effect on public administration in the not-too-distant future. They make yet further demands on the resilience and abilities of public servants. One thing is certain: on the basis of past experience, the system of public administration in Britain will illustrate its adaptability in order to meet the needs of changed circumstances.

Suggestions for further reading

T Dalyell, *Devolution: The End of Britain?*, Jonathan Cape, 1977
H Wallace, *National Government and the European Communities*, Chatham House PEP, 1973

Questions

1 Assess the impact of British membership of the European Community on central government.
2 What kind of organisation is the Post Office?
3 Why should participants in an organisation resent change?

Appendix 1
Assignments and projects

1   Write a letter explaining the importance of collective and individual Ministerial responsibility in answer to an enquiry from a member of the public.

2   Obtain an example of "delegated legislation". Who has delegated what to whom? What procedure has been followed in doing so? How is it brought into effect?

3   Prepare a list of the areas of administration over which the Parliamentary Commissioner for Administration has responsibility.

4   The Official Journal of the European Community of 4 June 1974 published Regulation 1392/74 covering the application of social security schemes to migrant workers. How would this be put into effect in the United Kingdom? Will it affect the island of Guernsey?

5   Which Government Department deals primarily with:

a)   safety at work?
b)   immigration?
c)   tourism?
d)   development of guided weapons?
e)   development of ports?
f)   the valuation of property for rating in England?
g)   local government in England?
h)   national libraries?
i)   the gas industry?
j)   universities?

6   The Minister of Transport is considering a proposal to increase the motorway speed limit. Prepare a list of interested parties he might consult before making a decision about this.

7   A visiting party of Russian health service workers has asked to be given a simple description of the working of the National Health Service in England. You have 20 minutes and an interpreter is available. Prepare a short paper which will help you to do this.

8   Examine a proposal to transfer direct responsibility for the running of the police force to the Home Office. Elect discussion leaders to speak for and against the proposal.

9   Draw up an organisation chart of the organisation in which you work. Consider any uses and possible disadvantages such a chart might have.

10   "It would be much better to present the budget and the Expenditure White Paper at the same time so that everyone could see a direct connection between the Government's income and expenditure." Discuss this view expressed recently in a leading national daily newspaper.

11   Discuss the advantages and disadvantages of allocating administrative responsibility for the postal and telecommunication services to

a)   a Government Department
b)   a public corporation.

Appendix 2
Useful statistical sources

A great variety of factual information concerning public administration is published each year in the form of statistics and may be purchased from Her Majesty's Stationery Office or else consulted in local libraries. All the major Government Departments have their own statistics divisions and these, together with the two collecting agencies—the Business Statistics Office and Office of Population Censuses and Surveys—comprise the Government Statistical Service. The Central Statistical Office co-ordinates the system. Some of the most useful publications include the following:

Annual Abstract of Statistics
Civil Service Statistics
Criminal Statistics, England and Wales
Department of Employment Gazette
Digest of Welsh Statistics
Economic Trends
Education Statistics for the UK
Eurostat: Basic Statistics of the Community
Family Expenditure Survey
Financial Statement and Budget Report
General Household Survey
Health and Personal Social Services Statistics, England
Local Government Financial Statistics
Monthly Digest of Statistics
National Income and Expenditure Blue Book
Northern Ireland Digest of Statistics
OPCS Monitors: free on request from the Information Branch (GS)
    Office of Population Censuses and Surveys, St Catherine's House,
    Kingsway, London, WC2B 6JP
Population Estimates, England and Wales
Public Expenditure White Paper

Scottish Abstract of Statistics
Social Security Statistics
Social Trends
Supply Estimates

Index